RANGER'S SOJOURN

ULYSSES NAMON

Copyright © 2023 by Ulysses Namon

Cover Design by Miblart.com

All rights reserved.

No part of this book may be reproduced in any form or by any electronic or mechanical means, including information storage and retrieval systems, without written permission from the author, except for the use of brief quotations in a book review.

1

THIS IS WHY WE DO THIS JOB

Outside the airlock of the Federation patrol ship known as the *Bass Reeves*, Tomi Ryan and her partner, Ranger Avery Healy, silently drifted across the empty void that separated them from the freighter, *Stella Warren*. Passive sensor sweeps indicated that both the freighter and the nearby pirate ship were powered down. Tomi thought it felt eerily calm in the vastness of space, considering that the freighter housed an active battle.

As Tomi and Healy drew nearer the *Stella Warren*, they kept the use of any repulsor thrusters to a minimum just in case there were any active proximity sensors, but so far all was quiet. She glanced toward the others—Federation Rangers and Space Patrol alike—as they made their way to their own infiltration points in pairs. Patrolmen Payne, Scotch, Maynard, and Leopold were all heading toward the freighter's bow for the crew quarters and the bridge. Rangers Watry and Zimmerman had paired up for the cargo hold, located midship.

As Tomi and Healy closed in on their destination, they each gave a short burst of braking thrust to slow their approach. The idea was that their knees should barely flex when their grip boots touched the ship's hull so as not to alert the pirates prematurely to their presence. Once they were securely planted on the hull, Healy came up to Tomi and touched his faceplate to hers so she could hear him—with their radios off, it would be a private conversation.

"Perfect ten-point landing, rookie. If you haven't already, turn your body cam on. Once inside, things could get real messy, real fast. We'll need good documentation of what went down. Now, let's get this hatch open—we'll have to do it manually so that no power indicators light up."

Tomi nodded in acknowledgment, trying to slow her heartbeat. Besides the expedition she'd recently come off, which had allowed her to fully understand the rangers' general disdain for the Survey Service, this was her first big mission as a Federation Ranger. She found it both thrilling and unsettling all at once.

She'd had plenty of training before this, and if she'd learned anything, the most important thing was to keep your cool in all situations. Improvise, adapt, overcome—that was the ranger motto. Although, next time she'd have to remember to pee first.

She took a deep breath and helped Healy assess the hatch. She didn't think they'd need to use a waldo or any other motorized tool for this job.

"I think something as simple as a rescue ax hooked into the hydraulic handwheel could turn it," she offered.

With Healy's approval, she managed to get the hatch to pop open without setting off any alarms. Once inside, they quietly resealed the airlock's exterior hatch and started the airlock cycle. Before opening the inner door, they drew their omniblasters, prepared for anything.

"Be sure to check your targets. We don't need to shoot any innocents," Healy warned. "I'll open the hatch; you send out the recon probes."

His warning was unnecessary; Tomi knew what to do. The probes she pulled out of her pouch could easily fit in the palm of her hand. With the push of a button, she activated each of them. Springing to life, the four probes hovered in place until Tomi instructed them to start their sensor sweep. Each probe flew in a different direction, conducting full-spectrum observations through the wall and taking environmental measurements.

As the data streamed in to her wrist comp, Tomi noticed there were two individuals in spacesuits moving, no, floating. Their movements indicated they were looking for something, but what?

"Not good," Healy said.

"It's not too bad. There's only two of them," Tomi observed.

"No, look at the environmental readings: temperature and oxygen levels are dropping while CO_2 is going up. They shut off life support. Add that to their little search pattern, and we can deduce that there are hostages hiding somewhere on the ship," Healy pointed out. "These bastards are making sure there are no witnesses."

Tomi was impressed. She had completely overlooked the environmental data. "So, what's the plan?" she asked.

"Simple—get in and take them down, nice and quick. Make sure to set your omniblaster to kill. Stun won't penetrate their spacesuits and we only get one chance. Any questions?" Healy was always simple and to the point.

"But Payne wants our blasters on stun," she reminded him.

Healy shook his head. "I don't care what Payne says. If anyone's gonna die today, it might as well be the bad guys." He didn't have patience for assholes like Payne.

After a brief pause, Tomi said, "Ready."

The airlock door slid open to the interior of the ship and the two rangers burst forth, using their grip boots to remain planted on the ground even with the lack of gravity. Preoccupied with checking storage lockers along the outside wall of the engineering space, it took the pirates a few critical seconds before they even noticed the two Federation Rangers had entered the compartment.

"Don't move! Federation Rangers!" Tomi and Healy yelled the

command simultaneously over their communicators and helmet speakers.

The two marauders startled, but they were not interested in surrendering, instead raising their weapons and taking aim.

The rangers didn't hesitate in firing their pistols before being shot upon. Healy hit the pirate on the right, hitting just below his helmet attachment collar. Enough of the jolt got through his suit to send the pirate into convulsions. Tomi hit her target right in the center of mass, but she'd made a critical mistake: her omniblaster beam width was set to wide, spreading across the pirate's entire torso. Instead of blasting a hole through him, the pirate was merely thrown backward, slamming into the bulkhead immediately behind him.

"Go check him," Healy ordered while he pushed his way through the atmosphere over to the engineering console.

As Healy powered up the ship's life support, Tomi scanned the pirate she had just shot. Despite her error, no vitals registered. His internal organs had been ruptured by her attack. Informing Healy the pirate was DOA, he then ordered her to watch the passageway.

As Tomi used her grip boots to secure herself back to the floor and walked to the other end of the compartment, she asked over her shoulder, "Why turn the artificial gravity off?"

"Didn't you notice? These guys are spacer parahumans. In free fall, they have the advantage."

Looking back over at the two pirates, she now noticed both of them had gloves on their feet instead of boots. Tomi shook her head; how had she completely missed that detail? Distracted by her shortcoming, she didn't notice the pirate coming down the passageway as he leveled his carbine's underslung grenade launcher directly at them.

Before Healy could turn the gravity back on, the pirate fired a concussion grenade between the two rangers. It was no bigger than a man's fist, but its detonation could be lethal if it was close enough. Fortunately for the rangers, it wasn't.

The explosion was loud and the concussion did hurt, but they survived the blast. The overpressure had pushed Tomi across the compartment, knocking her blaster from her grip. When she came to a stop, she got back to her feet, using her grip boots to clamp to the deck again as she looked around for her partner.

Healy had been pushed in the opposite direction and floated in the air. She let out her breath when she saw him move, but his blaster was over ten feet away. Relieved that he was okay, she realized she no longer held her own sidearm either. She began to look for it, locking eyes with the pirate who'd committed the assault.

Tomi narrowed her eyes, brought up her left arm, and activated her portable defense screen. Knowing the screen only covered her upper torso, she knelt down for maximum coverage as the pirate leveled his 10mm carbine at her.

"Die, motherfucker!" he screamed and pulled the trigger.

The carbine chattered as explosive-tipped bullets streamed toward Tomi. Only about half were even hitting her, and luckily, her screen held. Each bullet's impact fuse detonated prematurely as they struck the screen's plasma field. The thought briefly crossed her mind that this would be a really cool fireworks display if only she wasn't focused on staying alive.

What seemed like an eternity actually only lasted a few seconds. When the gun's magazine at last ran out of ammunition, the carbine made a click and stopped firing. The pirate had just enough time to say, "What the—?" when he was hit by Healy's grapple line.

Screaming, the pirate was dragged through the atmosphere to meet his enemy, whose plasma cutter was already lit and ready. As the pirate traveled past, Healy bisected him at the waist in one fluid motion. The result was a little smoke and the criminal falling silent as both halves of his body floated apart in the zero-gravity compartment.

"Get your blaster before more of them show up!" Healy yelled.

Tomi watched with envy as Healy activated his cordless lanyard, held out his hand, and his blaster flew back into his grip. Cordless lanyards were not standard issue—Tomi made a mental note to save up for one. For now, she had to chase over to the corner of the compartment to retrieve her weapon the old-fashioned way.

Unfortunately, the commotion had alerted another pirate to their presence, and before she could reach her pistol, he'd made his way into the engine room. His weapon of choice was known as the slicer: a general-purpose industrial cutting tool that, with modifications to its automatic blade changer, turned into a machine gun that fired nanofilament-edged circular saw blades. It was a unique weapon growing in popularity among the Star Demon Syndicate.

Seeing his dead comrades, the pirate aimed his slicer at Healy and screamed, "You'll pay for this, pig!"

He wasted no time in discharging his slicer and Healy didn't take any chances either. He dove for cover as the marauder's frenzied salvo cut equipment and the compartment's aft bulkhead to pieces.

The pirate hadn't noticed her yet, and Tomi had to act fast to keep the element of surprise. She didn't have time to get her pistol, so she grabbed the first weapon she could think of: her bush knife. Normally used for survival, it was a last-ditch weapon of choice for combat, but it still had its perks. While made from nanotech ceramic alloy, it did not require ammunition, power, or fuel, and its edge could cut through almost anything, given enough effort.

Remembering the hand-to-hand techniques taught during her training, Tomi came up behind the pirate and wrapped her arm around his helmet. He started flailing his arms at his unseen attacker, but before he could reach her, Tomi placed the tip of her knife against the weak point underneath the helmet's connection ring and pushed forcefully.

The knife's nanofilament edge slid through the layers of plastic with ease and smoothly into the pirate's neck. Tomi then removed the blade from his flesh and flicked the dark red liquid off before sheathing it. Her victim's blood gushed, but in free fall, it formed shiny red spheres instead of spraying all over the floor.

"Good work, rookie. Now retrieve your pistol and secure the compartment while I turn on the gravity," Healy snapped at her.

She understood what was eating at him—he didn't want any more surprises and neither did she. It was only luck that the pirate hadn't seen her, or else they'd both be stuck taking cover until their other partners found them. And hopefully, not too late.

Gravity now on, they heard a thud nearby. Healy used his drone controller to check where it came from. He saw a biosignature in a locker and said, "Ryan, get over here and cover me!"

Tomi complied, and as Healy yanked open the storage locker door, both of them yelled, "Federation Rangers!"

Inside was a man wearing coveralls marked with the name "Gallagher" on one side and the *Stella Warren* emblem on the other. He had his eyes squeezed shut and his hands waving frantically in front of him as he yelled, "Don't shoot! Don't shoot! I surrender!"

Healy relaxed, pulling the frightened man out of the locker right as they heard an explosion coming from the center of the ship—Watry and Zimmerman's assigned objective. Healy ordered the man to stay between the two rangers, and the group proceeded down the passageway to the ship's main loading bay. There they found even more devastation; one side of the bay was scorched with static discharges still flashing.

"What the hell happened?" Healy asked his rangers when they came into view.

"Crazy bastards tried to throw a plasma grenade," Watry answered.

"But I hit the guy just as he was winding up," Zimmerman added proudly. "As you can see, the grenade went off on their side of the bay instead of ours."

As the trio continued chatting, Tomi heard something. She held up her hand to get their attention. "Shhh..." The room grew silent as she tried to decipher the noise. "Can anybody hear that? It sounds like somebody is knocking."

Gallagher said, "I can hear it too! It's coming from the loading lock over there!"

Zimmerman walked over to an open control panel next to the loading lock door and pushed a button. The door hummed as it opened, Zimmerman and Watry pointing their guns at whoever may be waiting on the other side.

"Don't shoot, damn it!" one of them screamed.

They all wore the same *Stella Warren* emblem as Gallagher, and as the people climbed out, he exclaimed, "Croft! Abelson! You're still alive!"

Watry checked the ship's roster on his wrist comp and nodded. "This looks like the crew and ship's company of the *Stella Warren*."

Patrolman Payne's voice suddenly burst through their comm channel. "What are you rangers doing? Damn it, the perpetrators have gotten away!"

From the *Bass Reeves*, Captain Everly confirmed Payne's report over the comm. "The pirate skiff has departed."

"Pursue and take them out, Everly," Payne demanded.

"Hold that order, sir," Healy directed to Captain Everly. "We have survivors here in the loading bay."

"But the pirates—" Payne started to complain.

Everly spoke over him, "Roger. I'll maintain a holding position." Rangers always stuck together.

"Damn it! The pirates are getting away," Payne yelled through the comm, emphasizing every word.

"He's an idiot and an asshole," Watry whispered to anyone listening.

Everly could be heard making the final word on the matter. "We may come from different branches, Sergeant Payne, but as captain, I outrank you. I'm commanding you to shut the hell up!"

Tomi could understand Payne's disappointment. Something within also urged her to hunt the pirates down.

As if reading her mind, Healy put a hand on her shoulder. "We can serve justice to the pirates on a silver platter another day, rookie," he said. "But these people," he motion over to the freighter crew, "they are the reason we do this job."

2

WHY WOULD YOU WANT TO BE A RANGER?

Growing up on Earth in the days of the Terran Federation wasn't too bad, even for those with little money. The dystopian future of science fiction had been avoided, at least for most.

Some still complained that technology, particularly biotechnology, was an abomination of nature. Still, many of the nightmares that the extremists kept prophesizing hadn't yet materialized. With no proof, the extremists were ignored by the vast population. In fact, most sided with the benefits that came from that very biotechnology.

For parents who could afford it, getting genetic upgrades for their children was the new way to give their kids an advantage. Simply sending a child to a private school wasn't good enough anymore; a child's genetic foundation needed to be top notch as well. Unfortunately, it came with a hefty price tag. The fancier templates could cost as much as a house, and even the most basic of templates could be like buying a new car.

Despite that, Ted and Doris Ryan wanted what was best for their children and had vowed do whatever necessary to achieve that. They made sacrifices and saved up in order to invest in genetic upgrades for each of their children. Admittedly, the Ryans' choices were limited financially, but they were grateful that they at least had a choice.

The Ryans opted for an enhanced basic package that was guaranteed to result in a beautiful, healthy, athletic, and intelligent child. Therefore, even before she was born, Tomi's parents knew what she would look like as an adult, thanks to the genetic growth extrapolation: five-foot-nine, wavy brown hair, black eyes, and fair skin with a near-flawless complexion. This package worked a second time with Tomi's younger brother, Ted Jr., who came along two years later. He would grow to be two inches taller than his sister, with curly brown hair and green eyes.

To avoid the irrational hostility that those extremists felt toward those who received such genetic upgrades, the Ryans avoided telling anyone the truth about their children having them. They even waited to tell Tomi and Teddy the truth until they were old enough to understand. The judgment and need for secrecy seemed unfair when they were merely trying to give their children the best possible life, but the rhetoric they heard on the newsfeeds and, even worse, the public protests didn't simply concern them, it terrified them.

As the children grew older, Ted and Doris tried their best to treat them equally. Both had to partake in all chores, regardless whether it was a traditionally masculine or feminine task. But when it came to letting them experience typical teenage activities, Tomi noticed her brother didn't have to plead with Mom and Dad to hang out with his friends. As for Tomi, Ted and Doris always had their excuses lined up. "You're too young." "Concerts are dangerous." "What if you get stalked?" Blah, blah, blah...

Even her boyfriend, Olin, could be condescending in this matter. After making love one afternoon, she was still sitting on top of him while she complained about her parents' latest denial. As

Olin absent-mindedly massaged her C-cup-sized breasts, he made a dumb male comment that sent Tomi over the edge.

"It's a dangerous world out there, baby. Don't worry, I'll protect you."

Tomi rolled her eyes and heaved a big sigh as she pushed herself off him. She thought Olin must be getting his advice on how to talk to girls from some men's magazine. While some women may want a knight in shining armor to swoop in and rescue them, Tomi found this level of machismo to be quite insulting. She flopped down on the other side of the bed, ensuring that their bodies in no way touched.

She stared him down and asked, "And what am I supposed to do when you're not around? Curl up into a ball and cry?" She threw her arms up in frustration. "This is bullshit! I can take care of myself, thank you very much."

Olin had only been trying to be sweet, but he realized now that he'd really stepped in it. All he could do was try to smooth things over by complimenting her. He reached over to caress her shoulder only to have her push it off angrily.

Olin proceeded with caution. "I'm sorry, baby. Of course, you can do anything you set your mind to. I didn't mean it like that. You're beautiful, you're smart, you could be a model—"

"What? You think that's what all girls want to do, become models?"

Retreat! Retreat! Olin had naively forgotten that Tomi liked to be recognized for more than her outward appearance. She could never be satisfied in what she deemed the superficial world of sitting around and letting people take pictures of her. His intended compliment had only dug him in deeper.

She jumped out of bed, growling as she hunted around the room for her clothes. Olin racked his brain, desperately trying to think of another way to smooth things over, but by this time, Tomi had reached a full boil. He decided the best route was for him to remain silent and hope things cooled down eventually.

In his silence, he still made the crucial mistake of watching as Tomi bent over to pick up her panties, giving him a perfect view of her ass. Of course, she looked back at him right in that moment, and not in a sexy way. Her brows furrowed and her face instantly turned redder than it already was.

"Is that all I am to you? A piece of ass?" she yelled.

Olin widened his eyes and shook his head, throwing his hands up in a defensive gesture. Still, he couldn't help watching her butt cheeks move up and down as she stormed off to the bathroom to take a shower. When at last Tomi had shut the door, Olin lay back in bed and let out a deep sigh.

"Shit," he muttered in the empty room. He was horny again, but he knew after all of that, he wasn't going to get laid for at least a week.

It's said that some people were too smart for their own good. Tomi believed what they really meant was that whoever they were bitching about simply wasn't doing what they wanted them to do. She was realizing more and more that people didn't want you to stand up for yourself; they'd much prefer that you quietly acquiesced so their own lives would be simpler.

In Tomi's lifetime, there had been many occurrences when her parents or a teacher or someone in authority had tried to use some lame excuse to get her to do what they claimed was best. In reality, it was only best for them, not Tomi.

"Guidance, my ass," she would say to her brother and friends.

These oh-so-wise grown-ups were always trying to steer her toward what they knew, or rather, what they thought they knew. Whenever she had an opportunity to talk to any adults other than her parents or teachers, she got some unexpected answers.

"My job? I had no idea that it existed before I applied for it. I even had to ask the interviewer what his company did," one man had told her when she asked about his occupation. Another told her how he'd started out running a laundry business that later led to him becoming a senior manager at a casino. Who knew such a leap could be made?

Edward Lorenz certainly did when he theorized that seemingly unrelated events could come together to take a person through life, even mundane events or decisions. Therefore, Tomi decided that every decision she made should hold weight and be considered seriously. She also appreciated Isaac Newton's suggestion that humans should enjoy the unknown. "What we know is a drop. What we don't know is an ocean."

In Tomi's eyes, these two mathematicians were a lot smarter than any of the grown-ups in her life. Between Newton and Lorenz, Tomi determined that she would never settle for anything less than she desired, and she desired to learn and grow in ways untold, despite what protests others may proffer.

Reading about current events, Tomi had recently become passionate about the need to be free, which, ironically, tied into the need for law and order. Throughout history and even into her own time, there always seemed to be some pompous, self-righteous buffoon who thought they knew best how to run everyone else's lives. Whenever the political winds would change, some other pompous buffoon would decide that everyone not only already had rights but they were actually oppressed and needed even more.

It was one extreme or the other, and at first, Tomi was confused by all of this. It wasn't until one of her teachers laid out how things were supposed to work that she finally gained some clarity.

"The truth is the government is doing what it's supposed to be doing: very little," Mr. Malkamus would tell his students. "Government gridlock is a good thing. As long as the government isn't doing anything, it can't screw anything up. If they actually do something, it means it's truly necessary or people really want it."

When a student would counter from the point of view of control, Malkamus would counter right back that history has shown that every system with too many rules and too much control eventually strangled themselves politically, economically, and socially. If a student was on the other side of the argument, he would point out that to have rights merely meant the government couldn't arbitrarily take something from someone, not that the government had to provide anything to said someone.

"So, on one side, they want to scare the crap out of us so we'll hand over all the power to them, while the other side wants to give crap away so everyone will like them and keep them in power," Tomi opined during one of these exchanges.

"There you have it," Malkamus said with a wink. "Even among the elite, they have way too much time on their hands."

Luckily, society had not repeated too many of the mistakes of the past. It had already happened—Armageddon, that is—just not in the way it was always portrayed beforehand. It wasn't some giant asteroid hitting the planet or a nuclear war or any other major ecological disaster. All of those authors would have been sorely disappointed with the reality, which was not nearly as glamorous or dramatic as all that. Simply put, everyone ran their economies into the ground.

And it wasn't like they couldn't see it coming. So much money was being spent on projects and programs that anyone who bothered to check knew were a total waste, but it was done anyway because "it was the right thing to do" or "we need to be good stewards." All the while, there were plenty of problems that could have actually been solved, but were drowned out by the scare du jour of that particular week. Rather than affordable solutions with actual benefits, money was thrown away to chase after solutions that *might* work.

The world Tomi grew up in was the result of the aftermath of those mistakes. When whole bureaucracies collapsed and were no more, no one was inclined to resurrect them, especially since they were so expensive and benefited so very few. Not only the bureaucracies, but the organizations of people who supported those same bureaucracies had lost their influence right along with the leaders who ran them. That's the perk of starting a society from the ground up: you're open to trying different ideas since there was no establishment to argue with. It took over a hundred years of hard work, but at last, a better society had resulted.

This new society was able to sort through the ashes of the old and brought the best ideas together that allowed for a rapid recovery. Whole government departments were deemed obsolete or unnecessary and were left where they belonged—in the past. Even the department of education had been completely revamped.

It was too troublesome to recreate the bureaucracy and all of the political offices, so a student voucher system was set up in its place. Entities both public and private stepped in to set up the schools. The parents simply chose a school for their child and the funds followed the student. Unfortunately, some private schools could have exorbitant costs, and with a limit of 10,000 credits, parents who wanted more for their child had to pay the difference.

As society recovered, the desire to look to the stars was again under consideration. While some voiced their desire to make space endeavors exclusively about exploration and science, others realized that was unrealistic. Ultimately, humans were self-interested creatures. While some would be satisfied with altruistic pursuits, many others wanted more tangible rewards. Hence, early space exploration became about finding valuable minerals out in space.

With valuables on the line, there became a need for the law to follow the scientists into the unknown universe. And that was when the Federation Rangers were pioneered.

Tomi had been born centuries after the collapse, so neither she nor anyone she knew had to live through those difficult times, yet they were all able to reap the benefits. For the most part, life on Earth nowadays was peaceful, quiet, and dull. The biggest problem was dealing with biotechnology—mainly, engineering humans at the genetic level. Many still feared the unknown, and the older generations weren't too keen on this change that they believed interfered with Deus's creation. This meant Tomi and those like her had to keep quiet about their little leg up in life, unless they were ready to welcome hatred and opposition.

Thanks to a more efficient education system, Tomi was already a high school graduate by the time she had her driver's license. Being on the fast track, the issue of what she was going to do with her life came up more frequently. College, technical school, or trade school were the more obvious choices. At least in Tomi's day and age, there was some attempt to steer those who were not cut out for traditional college to go into a trade or something similar. After all, why waste one's time going to college just to wash out?

Tomi, however, did quite well in school and did qualify to go to college. Nevertheless, her scores weren't quite high enough to get a scholarship, and on paper, her parents made too much money to receive government aid. Her mom convinced Tomi that taking on loans would be worth it in the long run, and she did enroll at a two-year college at her parents' insistence. Still, Tomi couldn't help but feel guilty for the investment her parents had already made in her genetic upgrade.

To top it off, Tomi had found out through a little research that a degree was no guarantee of landing a good-paying job. There were too many people out there who went to the trouble of getting a degree only to find out there were no jobs that required that degree. She'd even met a woman with a master's degree in biology, which amazed her at first. But when she asked what kind of research she did, the woman gave her a blank stare before answering, "I make custom picture frames."

WHY WOULD YOU WANT TO BE A RANGER?

That gave Tomi pause. She was a year into her undergrad program to get a general degree in liberal arts and it seemed to be going nowhere. The pressure was mounting for her to decide what degree to pursue—the last thing she wanted to do was waste her parents' money. Since working at a garden center for the rest of her life didn't appeal to Tomi, she started looking elsewhere.

That was when she started looking into the various Federation services. It made sense with her passion for the balance between government and freedom, and for the first time, she felt a spark igniting deep in her belly. As she researched each branch, it was revealed that they all had their own advantages and disadvantages.

To gain clarity, she talked to recruiters to get an insider's view of what each service was like. This gave her insight into the perks and quirks of each service. Since Tomi was an intelligent female, she was a rarity among the Federation services. At least 90 percent of recruits were male, so each of the recruiters showed great interest in getting her to sign up for their particular branch.

While the Survey Service was not considered a military branch, they did get to travel, were more diverse in the personnel they recruited, and had their own kind of esprit de corps. But when Tomi looked at the requirements, she realized that wasn't going to work for her. People who joined the Survey Service were scientists, which required an advanced degree—i.e., lots of college. Science had never been her passion.

The Territorial Guard were the ground forces that each member planet got to keep for themselves. On one hand, the guard was more numerous when all units were counted together, but each unit had to stay on its home planet, so that meant limited travel. The recruiters Tomi talked to had bragged that the guard was where the action was since they were called up frequently to handle various emergencies, insurgencies, riots, natural disasters, and anything else the local authorities couldn't handle. But Tomi read between the lines—that meant facing down angry mobs pelting you with rocks and trash while never leaving Earth. No thank you.

The Federation Navy was by far the most expansive of the services since it had to cover all of the Federation's territory. The fleet was mostly composed of destroyers, frigates, and cruisers, but it was the carriers and battleships that were the pride of the Federation Navy fleet. While serving on one of the combat ships would be prestigious, the reality was a crewmember would most often find themselves assigned to a support ship or a naval base.

Either way, from what Tomi gleaned, the navy consisted of 99 percent boredom and the occasional 1 percent moment of sheer terror. With the main visual being a lot of outer space or crammed into the interior of a ship, liberty call would be the only highlight. And in that case, what was the point? Tomi checked them off her potential list.

The marines were a sub-branch of the navy, and thus, smaller. But because they were smaller, they were considered more elite than the other services. Acting as shipboard troops, the marines would wear combat armor and x-ray pulse laser carbines to conduct ship-boarding operations against enemy troops, pirates, or whatever strain of xenobiological insanity someone might encounter.

When required to go dirtside, the marines would don battlesuits: armored exoskeletons capable of carrying hundreds of pounds of weapons, which sounded exciting, but was rare. They were not an easy club to join and they had the lowest percentage of females. In the end, they were still a part of the navy, and because of this, Tomi wasn't so sure it was the route she wanted to go.

She had also heard about the Federation Intelligence Branch, or FIB. Whoever thought up that name must have had a sense of humor. Still, it was even more of a pipe dream than the Survey Service. No one ever applied for employment with Fed Intel—you didn't call them, they called you.

Stories abounded of prospects being approached in bars or parking lots and being asked if they were "looking for a job." If the prospect answered yes, that individual would swiftly disappear into the shadow world to play "cloak and dagger." Those who said, "I'll think about it," were later told, "We have no idea what you're talking about," when they tried to contact the FIB.

The Federation Space Patrol was similar to the navy, but instead of hurting people and breaking things, the job of the patrol was to enforce Federation law in the space lanes, spaceports, and the rest of Federation space. They were essentially glorified cops in blue and silver uniforms with shiny titanium badges embossed with the Space Patrol hologram. The spit-and-polish patrol took great pride in their duties, and while rarely seen on Earth, patrolmen were a common sight in spaceports from Earth to the remotest reaches of Federation space. It was kind of a tease to enter space, but only within arm's reach, and the concept seemed pretty mundane to Tomi.

The other side of the law enforcement coin were the Federation Rangers—a paramilitary force trained in combat, survival, and rescue on hostile and untamed worlds. Just as the Space Patrol kept law and order in the space lanes, the rangers provided the same out on frontier worlds, acting as interim sheriffs until those worlds managed to set up their own governments. The rangers also conducted search-and-rescue operations as well as escorted Survey Service expeditions. It is said that the rangers faced the most implacable enemy: nature itself.

In wartime, the rangers worked alongside the Federation Marines as pathfinders, snipers, and special forces. A long-held tradition was once a ranger completed a combat mission with a marine unit, that ranger was then presented and entitled to wear the marines' black beret. Rangers with that distinction were held in the highest regard, both among other rangers as well as the other Federation services.

With such a broad spectrum of missions and travel opportunities, plus the possibility of reaching the level of the elite, the marines and the rangers drew Tomi's interest more than any other branch. The choice was a toss-up until protests and violence against parahumans began making national news. The fact that fertility clinics were being vandalized and even bombed started to generate real fear among the general populace. When families with genetically upgraded children began being targeted and attacked, Tomi's own parents were on the verge of panic.

Tomi, on the other hand, was infuriated and it caused her desire to join up and defend the innocents from such unfair treatment all the more validated. The monsters who carried out these acts of terrorism may think of themselves as wise and concerned with the greater good, but in the end, they were nothing more than murderers and cowards.

Killing helpless children in their own homes was in no way courageous. They were not warriors, soldiers, or crusaders. No, these genetic purists were scum and deserved to spend the rest of their wretched lives locked away from society. When these radicals firebombed a bus full of students attending a school for those with genetic upgrades, it was the final straw. Public opinion turned completely against the purists and Tomi confirmed her decision to join the Federation Rangers.

3

JOINING UP

When she informed her family of her decision, Tomi's mother was beside herself with fear and emotions. Even her brother, Teddy, couldn't believe it. But it was her father who asked her if she was serious.

"You're not doing this because of the pressure your mom and I have been putting on you to get a job?" he asked her over the phone.

"No, Dad, I'm doing this because I want to...no, I need to. College is going nowhere and I don't want to spend all day grilling food or pruning plants. I want to do something meaningful."

To her surprise, he then offered his support. "I get it, Tomi. Just...be careful, okay?"

The final step should have been the easiest, yet when Tomi went to the recruiter's office, it seemed like he was on the side of her parents. He eyed her up and down, seemingly unimpressed.

"Why do you want to be a ranger?" the desk sergeant asked. "Wouldn't the navy or patrol be more to your liking?"

After all the other branches had fought for her signature, this irritated Tomi. He was just one more in a long line of people who thought they were so smart that they knew what was best for her. It took a little persistence to get the information on the requirements to become a ranger, but she finally convinced him she wasn't going anywhere without it.

"Well," he finally said, "seems you're in luck. We have new recruit testing beginning later this afternoon."

He passed Tomi a pile of paperwork to read over and fill out, emphasizing that they wouldn't start for several hours. When he suggested she take the time to rethink her decision, it only made her even more resolute. She had made up her mind and she was determined to see it through. To prove to the recruiter just how serious she was, she chose to stick around until the tests began.

Tomi sat down in the waiting room and began to fill out the forms and register for the required testing. Along with the usual aptitude test and physical exam, she would also need to pass the physical requirements test, obstacle course, vehicle simulators, and submit to a background check. It was a lot, and if Tomi's pride hadn't taken over, it may have been enough to change her mind.

She handed in the paperwork and checked the clock. Another hour to go. It was then that an overly friendly young man named Danny Royer walked into the waiting room.

"Hey, there! My name is Danny." He smiled and waved at Tomi. Between his naive eagerness and the fact that he chose the one seat out of many that happened to be right next to hers, this kid instantly got under Tomi's skin.

She managed a semi-friendly greeting. "Hey, Danny. I'm Tomi," she answered, not making eye contact.

"Your tag says you're going to be a ranger. So am I!" he proclaimed proudly.

Tomi looked him up and down, certain that he was joking. This kid wasn't just overweight, he was downright obese. He had exactly three chances of becoming a ranger: slim, fat, and none.

Danny continued to chatter and Tomi was certain she caught the recruiter smirking at her unfortunate situation. As others began to trickle in for the upcoming testing, she hoped Danny's attentions would be diverted, but no such luck. She thought about moving to another seat when, finally, their names were called.

The first several steps consisted mostly of paperwork, including the forms for the background check. After that, they began the testing, which started with the aptitude test since it was the shortest and, thus, the cheapest test to administer. That way, if anyone failed it would save the Federation a lot of money in further testing and training without anything to show for it.

At that point, the recruits were sent home for the night with no further instructions or information on whether they'd passed. Tomi had been concerned that she had missed some of the questions about mechanics—the price of not taking a shop class in high school. She later discovered she had nothing to worry about when she learned she had scored in the top five percentile.

The next day, all of the prospective recruits who had made it this far were awakened by an early morning phone call to come take their physicals. Her past experience with a physical did not compare to that given by the Federation Rangers. It started off pretty typical, consisting of eyesight and hearing tests as well as giving samples of blood, hair, and urine.

But then, each prospect took turns in a medical scanner.

Height, weight, body fat, and all sorts of information about the recruits' innards was on full display for the doctor's review. The examiner had even brought up how one kid had no arches on his feet. It seemed nothing could be hidden from them. If any problems or defects were detected with a recruit's skeleton, muscles, heart, lungs, or literally anything else, they were instantly disqualified.

It was nerve-racking for sure, but the thing Tomi found most disconcerting was having to strip down in front of everyone. This was deemed necessary in order to scan each prospect's exterior. With their group of thirty recruits only containing three other girls besides Tomi, she could feel several pairs of eyes performing an unwelcomed examination of their own. The only consolation was that the boys had to get naked too.

Tomi made the mistake of muttering something about this being the most unpleasant part so far. One of the female staff overheard and laughed at her as she approached.

"Darlin', you ain't seen nothing," she said with a hard smack on Tomi's back. "Back in the day, the examiner actually reached around inside to feel a woman's reproductive organs." Emphasizing her words with hand motions, she drew enjoyment when Tomi shuddered and curled her lips in disgust. "Aw, don't you worry yer perty little head, darlin'. They wore gloves!" She laughed again before at last walking away, much to Tomi's relief.

After being informed that Tomi had passed the physical, it was time to take the physical requirements test, or PRT for short. They started with push-ups, sit-ups, and pull-ups, followed by a 500-meter swim, and finished off with a 3,000-meter run.

Tomi was feeling more and more sorry for Royer. With each event he failed, the observers still let him continue to the next event, only to watch him fail again. How he passed the initial BMI requirements was beyond her, yet here they were. He was absolutely pathetic during the muscle-strength portion of the test, and when Royer walked out in his swim trunks, his whole body jiggled, man boobs and all. But the worst of it was during the run. He jiggled so much it was like watching the Pillsbury Doughboy take on intensive aerobics. *Hoo hoo!*

Tomi secretly hoped Danny would be disqualified at every turn to put him out of his misery if nothing else. Or maybe to put her out of her misery of her secondhand embarrassment. Still, Royer kept trying, certain he was going to pass. She wondered whether the testing officers were messing with him, which was confirmed when she saw them all whispering and exchanging money at one point—they must have had some sort of bet going at Danny's expense.

She felt bad for him, but she needed to worry about herself. She couldn't allow pity to bring her down right along with him. Unfortunately, Danny was on his own. Perhaps it was even a test for the other recruits to see who would maintain focus on the goal at hand and keep their emotions out of it.

The requirements for the rangers were more stringent than many of the other branches, so Tomi had to push herself harder, especially during the run. Upon hearing her finishing time of eleven minutes, she wished she had done better. Many others were still running toward the finish line, and Tomi briefly thought maybe she was being too hard on herself. But the truth was, she had to be better than good if she was going to be a female in the Federation Rangers.

Tomi continued walking to cool down and she saw Royer wheezing as he barely trotted along, not even keeping up with the navy or patrol candidates. She noticed several others poking fun at him, some to themselves and others quite rudely as they breezed past him with ease. Tomi decided not to partake in ostracizing him. She wouldn't let this test be the one she failed, but she certainly felt bad for the kid.

The third day, they arrived to see the obstacle course ready to roll. This exam was no longer about stamina, but the ability to overcome one's personal fears. With each obstacle, a candidate had to deal with darkness, enclosed spaces, heights, and all sorts of other common fears. Staff psychologists were on hand, evaluating each recruit's performance. The advice, particularly to those who aspired to become rangers, was to "push through no matter what."

The last thing the Federation Rangers needed was someone who was incapable of overcoming their own fears. Out on the wild frontier, there was no telling what sort of exotic and crazy situations a ranger would find themselves encountering. They'd need to withstand anything, or else they were worthless.

After the obstacle course, recruits were called over one at a time to receive their evaluation. Some didn't like what they were hearing, no doubt finding out that due to a certain phobia of theirs, they would not receiving the MOS they wanted, or possibly not even be able to join their service of choice.

Tomi's heart leaped when she heard her name called. Though she was freaking out internally, outwardly, she presented only confidence as she stood and approached the sergeant. Without looking up from his tablet, he read off his fill-in-the-blanks statement of findings.

"Ryan, Tomi: according our observations, you do not display any significant phobias or other psychological conditions at this time. You are cleared to continue on to the simulator phase. Report back in an hour."

Tomi let out a verbal celebration, which finally gained the man's full attention.

He looked directly at her and said, "You're not done yet. The simulators are no cakewalk."

Tomi regained her composure and returned to the waiting area until it was time to begin, surprised to see Royer still in the running to become a ranger.

The last phase of testing was the simulators. Different vehicles were represented, from infantry battlesuits to aerospace fighters, but Tomi was directed to some of the more exotic vehicles that only the rangers and survey scouts used. Flitters, hoverbikes, battlesuits, and multi-environment fliers were just a few that she had to demonstrate some level of aptitude with, even though she'd never used any of them before this point.

These simulators were not your childhood arcade games. Each one was configured to behave just like its real-world counterpart and were just as unforgiving if you made an error. Tomi watched as several recruits ahead of her were able to demonstrate some natural skill in at least one of the simulators, which gave them positive marks to go into a relevant MOS like battlesuit trooper or dropship pilot.

Two recruits even scored so high in the aerospace fighter, VTOL, and ground mecha that they got the attention of the bigwigs who usually couldn't be bothered to come out of their office during the testing phases. But as soon as these two recruits finished, an officer came right down from the control room, called their names, and instructed them to follow him.

When Tomi asked where they were being taken, one of the technicians commented, "Those two? They qualified to fly transforming fighters. It's not easy to find one out of thirty prospects, let alone two who meet the requirements."

"Yeah," another one added, "it's not unusual to process over 300 recruits in a day and get no more than half a dozen worthy of that position."

Tomi had heard that transforming fighters were considered the hottest and most difficult-to-master war machines in the Federation arsenal, but Tomi wasn't interested. From what she was able to research, it was not only a long shot to get your wings, but you likely wouldn't enjoy them for long. Life expectancy for those pilots was frighteningly low. Besides, she didn't aspire to be couped up in an armored shell.

When it was Tomi's turn, she became frustrated when she crashed during her first attempt with each simulator. But through her determination, by her second or third try, she managed to get the hang of it while other recruits were not so skilled or lucky. She noticed several who kept crashing over and over before eventually being told to head back to the main lounge. At least she wasn't one of them.

In fact, one of the technicians even tried to get her to test on the same simulators as the new pilot recruits. Though it did make her feel better about her results, Tomi was adamant about not giving up her ranger career track. She politely turned him down, and seeing that Tomi had her mind made up, he instructed her to report back to the main lounge and wait to be called.

Tomi waited and waited and waited. After a while, she got up and started walking around, antsy for something to happen. Moving helped to keep her awake and also allowed her to see what was going on in the different offices without appearing overly snoopy.

She paused when she noticed Danny Royer finishing up with the recruiter for the Federation Rangers. It was obvious he was not happy. She expected it to happen, but not quite this drawn out. Poor guy.

Royer stood angrily and walked out of the office. He kicked a garbage can that was in his path and cursed loudly.

Another recruiter saw this and yelled, "Hey! Don't hurt that trash receptacle. It didn't do anything to you!"

"Fuck off," Royer shot back.

Before he could leave, the ranger recruiter came out of his office. "If this is how you handle failure, then the Federation made the right call in turning you away. There's no one to blame for your shortcomings but yourself, son. Now get out!"

Though the recruiter was right, Tomi found herself wanting to stand up for the poor kid. It wasn't fun getting kicked when you were already down. Still, she wasn't finished with her own recruitment process yet, and she did not want to ruin her chances by pooling herself with someone who had not prepared properly.

She clenched her jaw shut, turning her head slightly away from him, and hoped Royer didn't see her sitting there. Just as he started to look in her direction, Tomi was greatly relieved to hear her name called. Talk about being saved by the bell.

"Ryan, Tomi!"

"That's me!" Tomi answered.

"Ah, my next victim," he declared. "Come on in!"

Stepping into the room and closing the door, Tomi took a seat in front of the recruiter's desk. He busied himself looking over her test results, creating an awkward silence. Finally, he turned to her.

"Impressive test results, Ryan. You have surpassed my initial expectations when you first walked in the door." He paused, still reading the information in front of him. "I see they couldn't convince you to sign up for fighter pilot or something else more glamorous."

"No, sir. I have already made up my mind—I want to be a ranger."

"Good, you're determined. You're going to need that because the tests you have passed so far will only get you in the front door." The recruiter leaned back in his chair. "The hard part is going to be the survival training before you're thrown into the field. You will be challenged physically, psychologically, and academically, and even so, it's all just a feeble attempt to get you ready for what you'll be facing out there on the wild frontier. Experience will be your toughest teacher," he warned.

"That's why I'm signing up with the rangers," Tomi stated confidently. "I want to get outside, not be couped up inside some shell."

"Oh, you'll be getting plenty of both," The recruiter countered. "I can guarantee that."

Tomi clenched her jaw. She was tired of people trying to scare her away from what she wanted to do. She said through her teeth, "I'm still doing it. You're not going to scare me away."

"I just want to make sure you know what you're getting yourself into. I can't promise you'll make it, but if you do, you won't come out of this the same person." A heaviness hung on the recruiter's words, but Tomi was still undaunted.

"Sign me up," she demanded.

The recruiter stared her down for a moment before letting a smile break through. "I like you, Ryan. You're gonna go places."

After completing the electronic documents and signing her full name a couple dozen times, Tomi was told to report back the next day to be sworn in.

When she did, she was taken into a large room with a podium at the front. There were several other recruits in the room, all from different branches. A Federation officer stood behind the podium and instructed everyone to face him, stand at attention, raise their right hands, and repeat after him.

Tomi did as instructed with seriousness and excitement. "I, Tomi Ryan, do solemnly swear that I will support and defend the Charter of the Terran Federation against all enemies, foreign and domestic; that I will bear true faith and allegiance to the same; and that I will obey the orders of the President of the Terran Federation and the orders of the officers appointed over me, according to regulations and the Federation Code of Military Justice."

When the room fell silent from the oath, the officer said, "Congratulations! Let me be the first to welcome all of you to the Terran Federation Armed Forces."

4

IMPROVISE, ADAPT, OVERCOME

Tomi planned to go visit her family and let them know she had passed, but first, she checked in with the recruiter one last time to ask him for any advice.

He simply smiled and said three words: "Improvise, adapt, overcome."

"Really? That's it? It sounds like something out of a movie or something," she said with a puzzled look.

"Ryan, out on the wild frontier, you will never know what's going to happen next, so expect anything. I could spend all day telling stories about the things I've seen and so could any other ranger. Even when you think things are boring, remind yourself not to become complacent. Adversity loves to follow complacency wherever it goes. You're a ranger now, Ryan. You've got this."

Many had chosen to ride one of the maglev cars to the recruiting station, but Tomi had opted to drive herself. One of her more impulsive decisions, she had recently bought a motorcycle. Since she couldn't afford a hoverbike, she had settled for a hubless model with a rotary engine. Fortunately for her, this bike's previous owner was moving out of town and couldn't take it with him, so he was willing to make her a deal.

The motor was only one liter, but it could still put out 175 horsepower. Olin referred to it as a "crotch rocket," and it was. It even had a custom paint job that Tomi actually liked, and it scored her some extra looks on the street.

As she reached her bike, she noticed several recruits, including an acquaintance from school, talking to a recruiter for the Space Patrol nearby.

Noticing Tomi, Amii called out, "Hey, Tomi!" She closed the gap to Tomi's bike. "Did you get into the rangers like you wanted?"

"Yep!" Tomi nodded.

Overhearing this, the patrol recruiter felt the need to comment. "Ranger, huh? Those are some loco bastards you'll be hanging out with." Tomi felt insulted, but before she could respond, he continued, "The rest of you pay attention because you'll be seeing her again someday. The patrol and the rangers may be polar opposites, but they're just different sides of the same badge. In the end, both want justice."

He stepped closer and spoke the last part just to Tomi. "You never heard me admit this, but the patrol and rangers do actually respect each other. Both our jobs are tough, dangerous, and most of all, thankless. It takes a certain mental fortitude to survive. Personally, I would rather stay on a nice clean ship than go dirtside, but that's my opinion."

Tomi thanked the recruiter for the perspective and then put her helmet on. As she started the motor, she noticed people out on the sidewalk on both sides of the street protesting. One group was carrying signs cheering on the Federation and protesting the loss of jobs, while the other group denounced war and demanded that nature be protected. Tomi recalled receiving her share of political rhetoric while in public school and college. At best, they were all vague or ambiguous, and at worst, they proposed unworkable ideas. Tomi wondered if she would ever find the answers.

The first misnomer of ranger school was that it's not a school, singular. It's actually a series of schools known in the military as the "pipeline." Thus, ranger school was officially called the Federation Ranger Training Pipeline. Regardless of what anyone called it, there was plenty of training that took place in different environments and on different planets.

The basic course lasted two months and consisted of textbook learning: law enforcement procedures, report writing, physical training, and other basic skills. While Tomi wasn't struggling physically yet, she still had to put in many hours of work every day to keep her scores up. She was eager to get out into the field and put this theory into practice.

With each school or training course, the current lessons built upon the previous. Once a skill was mastered, it had to be integrated with other skills, and it was during this point that their physical aptitude was put to the test and built up. They were made to perform calisthenics in full gear while being sprayed with a water hose or knee deep in mud or both. Then the recruits started training with the rangers' tools of choice: the EMG-8 4mm repulsor battle rifle, the PA-9A2 E3 heavy blaster pistol, and the K2 bush knife.

They favored the EMG-8 for simple reasons: it was rugged, reliable, versatile, accurate, and deadly. It had a muzzle velocity of 12,000 feet per second and muzzle energy of 28,000 joules, giving its 4mm projectiles tremendous reach and penetration. It could function perfectly well in the vacuum of space, the densest atmosphere, and even underwater.

It could also accept numerous attachments that allowed it to function as an assault rifle, sniper rifle, or even a light machine gun.

The rangers often made use of a HUD tactical LED scope linked to a multispectral smart scope, allowing both quick close-quarter sighting as well as distance shots. The smart scope used a ballistic computer coupled with gyroscopes, gravity sensors, and accelerometers to calculate long distance shots in any environment. A gyrostabilizer worked in concert with the smart scope to enable accurate shots regardless of the stability of the shooter stance or position, making it the most reliable weapon in any circumstance.

The PA-9A2 E3 was originally adopted to show solidarity with the Federation Space Patrol, though it turned out the spit-and-polish patrol could show some good judgment. The omniblaster, as it was more commonly known, was even more versatile than the repulsor rifle. Its power output could be adjusted from an electro-laser stun setting of 300 millijoules up to blaster settings maxing out at 10 kilojoules, capable of blasting a hole through ceramic armor. Beam width could be adjusted from a tight, armor-piercing beam to a cone as wide as a shotgun blast. The weapon used multispectral laser sights as its primary sighting system—infrared, visible, and ultraviolet—in addition to a holographic sight.

The K2 bush knife, on the other hand, looked like window dressing. Seemingly only there for looks, the instructor warned the rookie rangers to not be so dismissive about their most low-tech piece of equipment. Approximately eleven inches long with a six-inch blade, the whole thing was made of a single piece of boron carbide aluminum ceramic alloy, honed to a razor-sharp edge on one side and serrated on the other.

The knife's ability to take an edge and keep it was such that it could effortlessly slice through a hanging rope even after being torture tested on wood, bone, plastic, and even concrete. An ergonomic grip covered the tang with two holes in the cross guard and one in the pommel. It came with a Kydex plastic sheath that could be mounted in many different configurations.

The best and most important factor was that the bush knife didn't require power, fuel, or ammo to function; it didn't even need to be sharpened. When all else had failed, the ranger's bush knife would be his or her best friend. A good sharp knife could feed you, clothe you, and keep you warm and dry.

The guns were straightforward: take it apart, put it back together, make sure it worked, and then shoot the target you're supposed to hit. Though it proved to be easier said than done for some—a few recruits struggled with proper assembly or even hitting the target. One guy took five attempts to qualify using the pistol; he wound up doing many push-ups before the day was over. He was lucky to have finally passed though. Recruits who failed this portion washed out of the course completely.

After one such failed recruit left, one of the instructors told the rest of them, "Pay attention, boys and girls. Unlike what you see in the movies, failure is always an option. The only difference in failing here or in the wilderness is that here, you go home and cry. Out there on the wild frontier, you die."

While the recruits didn't learn how to use a knife in combat until survival training, they still had to carry their bush knife with them wherever they went. Failure to remember it resulted in push-ups for everyone in that person's squad. Tomi had found that out the hard way when she went to breakfast one morning without her bush knife. After the first week of being issued, everyone had learned to fasten it to the front of their uniforms so the instructors could see it clearly.

The next phase of class took them into extreme environment training, each course lasting one to two months. Tomi found the water operations course fun since she liked to swim. Plus, she felt pretty powerful when her male classmates admired her in her swimsuit even though she only wore a standard-issue one-piece in solid black.

While in the pool, students learned how to use such equipment as scuba, a rebreather, and an artificial gill. Being water-adapted, a triton parahuman named Zimmerman didn't need any equipment, which Tomi thought was pretty awesome. Still, he had to participate in order to work as a team with other rangers.

Before they went into open water, the candidates were fitted with their exploration suits: a complex layering of nanoweave compound fiber mesh, a thermocouple layer, and a nanoscale vent layer that would let air circulate while keeping water and contaminates out. The exosuit was the single most advanced and important piece of equipment they would ever be issued. The instructors told them to make sure their suits fit perfectly since it would be protecting them underwater, in space, and many other hostile environments.

When they finally did go out into open water, the students learned to use various surface and submersible vehicles, as well as how to navigate underwater. Tomi even finally found a use for her bush knife when her dive buddy got himself tangled in an abandoned fishing net and she had to cut him loose. While learning marine orienteering, the students discovered how to use underwater sensors like a handheld sonar and magnetic and gravitic sensors to help them see more clearly. Even Zimmerman was impressed with all of this technology, since seeing through murky water was practically impossible with the naked eye.

Next, they went up to a space station to learn shipboard operations, emergency procedures, and how to move in free fall. After a few days, the class was finally sent to their first training outside of Earth. Tomi was ecstatic to finally see her home planet from lightyears away. The only downside was they were sent to Olympus's binary twin: the planet Hades.

Hades, in so many ways, was the polar opposite of Olympus. Where Olympus was said to have a beautiful and pleasant environment, Hades lived up to its name. Even from orbit, it looked like hell itself. Constant volcanism meant rivers of lava flowing across the planet's surface. In other places, boiling water geysers bubbled up from below. The end result were rivers and lakes full of microbes of every color. The terrain was so impressive, people who had visited referred to it as "beautiful desolation."

Despite the harsh environment, or perhaps because of it, Hades was the perfect planet for the training they were due for. While there, the students learned different methods of survival: locating and avoiding hot spots and gas clouds, how to test and purify mineral-laden water, and how to navigate in terrain rich in large concentrations of magnetic-compass-disrupting metal.

The last of their basic training involved parachuting. The trainees spent two months learning basic static-line jumps, and then transitioned to repulsor wing rigs similar to the models used in the SEAL triathlon. When they mastered high-altitude jumping, they finished off with an orbital insertion. Each trainee was launched from a training ship with a personal defense screen for reentry. Upon completing reentry, the shield was powered down and the student completed an otherwise normal free-fall parachute jump.

Taking notice of how nervous the trainees were the entire time during jump training, the jumpmaster constantly emphasized, "Remember your motion sickness bags."

This part of the training came easily for Tomi. While her classmates were green, pale, or visibly shaking, she was calm and even tried chatting with other trainees before each jump. During one of these jumps, the jumpmaster noticed this and walked up to her.

"What are you, an adrenaline junky?" he asked. "Aren't you even a little bit scared?" When Tomi told the jumpmaster about her triathlon, he perked up and exclaimed, "You were in a SEAL triathlon too?"

He started to tell her about his triathlon days when a trainee behind him puked up his breakfast. The jumpmaster heaved a heavy sigh and told Tomi, "Maybe I can tell you the story some other time."

He turned to the trainee who was now wiping his mouth with his sleeve and scolded, "How many times do I have to say it, scrub? Use your barf bag! Clean that up and try again."

As the jumpmaster walked away, the trainee sitting next to Tomi started searching through his pockets. She was grateful when he found his bag just in time.

When the instructors finally congratulated the trainees upon graduation from basic training, they mentioned graduate school being the next step.

Tomi gaped and said out loud, "There's more?"

Advanced training for the rangers dealt with survival on the various environments they might have to deal with while enlisted. Whether desert or tundra, swamps or barren mountains, rangers had to know not only how to survive but also operate and actually accomplish their missions. This required exposure to various planets.

The whole class was transported to a temperate forest on Olympus to learn fieldcraft. Before they departed, the trainees were issued their last piece of important equipment: the chameleon cloak. Like a hooded robe, it completely covered the wearer. The cloak had a layer of nanoscale sensors that saw the surrounding scenery. The nanoscale color cells would imitate that scenery, resulting in camouflage so accurate that the ranger wearing it literally became invisible. It worked so well that the only time a hiding ranger was located during practice was if he either made noise or somebody stepped on him.

Along with all of the hiding in the woods and sneaking around, everyone practiced building lean-tos, setting snares, chopping firewood, and became well acquainted with their bush knife. Tomi even found out what the holes in the knife's hilt were for—to tie the knife to a stick so it could be used as a spear for hunting, fishing, and defense.

When reconnaissance and target acquisition were taught, Tomi became a little suspicious and asked, "Are we going to war or something?"

"Improvise, adapt, overcome," was the instructor's vague answer. Then he started talking about his own experiences with combat.

What he meant was while rangers were mostly concerned with rescue and law enforcement, they did also sometimes go to war. With all of their skills in stealth, surveillance, and survival, it turned out that rangers made great pathfinders for the marines and excellent forward observers for the navy. In small and highly skilled teams, rangers could also penetrate deep into enemy territory and rescue downed pilots without ever being seen.

At long last, Tomi finished graduate school and she and her classmates were about to receive their final scores. Those with enough points would graduate, while those without would be recycled and sent back to redo the portions they failed. It was not easy to tell how they were doing. Many exercises were pass/fail with no room for error, and the instructors kept student evaluations confidential until the very end. This was intended to prevent any cheating and was done to the point that they even kept failing cadets around to throw off the others.

In her moment of anticipation, Tomi wished she had one of those sick bags handy. However, when she received her scores, she was hugely relieved to discover that not only did she pass but she actually did quite well. Tomi released all her nerves in a long sigh. After nearly a year, she had successfully completed all her training and could now be assigned to her first real mission, just as soon as the graduation ceremony was over.

The ceremony was dominated by the usual pomp and circumstance. Tomi hadn't been this excited since graduating from high school. It was great to see her family—her mom and dad showed up, but Teddy was now in college and couldn't make it. Still, it had been such a long time since she'd seen her parents and it was nice to spend some time with them, have a meal together, and see the local sites. Tomi decided she would just have to give her brother a ration of crap later.

After the break concluded and all the family members had bid their graduates farewell, the rookie rangers learned they would be receiving their first assignments immediately. Tomi eagerly waited for her turn as other graduates were informed of their first command to report to. She was hoping for some far-off exotic planet with lots of action and excitement, but when she and Zimmerman were called into the office together, she was left feeling disappointed.

"You'll be reporting to a ranger detachment station on an asteroid mining colony," the officer informed them.

Noticing that Zimmerman didn't seem too thrilled either, Tomi said as they left the office, "Oh great, we've been sent to patrol a rock floating in space."

He nodded. "It seems like command is just plugging holes, but what can we do?"

On the day of departure, the graduates boarded their respective transports. Tomi looked at her itinerary and noticed it wasn't a straight shot. She and Zimmerman would have some extra connecting flights. Looked like she wasn't going to get much sleep on the way there.

When they finally arrived at the colony's space dock, they noticed that the Chateau Rouge mining colony was so small that it didn't even have a proper spaceport. Rather, it simply had a space dock with four berths for ships. Looking around as she stepped through the passage tube, Tomi was not impressed; the facility had clearly seen better days. Tomi had also been unimpressed with the passenger liner when the idiots lost her luggage.

After collecting Zimmerman's bags, they went over to the dock's assistance kiosk and activated it. When it dinged in response, Tomi took the lead.

"Hello, Ranger Ryan and Ranger Zimmerman reporting in. Can you direct us to the ranger's office?" Tomi asked.

The colony's central computer answered, "The ranger colonial office has been notified of your arrival. Directions to the office have been sent to your personal wrist comps."

They made their way to the office in silence, both still fuming over their lackluster assignment. After walking in and introducing themselves, Tomi noticed the ranger sitting behind the duty desk appeared to be mere few years older than she.

"What? They're still sending noobs here? Unbelievable!" he shouted.

"What do you mean by that?" Zimmerman asked.

"This facility has been slated for decommissioning. Management has already started the process of shipping all of the mining equipment out of here. No worries, though. I'll let the LT know that you're here. You'll likely be reassigned."

"Well, maybe we'll get a more exciting assignment this time," Zimmerman offered when they were directed to their temporary private quarters.

About a half hour later, a knock came at Tomi's door.

"Ranger Ryan, your reassignment has been delayed," the commanding officer informed her. "Looks like you can settle in for a few days."

"Settle in? Has there been news of my luggage?" Tomi thought he was implying that it had been found, but no such luck.

She'd barely shut the door and walked back to the bed when another knock came at her door. Expecting to see the lieutenant again, she was instead met by Zimmerman's smiling mug.

"Greetings, Ryan. Did you get your reassignment?"

"Not yet. Did you?"

"Yeah, I'll be helping escort a survey mission on some frontier world."

"Sounds more exciting than this rock. I'm happy for you, Zimmerman. Only thing I've heard so far is that I might be stuck here for a few days," Tomi said rolling her eyes.

"That sucks. At least you can relax for a few days. I won't even have time to unpack my stuff. They have me shipping out tomorrow morning."

Tomi was frustrated at the difference in their first experience as a ranger. "I can't even unpack!" she yelled in frustration. "My luggage still hasn't been found."

As promised, Zimmerman shipped out early the next morning. So early in fact, he was gone before Tomi even woke up. Without him around, she didn't have anyone to talk to and the next few days became as monotonous as they were routine: wake up, shower, eat, wait around in the ranger office, eat, work out, shower again, eat again, go to the common area to watch videos, and go to bed just to start it all over again the next day.

On the third morning, Tomi finally got what she was waiting for when she was ordered to report to the lieutenant to receive her new assignment. She eagerly showered and dressed and then headed to his office. In front of his door, Tomi activated the chime and entered when she heard him answer, "Come in."

Inside the office, Lieutenant Vo sat behind his desk. Tomi dutifully sounded off.

"Ranger Tomi Ryan reporting—"

"Okay, okay, kid. That's enough of that. I know who you are. Listen, we finally got your orders. You are to rendezvous with the *Bass Reeves*."

Another dumb assignment? Tomi angrily blurted out, "What will I be doing on this ship?"

Looking her straight in the eye and daring her to argue further, Lieutenant Vo said, "Whatever they want you to do."

Tomi knew better than to open her mouth again, but she couldn't hide her disappointed. She was going to be stuck inside a metal box, exactly the reason she'd opted not to join the navy. And maybe worse, she still had no idea exactly what she would be doing.

Reading the expression on her face, Lieutenant Vo asked, "What's the matter, Ryan? Rangers are supposed to like jumping into the unknown."

Looking at her itinerary later, jumping into the unknown was a good description. She had never heard of half of the spaceports she would be traveling through. Her final destination where she was to meet up with the *Bass Reeves* was listed as New Aarhus—where the hell was that?

Tomi could still hear the rangers' unofficial motto ringing in her ears: "Improvise, adapt, overcome."

5

VIRGIN TERRITORY

Bouncing from port to port was just as fun to Tomi as it was the first time—not at all. But at least this time, she'd received her luggage at the end of each flight. Since she had no idea what New Aarhus was like, she wore her civilian clothes for the trip.

When at last she arrived, it was only to find out that she was a day late—the *Bass Reeves* had already left port without her.

"Arrrggh!"

She had always laughed at the comedies where people had everything go wrong while traveling. Now that she was experiencing it for herself, she wasn't laughing any longer. She located a patrol officer and asked him to check into the situation.

"There's a ranger from the *Bass Reeves* who is still on station. I'll direct you to meet up with him, since he'll likely be heading to the *BR* himself at some point."

The whole experience was exasperating, but at least she was finally getting somewhere. She followed the directions that the officer sent to her wrist comp and wound up at the one of the spaceport's nicer hotels. Walking into the lobby, she handed her luggage over to an AI porter and then pinged her contact's communicator.

"Over here," a man in his midtwenties called to her as he stood from his barstool.

Tomi got a good look at him: six feet tall, ruggedly handsome, brown hair and eyes, and even a mustache. Tomi approved—at least he looked like a man's man. She approached and they shook hands.

"Corporal Avery Healy. Join me for dinner, Ranger...?"

"Ryan. Tomi Ryan," she answered his implied question.

"Ranger Ryan," he repeated her name to commit it to memory.

"What are you still doing in New Aarhus?" she asked. "Why didn't you board the *Bass Reeves*?"

"Someone had to stay behind and make sure the rookie knew where to go." Tomi tried to ignore the suggestion that she was incapable of finding her own way. Healy continued, "Let me give you the rundown on what to expect."

Hardly able to wait, Tomi was wiggling in her seat. This detail was not lost on Healy.

"You're going to love it," he said, smiling at her. "None of that sitting in some office on a remote mining colony." Healy must have heard where she came from. "Instead, we'll be enjoying the great outdoors with a bunch of eggheads."

Tomi raised her eyebrows. "You mean—"

"That's right," he nodded. "We'll be escorting a Survey Service mission. Don't be too upset though. At least we'll be on a barely explored planet. Terra incognita—even I don't know what to expect. So, eat up, buttercup. It's going to be a busy day tomorrow."

Tomi noticed that Healy seemed to think she should be dreading joining a survey mission. She had heard that the rangers and the Survey Service didn't always get along, but she didn't see what the big deal was. At least she'd be going somewhere new and exciting, somewhere other than a floating rock in the middle of nowhere.

Hitching a ride on a cargo shuttle the next morning, the two rangers traveled out to rendezvous with the *Bass Reeves*. Jensen, the shuttle captain, informed them that it would be several hours before they would meet up with their ship. He invited Tomi and Healy to have some lunch: sandwiches paired with very strong coffee. Tomi took a sip and cringed at the bitterness.

"So, how's the coffee taste?" Jensen asked.

"Strong," she answered honestly. Tomi wasn't used to such heavily caffeinated beverages, but even Healy seemed to agree.

Laughing, he added, "This stuff will definitely ignite your reactor!"

Jensen nodded in approval. "Just the way it should be."

Several hours later when the shuttle synchronized course and velocity with the *Bass Reeves*, Jensen called over the comm to the ship, "What do you want to transfer first, the trash or the passengers?"

A voice aboard the *BR* answered unceremoniously, "Trash."

Tomi felt slighted. Was the trash more important than people? She was eager to get started and also to locate her private quarters. No matter, once the cargo containers were transferred, it was finally their turn.

Jensen turned to them and said, "Good. Now suit up. We'll transfer you two next."

Tomi thought at first that the guy had to be kidding, but looking at his face, she could tell he wasn't. Guess the transfer meant floating in space between the two ships. She suddenly felt a little nervous, but she noticed Healy already getting his exploration suit on. Not wanting to fall behind or appear incompetent, she unpacked her own exosuit and started to put it on.

Aboard the *Bass Reeves* at long last, Tomi was just settling into her stateroom when it was announced that there would be a meeting in the common room for the rangers. When she arrived, Tomi saw Healy, two rangers she hadn't met yet, and the familiar face of a water-breathing parahuman.

"Zimmerman!" she exclaimed. "You're here?" Tomi was confused why she hadn't received her reassignment when he had if they were being sent to the same mission. Was she being tested?

"Ryan? When did they assign you to the *Bass Reeves*?" Zimmerman seemed just as confused.

"Like three days after you left me alone on that boring rock!"

Healy interrupted them. "You two lovebirds will have to catch up later." He motioned toward the captain who was glaring at them. "It's time for the mission briefing, and Captain Everly doesn't like to be kept waiting."

It was just as Healy had said: the planet Abraxis was so far mostly unexplored. Only one of its three continents had been thoroughly surveyed, one partially explored, and the third had only orbital observations and scans conducted. At the urging of a major university, the Survey Service decided to mount a surface expedition and the lucky rangers aboard the *Bass Reeves* were to be their escorts.

The ranger she didn't know blurted out, "I knew it! We're babysitting again."

"Watch it, Watry. I'm not thrilled with this either, but you know as well as I do that it's a part of the job." After his warning to Watry, Captain Everly continued, "Lieutenant Elba will be the lead ranger for your team while dirtside. He should be there by the time we arrive and I will come pick you up once the expedition ends."

"You're not coming, Captain Everly?" Zimmerman asked.

Everly shook his head. "The captain of any Federation ship is required by regulations to stay aboard the ship at all times. In case anything goes down, I can get the *BR* wherever it's needed in a hurry. But I assure you Elba is a top-notch ranger."

Healy nodded. "Watry and I have worked with him before," he told Tomi and Zimmerman. "He's a no-nonsense guy, but he is an excellent ranger."

Everly directed his final instructions to the two novice rangers. "Even though we have one of the fastest Alcubierre warp drives, it will take almost a week to get there, so spend your time studying the info packet HQ sent along with your orders. The more you know, the less you'll be surprised."

Without realizing she was speaking audibly, Tomi repeated a saying she'd once read, "Fools find life full of surprises; among them, death."

Healy laughed and said, "Be sure to remember that when we get dirtside."

It's quite an experience setting foot on an alien world. Tomi thought about how the Federation Rangers had an advantage on the scientists in this respect. Since rangers undergo their survival training on planets other than Earth, it was not quite as overwhelming for them as it was for the first-time scientists on the team. But like other planets, Abraxis had significant differences that any first-time visitor would notice, seasoned or otherwise.

First and foremost were the dual suns—a glaringly bright F-class and a dim red dwarf. But unlike most binary systems, Abraxis sat right between the two stars, directly at the center of gravity. In this star system, the suns circled the planet rather than the other way around, but at distances such that the planet was still habitable. While Abraxis did rotate on its axis, both hemispheres were awash in light from at least one of the stars at any given time, meaning there was never any true nightfall.

Stepping off the dropship's cargo ramp, Tomi was taken aback by how dim it was. Everything had a reddish cast to it. She looked up and noticed the sky was a pale-yellow color, but her thoughts were interrupted as Everly and the *Bass Reeves* departed. She watched the ship lift off and disappear into the stars as a man came toward them.

"Healy! Watry! How the hell have you two been?"

"Lieutenant Elba!" Healy acknowledged with a smile. Motioning toward Tomi and Zim, he said, "These our are new recruits, Ryan and Zimmerman. Go easy on them."

There was a pause and then Healy, Watry, and Elba all started laughing.

Another man approached in that moment and introduced himself. "I'm Ota, the expedition leader. I do not intend to interrupt your reunion, but we need to get moving on our camp setup. Place your gear over there. We need to unload the heavy robots and the habitat parts."

The thrill of the unknown called to Tomi as she began helping with the mundane task of unloading the scientists' cargo. Along with the two construction robots, otherwise known as heavies, four flitters for the rangers also came down the ramp. More than just hoverbikes, the flitters were more akin to a VTOL—each one capable of flying to altitudes of over 10,000 feet thanks to a fusion turbine and repulsor impellers in its wings. Tomi couldn't wait to hop on one of those bad boys.

Since Tomi and Zimmerman were the rookies, they were tasked with pulling their vehicles over to the ranger's assembly area. The flitters had wheeled landing gear, so they rolled off the cargo pallets and across the firm soil of the plateau with ease. Healy instructed them to line them up nicely since there were more vehicles on their way down.

With the help of the heavies and prefab components, assembly of the habitat went fast. In no time flat, the team had sleeping quarters, a galley, a lounge, and even a shower. As other modules arrived, labs, workshops, a med center, and offices also came online, allowing the expedition to get down to business.

Ota announced over everyone's comm devices that there would be a mandatory meeting for everyone taking place in the lounge in a few minutes.

Tomi went over to get her gear and noticed David, the red dwarf, setting on the horizon. Missing the detail of the dual suns in the mission briefing, she commented how they'd finished setting up camp just in time, implying that night was about to fall. Without a word, Watry laughed and pointed in the opposite direction of the dwarf's sunset. Tomi turned and saw the beginning of a glaringly bright sunrise—the big F-class star known as Goliath.

Having witnessed the exchange, Healy put a hand on her shoulder. "It's important to read your mission briefing, rookie."

Tomi tried to hide her blushing cheeks as Healy motioned to his polarized goggles. Putting them on, he signaled that she should do the same just as the star's light intensified. Tomi promised herself she'd never neglect to read another mission briefing going forward. She wasn't going to be caught sounding stupid ever again.

Ota began the meeting with a rundown of rules, regulations, schedules, and whatnot before turning the floor over to Lieutenant Elba. On his signal, Tomi and the other rangers fell in line behind him.

"For those who do not know me, my name is Lieutenant Eduardo Elba, and standing behind me are rangers Watry, Healy, Zimmerman, and Ryan. So to not take up too much of your precious time, I'll get straight to the point. Dr. Ota may be in charge of this expedition, but when it comes down to safety and security, my word is law." Lieutenant Elba paused for dramatic effect, almost as if daring anyone to say otherwise.

Satisfied with the silence, he continued as he counted his own rules off on his fingers, "First, since we are all adults, your safety will be up to each one of you. That being said, if I or any of my rangers see an unsafe situation, we have full authority to call any of you on it, and you had better listen.

"Second, even though we are out on the wild frontier, this is still a Federation expedition on a Federation planet, so Federation law will be in full effect. That means all rangers have full legal enforcement powers and have the authority to place anyone under arrest for breaking Federation law.

"Which brings me to my final point: if an evacuation alert goes out, I expect everyone to muster immediately at the evacuation point. No exceptions, no excuses. There will be a drill—unannounced, of course. Show up like you're supposed to, and things will go easy. Test me, and we will keep drilling until we get it right. Those who can't get with the program will be kicked off the expedition, period." He paused again, very briefly, and then concluded his speech. "Have a pleasant stay here on Abraxis. That is all."

Tomi had to admit, Elba was exactly who she aspired to one day become. He simply oozed authority and confidence, and it seemed so effortless. She would love to witness one of the scientists falling out of line just to see what became of them under Elba's law. Tomi held back her chuckle when she noticed some of the younger science team members' eyes bugging out. She saw a few others who rolled theirs instead.

Healy leaned over and said, "Welcome to Babysitting 101, rookie. We'll need to keep an eye on the ones showing an attitude."

6

GOVERNANCE

The evacuation drill went off without a hitch. The more experienced science team members knew that if it did, the rangers wouldn't keep the researchers on such a short leash and they had warned the newer scientists to obey now for more freedom later. After that, everything went just as expected, with the survey scientists going about their research projects.

Tomi made the mistake of almost becoming complacent as the end of the first month approached. The only hiccup was when one scientist was discovered to be making illegal drugs in his lab. When they were stolen, he was dumb enough to report it. *So much for having a PhD,* Tomi thought. Other than that, nothing of note happened until the second month came to a close.

It was then that one of the geologists decided it would be a good idea to climb down into a ravine to collect a sample. After getting his prized sample, he discovered that climbing out was going to be a bigger effort than he'd anticipated, especially one-handed. It would have been possible if he had climbing gear with him. Because he didn't have that forethought, he quickly found himself stuck in the ravine, refusing to let go of his precious sample.

With the barometric pressure dropping, his partner had no choice but to put in an emergency call to the rangers.

"Trapped on the side of a cliff?" Healy was in disbelief at the stupidity of these guys.

"Yes, sir. We need assistance."

Healy rolled his eyes. "What a dumbass!" He turned toward Tomi and said, "Ryan, you're with me. Be sure your climbing gear is working because I have a feeling this isn't going to be easy."

Tomi was already ahead of him; she had not only checked her climbing gear but also her survival kit and medical bag. Both seemed prudent since the weather was getting worse and she had no idea what condition the victim was in or how long this rescue mission would take.

Mounting their flitters, Tomi and Healy took off, traveling toward the coordinates given by the distress beacon. Healy motioned toward the approaching storm front as they rode. The flitters were fast, but at the rate the storm was moving, they would be lucky to complete the rescue and return to base before it hit. Flying in such a storm would be suicide, but truthfully, neither Tomi nor Healy looked forward to weathering it out in the field either.

Nearing the coordinates, Tomi spotted the aerocar that the two academics had used to fly to their location. Landing next to the bulbous aircraft with its wings folded, the rangers were greeted by a panicked scientist. Mathers, a paleogeologist, ran out from behind the airship waving his arms as though they might not see him.

"Hurry!" he shouted. "I don't know how much longer Albertson can hold on."

"Is he injured?" Tomi asked.

"How should I know? I'm not stupid enough to climb down there."

"At least one of you isn't," Healy said, annoyed.

Walking over to the edge of the cliff, Tomi and Healy looked down into the ravine and noticed why Albertson was having such a difficult time holding on.

"Like I said, dumbass," Healy said to Tomi, motioning down at him.

Gearing up with their gecko gloves and grapple lines, Tomi and Healy anchored their safety lines at the top of the cliff. They then rappelled down to Albertson. Tomi secured Healy while Healy attempted to tie ropes around Albertson.

"Albertson, you idiot. If you would just let go of that sample bag it would be so much easier to rig a safety harness to you," Healy lamented.

"No! These samples are the discovery of a lifetime. You rangers just don't understand." Albertson rolled his eyes, but it wasn't his smartest idea. Though, it wasn't as dumb as his follow-up demand. "I've got to get this back to the lab. Hurry up!"

This was a foolish response and attitude, Tomi noted. If Elba found out about this, he'd send Albertson packing for sure. That is, if Albertson survived Healy's wrath first.

With the safety ropes in place, Tomi and Healy climbed back to the top of the cliff and threaded the rope through a come-along. Not very high tech, but it did the job. Tomi was quickly learning that being the rookie meant getting all the lowly jobs. This time, she was tasked with turning the crank to lift Albertson back to the surface. From his screaming and yelling along with the plethora of profanities, she secretly took pleasure in knowing Albertson was being dragged up the cliff face. It was his own fault for refusing to use his hands or feet. Healy was right: these guys were dumbasses.

Albertson finally crested the top of the cliff. *About time*, Tomi thought. Her arms were getting tired. Healy went over and pulled Albertson up to his feet, still clutching his samples. Tomi bet Healy wished he could knock them right out of Albertson's hand and down into the ravine. Probably wasn't worth having to deal with Ota though, but Healy still got to yell at him a bit.

"You can let go of your fucking rocks, jackass. You're on flat ground," Healy chided.

Albertson huffed, but didn't say anything, simply heading straight to his aerocar. As he walked past his partner, Mathers asked if he was going to thank the rangers for saving his ass. Albertson didn't like that.

"Everyone, just shut up and get me back to base!" he yelled.

Healy wasn't interested in Albertson's pissy mood. Instead, he was focused on the distance. Slightly more aware than his fellow geologist, Mathers took notice.

"What are you looking at?" he asked.

"The mountains."

"What mountains?"

"Exactly," Healy said. Turning to Tomi, he added, "Get the survival shelters out. That storm," he jerked his thumb toward the approaching storm front, "will be here in less than ten minutes."

Tomi immediately unpacked the shelters. Mathers surprised them both by offering to assist, but Albertson, having put his samples in the airship, had come back out only to complain.

"Why aren't we leaving?" Seeing that everyone had set up the geodesic shelter domes and was now anchoring them into the ground, Albertson started pleading. "No, no, no! Forget about the fucking shelters! Let's just get back to base where we already have better shelters and food and—"

Healy chastised, "There is no way we're flying in that storm. It'd be a suicide mission. If you know what's good for you, you will join us and get your shelter up." When Albertson just gaped at him without moving, Healy yelled, "Now, you fucking moron!"

Albertson's ears turned red. "How dare you tell me what to do, you jackbooted thug! You are merely a ranger—an order follower with no original thoughts of your own. While I...I am on the verge of a scientific breakthrough."

After puffing out his chest for a brief second, Albertson suddenly pulled his K_2 bush knife, just like the one the rangers were issued, and rushed over to Mathers's shelter. Before anyone could react, he slashed it open from one side to the other. He proceeded to the next one and began slashing Tomi's shelter open as well.

Albertson was almost to Healy's shelter when Tomi gave him a great shove like an offensive lineman, knocking him to the ground. She yelled, "Albertson, what the hell are you doing?"

Albertson regained his footing and started waving his knife around frantically, yelling, "Get back! You assholes will not keep me from making the discovery of the century!"

Keeping her distance, Tomi pulled her omniblaster, set it to stun, flipped off the safety, aimed, and fired. At a high fraction of the speed of light, the blaster bolt hit Albertson square in the solar plexus. All of his muscles locked up as his nervous system was swamped with electrical current. The instant Tomi released her trigger, Albertson's body relaxed, dropping his knife as he fell in a heap right where he had been standing.

In an effort to distance himself from the other scientist, Mathers said, "Damn, Albertson went loco on us!"

Healy went over to Albertson and checked his vitals. "Good work, rookie. He's still alive." He signaled for Tomi to holster her sidearm.

"What are we going to do? We only have two shelters and four people." Tomi pointed out.

"What's the ranger motto, rookie?"

"Improvise, adapt, overcome," Tomi dutifully repeated to Healy's approval.

"Improvise? How do we do that, Healy? The math just doesn't check out," Mathers questioned.

"Not math. Geometry. You and Ryan can share a shelter, and I'm the lucky winner who gets to share with your buddy. It will be a tight fit, but it should do the trick. Let's make sure we've taken anything Albertson could use as a weapon and tie him up."

Mathers commented under his breath about how crazy Healy

was, and Tomi had to restrain a snicker. She used the opportunity to poke a little fun at the saner of the two scientists.

"No funny business, dude, or I'll stun you too." Tomi wiggled her omniblaster in its holster, but Mathers didn't laugh.

They barely squeezed into the two remaining shelters just before the storm hit. There were high winds and rain that then turned into high winds and sleet as the temperature dropped below freezing. Tomi checked to make sure her exploration suit's power cells were fully charged. She was beginning to love this suit.

As crisis situations often go, the storm was like many—frightening as hell going through it, but once it passed, one wondered what the big deal was. That was, until the next crisis came along.

Wriggling out from the cramped shelter, Tomi stood up and stretched. It felt good to get out under clear sky and in fresh air. By now, Goliath had started to set as David was rising. Mathers crawled out behind her and they heard the sounds of a struggle coming from the other shelter.

"Get your ass out here!" they heard Healy yell. "Consider yourself under arrest."

A moment later, Healy dragged Albertson out of the shelter who was throwing a full-blown toddler tantrum. *Ah, babysitting,* Tomi realized. She had never seen such a highly educated adult act the way Albertson was. Everyone had their moments, but this guy just wasn't cooling off. She looked over at Mathers, who rolled his eyes in embarrassment. It was clear he did not want to be grouped with Albertson in the rangers' eyes.

"Do you know who I am?" Albertson shouted at Healy. "I'll have your badge! Your career is over, motherfucker."

Now Healy's patience had run out. Wrestling Albertson to the ground, he checked the ties on his hands and feet, tossed the scientist over his shoulder, and lashed him to the flitter's rear seat like a bagged kill.

"Grab your gear. We're heading back to base," Healy told the others.

Facing a raging storm was scary, but facing Ranger Elba's wrath was terrifying. Tomi was grateful she wasn't the target of his anger. All of the rangers, along with Ota, were present to witness the proceedings. Even though Tomi and Healy were not the subjects of the inquiry, it was still not fun to experience the man's righteous anger. After hearing Healy's report followed by testimony from both Tomi and Mathers, Elba didn't hold anything back.

"Of all of the stupid, suckhead stunts I have heard of, this takes the shittiest cake of all! It's bad enough you endangered your own life, but you then proceeded to sabotage survival gear intended for others. Never have I seen such a callous disregard for life, especially from someone with a PhD!"

Albertson tried to interrupt Elba. "The rangers had no right to interfere! I was—"

"Shut up, you filthy maggot!" Elba's rebuke was swift. "I can't imagine you have the gall to complain about your rights being violated, considering how many rights you disregarded."

Albertson tried to object once more, but Elba wasn't hearing it. "My decision is final. You're off the expedition. You will be spending the duration aboard the survey ship until your shuttle arrives."

Elba turned to his rangers. "Watry, Zimmerman, make sure this man is on the next flight off planet." Then, addressing everyone present, he finalized the so-called hearing. "There is nothing more to say."

Albertson tried to speak, but Watry cut him off. "Forget it, college boy. Lieutenant Elba's word is law here. Your ass is gone."

He and Zimmerman each grabbed one of Albertson's arms, his hands still tied behind his back, and they led the disgraced scientist outside to the survey ship.

Tomi laughed at Watry's insulting nickname for the scientist. She'd have to remember that one.

It wasn't long before the dropship arrived. Zimmerman carried a duffle bag full of Albertson's clothes. Elba didn't even let him leave the survey ship long enough to gather his samples—one of his colleagues would have to take care of that. While Tomi watched in relief as Watry shoved Albertson aboard his chariot, Dr. Ota walked up next to her.

"In case my...*ahem*...subordinate didn't already, I just wanted to say thank you for what you did out there in that ravine, Ranger Ryan. If you hadn't shown up when you did, both Albertson and Mathers would have certainly died in that storm."

Surprised, Tomi turned to the expedition leader. "You're welcome, but really, I was just doing my job."

Ota chuckled. "Good ole ranger modesty. I know you're just doing your duty, but even I agree there is no room for an obstinate ass like Albertson on an expedition. Those bush knives have a nanofiber edge; he could have easily maimed or killed someone or even harmed himself, for that matter. If anything, I'm glad all of you made it back in one piece. Being expedition leader means I am ultimately responsible for what happens to everyone, including you rangers."

Tomi looked at Ota, a college professor who had the thankless job of keeping an expedition composed of dozens of big egos working together like well-oiled machinery. She certainly did not envy him.

"Must be tough keeping dozens of personalities with conflicting ideas working as a team," she acknowledged.

Dr. Ota laughed. "I'm the one who insisted on mounting this expedition in the first place. When no one else would volunteer, I had to step up to lead it. Traveling here and getting the research done is my reward, even if I don't get to do much hands-on science myself. The end goal is that we gather some breakthrough findings to share with the world."

Though Tomi now understood why the rangers didn't like going on Survey Service expeditions, she did find herself gaining a new respect for Dr. Ota when she recognized his motivations as some of the very reasons she'd joined the Federation Rangers. Sometimes it was about being a part of something far greater than yourself.

7

FOUL HARVEST

On the far side of the red dwarf, David, a small ship dropped out of warp very close to the star's photosphere. Barely big enough to carry three men, the ship's small size coupled with the proximity to the star effectively made the ship undetectable. Nonetheless, one of the ship's passengers did not like being so close to something so volatile.

"Holy shit, Sutter! Could you have gotten us any closer?" complained Jericho, assistant to Jobe, the lead hunter on their illegal expedition.

"Hey, mud stomper, I don't tell you how to shoot animals, you don't tell me how to fly," Sutter shot back.

Jobe was getting irritated with the two men bickering. "Shut up, both of you! Sutter, hurry up and get us dirtside. I'm not paying you to go sightseeing."

Sutter was about to make another smartass remark but thought better of it. He believed Jericho to be a snot-nosed punk and that he could easily take him. But Jobe, on the other hand, looked like he ate titanium alloy and shit antimatter—not one to mess with. Sutter quickly got down to business plotting a course. With the transit around the star completed, he chose a meandering course in order to avoid detection by any of the other ships that he'd noticed around Abraxis.

"Just a heads up, there are ships in orbit around the planet that I can't identify from this range," Sutter informed Jobe.

"I don't give a shit. Just get this pig dirtside."

Jobe didn't seem interested in such details of space travel, but it was no surprise. He'd made that abundantly clear when he hired Sutter. "You're being paid to fly us there and back, no questions asked," he had said. Not exactly a details man; just somebody who kept his eye on the prize.

Sutter piloted the hunting skiff into a steep approach vector. Their ship needed to be out of orbit, through the atmosphere, and down to the planet's surface before any of the orbiting ships could detect them. Dropping almost straight down did the trick, though it made for a bumpy ride. The skiff settled down on its landing gear with only the local wildlife taking notice.

The rear ramp opened and Jobe strode out. Sniffing the air, he said, "You smell that?" When the other two gave him blank stares, he added, "Smells like a shitload of money out there. Let's go get it!"

A month after Albertson's departure, the expedition seemed much quieter. Still, Tomi sensed something elusive simmering under the surface. Standing in the middle of their camp, she searched around for anything amiss. The scientists were busy doing their research and scouts were conducting surveys—everyone seemed to be civil toward each other. Tomi couldn't quite put her finger on it, but she knew something was in the air.

When she saw some strained, almost hostile body language

between Healy and three of the biologists, she knew she had to ask. As they walked away, she approached.

"What was that all about?"

"Ryan, do you know what the sentience/abstract cognition test is?"

She hated it when someone answered a question with a question, but she was interested in getting to the bottom of this mystery, so she played along. "When a newly discovered species displays signs of both intelligence and organization, the test is administered to see if the species is capable of abstract reasoning."

"And?" he prompted.

Tomi gave it some thought. What *did* happen if a new species passed the test? Celebration? No, only if the species had FTL (Faster Than Light) capabilities were they welcomed into interstellar society. Then she remembered an idea known as the zoo hypothesis.

"Oh! Once a new species is determined to be sentient but not FTL capable, the planet and even the star system they live in becomes off-limits to all harvesting, extraction, and/or development."

Healy smiled when he saw the realization on Tomi's face, but she was still confused about what he was implying.

"But nobody has seen anything on this planet that meets the test's criteria, let alone is capable of passing it. Why the big deal?" she questioned.

"A little birdy told me Professor Weingarten and his two acolytes have gotten positive results from an uncatalogued species allegedly native to Abraxis," Healy admitted.

Tomi's jaw dropped. "Why haven't they told anyone?"

Healy shook his head and shrugged his shoulders. "Strange, isn't it? A discovery like that, you would think they would be announcing it to the whole universe, but instead they're sneaking around and having confidential meetings. All I have seen so far is exactly nothing: no photos, video, audio, biometrics, lab analysis, nothing. I did manage to catch a glimpse of some of the test results, but that's it."

Tomi didn't know whether to be flabbergasted or outraged. Weingarten was supposed to be a dispassionate scientist, not some radical activist. The lack of proof seemed rather suspicious, and Tomi wondered what was really up their sleeves. She too would have to keep a close eye on the professor and his little minions.

The horned juggernaut plodded along with the rest of the herd looking for fresh pastures to graze. The beast's eyesight was as good as human, but with a large horn jutting out from each shoulder, its field of view was a little limited. The creature's nose and ears, on the other hand, were quite keen. A would-be predator would have to approach from downwind and either be as silent as death itself or as swift as lightning. Unfortunately for this herd, they were being stalked by a predator both swift and silent.

Jobe watched the bird's-eye view provided by his drone. As expected, the herd of horned juggernauts were heading to greener pastures—such big creatures could certainly eat. Most people would be surprised that Jobe knew so much about zoology, forestry, law, and economics, but in order to be successful at what he did, he needed to. To be able to harvest the right animals, know where to sell them and to whom, all without being caught, required an extensive skill set. All his knowledge told him that now was the time to reap.

Unlike big-game hunters of yore, Jobe's tool of choice was a maser. It worked just like a laser, except it used microwaves instead of light. The maser focused those microwaves on the vulnerable parts of its prey. For the horned juggernauts he was hunting, Jobe targeted the brain. Not only were these animals big and strong but they also had two hearts and thick skin. With all of that redundancy, going for the vitals would not ensure a quick enough kill, but targeting the brain did.

Jobe wasn't a sportsman. Only interested in the financial outcome, he used numerous cheats. His maser produced no flash and no report so it wouldn't spook the nearby prey. Plus, a tripod mount made it ultra-stable, and being slaved to its multi-band scope made it ultra-accurate. The scope came equipped with both a fire control computer and auto tracking; all Jobe had to do was select the exact location on the animal he wanted to shoot, and then tell the gun to start shooting. The best part was that he could select multiple animals at once.

With all of the desirable animals selected, Jobe pushed the button marked "execute" and watched as his beamer hummed to life and started dispatching the beasts. As each target dropped, Jobe smiled and imagined he saw dollar signs.

Tomi was casually hanging around Weingarten's flunkies as they went about their work—two grad students named Bogar and Smiley. She was keeping an eye on them to see what she could learn. Was Healy correct in his assumptions? It looked to Tomi as though they were going about legitimate science.

Even so, she was particularly put off by the girl named Bogar. For some reason, the young biologist was hostile toward Tomi and she didn't know why. They had yet to exchange a single word, and there was no way Bogar could know she was looking for signs of them falsifying reports. Could she?

Tomi's communicator chirped. "Ryan, I need you to grab a full forensic loadout and get your ass to my coordinates, like yesterday!"

By the tone of Healy's voice, Tomi could tell something serious had gone down. Perhaps something warranting a full criminal investigation. She was tempted to ask for details, but instead acknowledged his orders. She figured she would find out what the big deal was when she got there. Asking would likely only earn her a scolding.

Running to her flitter, she started it up and flew off to get the equipment Healy had asked for. What she didn't realize was that Bogar and Smiley had overheard her conversation and had concerns of their own. They immediately went to catch Weingarten up to speed.

"Holy shit!" Tomi exclaimed.

When she'd gotten within 1,000 yards of Healy's location, she could already see why he had called her. There were carcasses of several large animals covering an immense area. She began to count, estimating dozens of the dead creatures, maybe even closer to a hundred. Looking like a cross between a gorilla and a rhinoceros, each one likely weighed in around two tons or more.

Landing near Healy, Tomi could see why she didn't recognize the species at first. The horned juggernauts were missing their most well-known feature: their dual horns. Dismounting her flitter, Tomi opened the cargo compartment and pulled out two large bags containing a whole assortment of forensic technology and carried it toward Healy's location where he was talking with Moore, one of the expedition's lead ecologists.

"Here's the gear," Tomi said. "Where do you want it?"

"We'll start on this one right here." Healy pointed at the rust-colored animal lying near his feet.

It had stubs on its shoulders from the excised horns and an incision on its side. Other than that, nothing looked out of place. The so-called surgeries would have been performed postmortem, but Tomi couldn't tell how the beasts had died. What weapon was capable of mass destruction without a trace?

"What killed it, Healy?"

"You tell me, rookie."

Tomi pulled out and activated different sensor drones. Each one sprang up into the air and circled around the nearest dead beast, some scanning in different spectra of electromagnetic radiation while others used ultrasound or scanned for chemicals. On her HUD, a detailed picture emerged from the data fusion: a virtual necropsy.

"That's weird," Tomi said out loud. Although the juggernaut's head seemed untouched externally, internally was a different story entirely. "The creature's brain looks like jelly and the brain case is fractured from all directions." Looking closer, she noticed that there was disrupted tissue from the juggernaut's brain case through its body in straight line. She furrowed her brow and told Healy, "Whatever killed the beast traveled in a perfectly straight line and caused no kinetic trauma."

Moore moved to look at the data over Tomi's shoulder. "Looks like a radiation beam of some kind. The tissues affected were cooked into a jelly-like substance."

"Definitely the work of a professional," Healy agreed. "His method killed without damaging the valuable parts. Even more, it left no obvious traces behind."

Looking at the chemical and bioscans, Tomi could see Healy was right. Besides not having any outward signs of trauma to their heads, not a single chemical trace was detected. She didn't have any words for what she was feeling except utter disgust. These generally peaceful creatures were simply going about their lives only to be maliciously slaughtered for some wholesale body parts.

Tomi ordered one of the camera drones to pan around and take an official count. The entire herd was downed; ninety-three in total lay lifeless in the meadow before them.

"Why?" was all Tomi could manage to say.

"Supply and demand," Moore answered with a shrug. "There are people out there willing to pay good money for a horned juggernaut's horns and gallbladder, and there are unscrupulous people willing to take the money and the risk to fill that demand."

"So, now what? We hunt the poachers down and haul them off to jail? It won't help these juggernauts—they'll still be dead," Tomi pointed out.

"I understand how you feel," Moore said gently. "The way the law is now, it's in no one's interest to protect the animals. It's impossible to get a license to hunt these creatures, which makes the activists think they've won. But in reality, all it really does is encourage the illegal poaching of the poor creatures."

Tomi thought it sounded so absurd. "Why would the animal rights activists be happy about that? Nothing has been accomplished. The animals are still dying."

Moore nodded. "And therein lies the problem."

"So then, what *should* be done?"

"I may be an ecologist by training, but I'm also a conservationist. I truly care for life, but I'm a realist as well. We need to do whatever will actually protect a species in the long run, and if that means a few are harvested by hunters, then so be it. Those who want to ban hunting are living in a fantasy world."

Tomi was surprised to be hearing this from an ecologist.

Moore motioned to the dead juggernauts. "The animals you're looking at would have eventually died someday, but if they can live long enough to reproduce and raise their young before they kick the bucket, the species survives. If those hunting them are doing so under the radar, there's no liability—they'll take out the females and young right along with the rest."

Tomi was beginning to see what Moore meant and she concluded for him, "But if hunting permits were available, at least the hunters would be monitored and held accountable by the rules and limitations."

"Now you're catching on," he said.

Healy was in the meadow, moving from kill to kill, checking the results from each scan plotted on a virtual map. He had discovered how the kills related to each other. Rejoining Moore and Tomi, Healy held out his wrist comp to show her the data.

"You see it, Ryan?" Healy asked her.

"The weapon only required one shot," she acknowledged. "It jumped from beast to beast. The wound tracks in all of the kills converge to one location." Tomi looked in the direction it seemed to originate from and noticed a small rise over 200 yards away that would make for an ideal shooting position. "There!" she shouted.

Scans of the ground showed foot traffic from one robot: a utility model. It probably did the actual cutting to obtain the prized parts. Other prints indicated at least two general-purpose androids, but no vehicles. More than likely, they arrived in a hover truck of some kind. Only when the rangers walked up to the rise did they locate any human tracks.

"I count two, no, three sets of tracks," Healy observed. "About what one would expect: enough to get the job done, but not so many paychecks."

Tomi located what looked like prints from a tripod, and judging by its measurements, it could have mounted a sizable weapon. But what was this mystery weapon?

Just as the rangers were finishing up, Dr. Weingarten arrived in an aerocar with Smiley and Bogar. He'd barely exited the vehicle before launching into a verbal assault.

"This carnage is an outrage! These animals are supposed to be under Federation protection." Walking up to Tomi, Weingarten pointed his finger in her face and bellowed, "I want your name. I want your badge number. You *will* be held responsible! This is a dereliction of duty."

"Weingarten, you do your job, and we'll do ours," Healy said, stepping between them. "If you have a problem with the way the Federation Rangers are handling things, you can take it up with Elba. Otherwise, shut up and get out our way."

Tomi stepped away to receive an incoming call from

Zimmerman. As they caught each other up on their findings, she watched Weingarten's ears turn red, before he huffed and walked back to the aerocar where his assistants were already waiting. Neither Tomi nor Healy noticed when Bogar concealed a tracking beacon on Healy's flitter before departing.

After Weingarten was out of earshot and Zimmerman ended their chat, Tomi walked back over to Healy. "I just heard from Zimmerman. He and Watry found another group of these juggernauts. Sounded like they were almost as numerous as this herd. What are we going to do, Healy?"

Healy didn't say a word as he activated a conference call on the rangers' comm system. Within thirty seconds, Watry, Zimmerman, and even Elba had all joined in.

Elba took control of the impromptu meeting. "I've just gotten word from Ota that another kill site has been located."

The air felt thick and heavy as a brief silence was shared by the rangers.

Elba sighed. "Let's cut to the chase. We have about three poachers loose that we know of, and we now have three separate confirmed sites with a total number of 273 kills. What are you rangers going to do to stop these bastards?"

Watry offered an idea. "I'll take Zimmerman and find their ship. Since it's their only way off this mudball, it's guaranteed they will return to it. If we can find it first, they're toast."

Elba countered, "That's a lot of real estate to cover. You have an idea how to do it quickly?"

"The three sites are spread out pretty evenly. They've got to be hiding their ship somewhere in the middle here," he said.

Healy cut in, "Good, you two head to the ship, and I'll take Ryan and stop those bastards before they strike again. Some of the expedition zoologists have been tracking these horned juggernaut herds. All we'll have to do is check on the nearest bunch. I bet that's where we'll find them."

"Excellent!" Elba said with a rare sampling of praise. "I knew there was a reason I keep you bastards around. Now, how about all of you get out there and catch those assholes in the act? Bring 'em in and I'll buy the first round."

None of the rangers could object to that, so all four gave an enthusiastic, "Yes, sir!"

Flying low, Tomi was driving with Healy riding behind her. The rangers used an uplink to one of the expedition's high-altitude drones to find and observe the nearby herds of horned juggernauts. They had come across two separate herds fairly close to the previous kill sites, but neither of them counted over thirty head. Healy insisted they keep looking further out for a larger group.

As they kept moving and using the drone to scan more territory, the rangers eventually discovered a particularly large herd moving east at a steady pace. By now, they were at least twenty miles from any of the previous kill sites, but Healy was emphatic that this would be the herd the poachers would go after.

"But why not take the herds that are closer?" Tomi asked.

"In order to make their trip worth the cost and risk, they need to get the largest number of kills in the shortest possible time. Stopping to get these smaller herds only slows them down with not enough profit to show for it, but at least this way of thinking makes them fairly predictable."

Jobe barked orders at his robots to get his maser set up. This spot was perfect. It was downwind and elevated with a wide field of fire. Yet, it would all be useless if they were still making noise when the prey arrived. The herd of juggernauts was heading quickly in their direction and the damn beasts could just about hear a mouse fart at

1,000 feet with all of those ears along their backs. They needed to hurry.

Like clockwork, the robots had just finished setting up when the poachers could hear the ground rumbling.

"Get your asses in into the hides now. Quickly!" Jobe yelled to both human and robot alike.

As he took cover, Jobe smiled once again. This had been a bountiful day and he couldn't wait to cash it all in.

8

PREDATOR AND PREY

"Okay, hold here a moment," Healy told Tomi as she slowed their flitter to a standstill.

Now that they'd found the golden herd, Healy had begun muttering to himself. "Where might they set up?" He glanced between the map and their physical surroundings.

Tomi didn't dare interrupt him as he rattled off his notes to himself about the direction of the wind and good hiding places. It sounded like he was trying to get into the poachers' heads.

"There," he finally said, indicating a point on the map. "Take us to these coordinates."

Checking the location on her HUD, Tomi was puzzled. "That's in the middle of the forest, hundreds of yards from where the herd is traveling."

"Don't you remember your training, Ryan? When you're dealing with prey that has good hearing, you need to be as silent as a gentle breeze. I've identified the perfect place for the poachers to ambush the juggernaut herd, but we can't spook them before we're ready. We need to catch the poachers red-handed, which is why we're going to hide over here." Healy firmly indicated to the same location on the map he'd already directed her to go.

Elba did say to capture them in the act, Tomi remembered. She nodded, gunning the throttle.

When the rangers came to the boundary where the woods turned to brush followed by open meadow, Tomi no longer needed her motion tracker to locate the herd. Already, they could hear and feel the horned juggernaut herd approaching. It was the moment of truth.

Tomi and Healy both dismounted the flitter and pulled on the hoods of their chameleon cloaks. Nearly invisible, Tomi scanned the area and spotted something.

"Healy, over there," she whispered. "It looks like some type of beamer mounted on a tripod."

Healy looked where she was pointing. Using his rifle scope, he could see both the beamer and the poachers.

"Bingo," he whispered back. "Good eye, rookie." Now that the rangers knew where all of the players were located, Healy instructed Tomi, "Get ready. It's show time."

She pulled her sidearm and set it to stun, but before they could move, the sound of an approaching aerocar disrupted the tension. It landed out in the meadow, and Bogar and Smiley jumped out, Weingarten no longer with them. *So, he likes to send his minions out to do the real dirty work,* Tomi thought.

Oblivious to the fact that the aerocar had put the juggernauts on high alert, the two scientists ran toward the poachers waving their hands in the air and yelling, "Stop!"

Coming to a halt in front of the maser to block the poachers' line of fire, the grad students assumed that the poachers would not shoot another sentient. They assumed wrong. Jobe selected Bogar with the beamer and ordered it to execute. It swiveled on its tripod, pointing right at her, and fired without warning.

There was no flash, no report, just the sound of the beamer powering up and the subsequent thud of Bogar's body hitting the ground. The heating effect was so intense, it had traumatized Bogar's heart in that brief instant, sending her into cardiac arrest. She died before she even hit the ground.

Smiley screamed as Jobe selected her next. Realizing their mistake, Smiley tried to run away. Fortunately for her, Tomi and Healy were already on the move, and before Jobe could tell his maser to execute, the rangers had closed in.

"Federation Rangers! Don't move!"

The overconfident poachers turned their attention toward the rangers, panic striking their countenances. Smiley used the opportunity to slip away, unnoticed by anyone.

"Fuck! It's the rangers!" Jericho screamed while Sutter looked dumbfounded.

"Don't just stand there! Attack!" Jobe ordered his robot minions, who promptly swung into action. Jobe, Sutter, and Jericho turned and ran to their hover sled.

"Take out the robots," Healy told Tomi.

Flipping her omniblaster to disintegrate, she fired at the android coming at her. Her shot was a little to the right and took its arm off. She corrected, and her second shot went through the android's power cell located in its chest. There was a bright flash and an explosion of sparks, and the android was knocked over backward.

Healy engaged the utility robot that was used for the cadaver cutting. His shot disabled its left side, but it continued charging. He flipped his blaster to maximum and fired several times into different parts of the robot, knocking pieces off and finally bringing it to a halt.

Hitting her stride, Tomi took out the third robot with a shot to its head. Clearing the scene, she saw the poachers speeding away on their hover sled before catching sight of Smiley.

"Damn it!" Tomi cursed.

The scientist was slowly heading straight toward one of the horned juggernauts, hand out in front of her as though she were planning to pet it like some damned fairy tale princess. *What in the hell is she doing?* Tomi wondered.

Being herbivores, the horned juggernauts were typically rather peaceful, but like some terrestrial herbivores such as the elephant or moose, juggernauts tended to fight when startled rather than flee. Whatever Smiley's goal, she seemed oblivious to the clear signs the juggernauts were giving her to back off: heads held high, muscles tensed, snorting and snuffing. The bull easily weighed in over two tons and was ready to defend his family.

When Smiley didn't back down, he began pawing the ground. The juggernaut didn't know what was exactly was approaching or why, but instinct already had an answer: attack. Letting out a deafening bellow that permeated the air, the mighty juggernaut pounded its front feet into the ground, creating an even stronger energy. The humans could feel it vibrate in their very core, triggering their own fight or flight responses with an adrenaline rush.

Realizing her second big mistake of the day, Smiley stopped in her tracks, but it was too little, too late. Only fifty yards from the juggernaut, the creature locked eyes with her. With a sudden and continuous roar, it leveled one of its three-foot-long horns at the human female and charged.

Tomi watched all of this unfold before her eyes, momentarily rooted to her spot. She didn't have to be an expert in animal behavior to know that even if she ran to the scientist, Smiley would be run down and trampled in a matter of seconds, well before Tomi reached her. Besides that, Tomi would never be able to stop its attack—she'd merely become another casualty.

No other options, Tomi holstered her pistol and brought her

long rifle to her shoulder. The weapon's gyro stabilization system was already spun up. Peering through the scope, she could see everything across the spectrum from microwaves to ultraviolet. The internal ballistic computer had already calculated a firing solution to hit the juggernaut center of mass. She was so focused she couldn't even hear Healy shouting at her to take the shot.

Flipping the rifle's selector switch to semi-automatic, Tomi took a breath, let it halfway out, and squeezed the trigger. There was no flash or report and barely any recoil, just a loud crack as the rifle's repulsor coils accelerated a projectile to over two miles per second. The bullet, looking more like a 4mm headless nail, covered the distance of over 200 yards faster than a human could blink, striking a mere tenth of an inch from where Tomi had aimed.

There was no explosion or blood spray, just a cloud of pink mist behind the juggernaut as it was knocked down. But it wasn't enough to kill it or deter it. Getting back to its feet, the animal roared angrily, rearing up on its hind legs before dropping back to its feet, and resumed the charge.

Tomi's mind raced for solutions. Making sure the juggernaut was still targeted, she squeezed off another shot. In her haste to fire again, this projectile went high and struck the creature in its spine, proving that while the beast was truly mighty, it was not unstoppable as its name suggested.

This second shot knocked the mighty beast the ground once again, and this time, it didn't get up. Partially paralyzed but still alive, the juggernaut dragged itself along with its front legs, determined to protect its family however possible from the threat known as Smiley. Tomi was about to line up another rapid-fire shot when Healy came up behind her.

"Take your time, Ryan. You severed its spinal cord; it's done for." Healy went on to inform Tomi that the juggernaut had redundant organs, so it would be quicker to shoot the animal in the braincase to end its suffering.

She nodded and slowly aimed one last time. When she pulled

the trigger, the beast drew its last breath and closed its eyes. Seeing their bull silenced, the remaining juggernauts turned and fled from the mysterious attackers.

Once the thundering herd faded away, the rangers closed the distance to Smiley and found her lying flat on her belly.

"Don't shoot! Don't shoot me!" she yelled at them.

Healy looked at Ryan and shook his head. He took the young grad student by her left arm and helped her up. She was quite filthy and from the mud on her face, it appeared she had been crying.

"You could have killed me, you fucking bitch!" she half screamed and half sobbed at Tomi.

Trying to keep her composure, Tomi simply answered, "You're welcome."

Smiley started throwing a fit. "You're welcome? Really? You jackbooted asshole! You killed an innocent, majestic creature. I hope your uterus shrivels and your ovaries rot!"

Tomi's patience finally ran out and she punched Smiley in the face, giving her a bloody nose. "Shut up, you self-righteous cunt!" Tomi screamed. "It's because of you I had to kill this creature in the first place, not to mention it's your fault those damn poachers got away."

"That's enough!" Healy shouted, stepping between them.

Still choking on the blood running out of her nose, Smiley ignored him as she cursed at Tomi some more. "Damn you to perdition, pig! I'm going to sue you! I'm—"

"You are under arrest," Healy said, spinning her around and snapping restraints on her.

"What? I didn't do anything wrong. You can't do this!" she protested.

"Yes, I can. You interfered with an official ranger operation. That is both a crime and a violation of your contract, and now, you are under arrest."

Smiley's screaming turned into full-blown sobs as Healy contacted Elba with an update. It was a foregone situation; yet another scientist would be kicked off the expedition by the end of the day, plus another dead.

Walking Smiley back to the poacher's hide, Healy made her stop at Bogar's body. "Consider yourself lucky that you get to go home. Your poor choices led your friend to her death."

After securing Smiley, Healy went over to check on his partner. "You okay?" he asked.

Tomi nodded noncommittally.

"You should be proud of yourself, you know," he added. "Despite the clusterfuck that occurred, you did good. You saved a whole herd of innocent animals, minus a bull, which is a lot more than what those glorified sorority sisters have done."

Tomi laughed and then pointed out one problem. "Yeah, but the poachers still got away."

"Tomi Ryan, why do you think rangers work in teams? I'll bet you drinks tonight that those poachers aren't home free just yet."

Jobe raced the repulsor sled to the point that its power system redlined. Jericho and Sutter kept looking back to see if anyone was following them, but so far, so good.

"Shouldn't we slow down?" Sutter finally asked. "You're gonna burn up one of the repulsor units or overheat the fusion cell."

"Shut the fuck up, space monkey!"

Jobe wasn't interested in listening to anyone's bullshit. All he knew was the fucking Federation Rangers were dirtside and somehow privy to their operation. They were so dialed in, the pigs had even known exactly where to ambush him. Jobe couldn't believe he had become the one being hunted. And what that dumbass Sutter didn't realize was if the rangers could locate them out in the field, they sure as hell could locate their ship. Their only hope was to get there first.

When it came into view, Jobe didn't even slow down. He

jumped off as soon as they neared, leaving Jericho and Sutter behind to fend for themselves. Cursing, Sutter grabbed the sled's controls and managed to stop it just before it careened into a tree. The dashboard displayed numerous warning lights flashing and there was smoke coming from the power cell compartment.

"Well, this rig is fucked," Sutter commented. When he didn't get a response, he noticed Jericho had already bailed as well.

"Get your ass in here, Sutter. We are leaving now!" Jobe yelled at the top of his lungs, his voice cracking.

Now Sutter was even more scared than when the rangers had first showed up. It was never a good sign when even the great white hunter was panicking. Sutter bolted inside and rushed through the checklist for liftoff. As the console lit up, showing the ship's systems coming online, he heard a warning alarm.

"What the fuck?" he said as he looked at the indicator.

"What the hell is wrong, Sutter? We should have left five minutes ago," Jobe demanded.

The display showed a malfunction in the fusion reactor's control system, which didn't make any sense. The ship's fusion reactor had no moving parts and could run without maintenance for decades. Why would it be malfunctioning now when they needed to get away quickly?

Without answering his superior, Sutter ran back toward the reactor's access panels and looked for the specific control board that was acting up. Opening the third panel, he jumped down into the crawl space and found the board bay he was looking for. He opened it and was immediately dumbfounded by what he saw—the control board was missing with a note in its place.

He read the note that only consisted of two words: "Look up." When he did, Sutter found himself staring at the muzzle of an omniblaster.

"Hello. I am with the Federation Rangers," Watry said casually. "You are under arrest for poaching." He fired his pistol, stunning Sutter.

A couple seconds later, Jobe and Jericho rounded the corner to the access panels to see what was taking Sutter so long. Seeing Watry standing over the open panel, Jobe pushed Jericho toward the ranger and turned on his heels to flee. Unfortunately for him, Zimmerman was ready and waiting.

Jobe stopped short of the barrel of Zimmerman's omniblaster when a stun bolt hit him, sending Jobe to the deck. Jericho turned around and saw him convulsing and another ranger present. Jericho just managed to get his laser pistol out of its holster before Zimmerman stunned him as well.

"Nice shooting, Zimmerman," Watry said.

"Thank you, sir. But I'm just amazed that you knew where to look for the ship," Zimmerman complimented back.

Watry shook his head. "It's not that I'm that smart. These crooks are just that stupid," he said with a laugh. "Now help me cuff them while they're down. Then we get the pleasant task of processing and inventorying this whole ship."

Back at base camp, the expedition members were irritated. They had been promised if their first evacuation drill was successful, there wouldn't be any more for the rest of the mission. Yet, here they were, an alarm signaling for them to evac. Several grumbled about having to stop their research and one said, "There had better be a motherfucking emergency."

Elba sobered them all up fast when he broke the news. "Thank you all for responding so quickly. It is with deepest sympathies that I must inform you that one of your fellow scientists was killed by poachers earlier today. Julie Bogar's body is being brought back by Federation Rangers as we speak. You'll notice Judith Smiley is also missing from our meeting. Rest assured, she is alive and well, and is on her way back with the rangers."

For now, Elba decided it was best to leave out the fact that Smiley was under arrest. He still needed to secure the two scientists' quarters and lab area, and he didn't want to let on to Weingarten or any other coconspirators that the rangers suspected the two biologists of malfeasance.

As the arriving aerocar pulled everyone's attention, Elba never officially ended the meeting, using the distraction to slip away and conduct his investigation.

When the aerocar landed, the gravity of the situation hit home for the other expedition members. While several started to cry as Bogar's body was carried to the morgue by Watry and Zimmerman, Weingarten simply watched with pursed lips. Grief then turned to shock as they watched Tomi and Healy escort Smiley in restraints to the ranger's office.

These events involving his followers did not tug on Weingarten's heartstrings as one might imagine. Instead, he was merely concerned for the cause and for himself. He quietly made his way to their quarters. Bogar's death might not have triggered an investigation, but Smiley's arrest certainly would, and Weingarten was hoping to retrieve any incriminating evidence before the rangers found it.

He stopped abruptly when he saw Elba securing the door to his acolytes' personal quarters. He was too late.

"Hello, professor. What brings you this way?" greeted the lead ranger.

Weingarten could tell by the man's facial expression alone that the rangers knew about the false test results Bogar and Smiley had concocted. *Stupid cows,* he thought. Their carelessness had gotten them caught. Weingarten had warned them time and time again to be discreet; it's a ranger's job to notice things such as this.

No matter, the rangers shouldn't find anything that tied him to their efforts. He'd simply have to come up with something else to stop the exploitation of this planet.

Saying nothing, Weingarten walked away.

Of all the situations and incidents Tomi had to deal with, it was the least violent and least dangerous of them that seemed to cause the most trouble. Rescues, medical emergencies, chasing poachers, and even weathering storms on foreign planets were quite easy to deal with compared to the scandal Bogar and Smiley had caused.

Because of Smiley's arrest, Elba had the authority to legally search her quarters and work areas. Plus, since Bogar was also interfering with the rangers' ability to carry out their duties, hers were liable to be searched as well. The result was discovering all of the sentience tests they had faked and were about to submit. The lingering question was why?

A background check revealed that both women were members of various radical organizations determined to stop bioresearch, harvesting, extraction, and development on any and all newly discovered planets, including Abraxis. Tomi could only shake her head. Such a shame that not all scientists were like Dr. Ota: objective and dispassionate with his only agenda being the pure pursuit of knowledge.

"With such self-destructive behavior, the very animals they seek to protect will only be put at greater risk," Ota confided in the rangers, shaking his head. "Not to mention, their actions now call into question the validity of any future research dealing with newly discovered sentient species."

"It's a real can of worms, that's for sure," Watry said.

The other expedition members were questioned regarding what they knew of Smiley and Bogar. Those who knew of their politics admitted they thought they were a little radical, but otherwise stated that they seemed to be intelligent and conscientious. However, several also claimed that the two were very tight and didn't reveal much about what they were really thinking. Except, that is, to the great Dr. Weingarten.

"They act like he's the expedition leader," one of them stated. The rangers already had their suspicions of the professor, so these sorts of statements only further proved them right. Ota had even shared with Elba his discovery of the articles written and speeches given by Dr. Weingarten about using any and all means available to stop the "rape of virgin worlds."

Unfortunately, he had left when they told him to, and he smartly had not returned with Bogar and Smiley to the second site. So, without any solid leads tying him to the false reports, the rangers couldn't take much action without a confession. Weingarten proved to be as uncooperative as Smiley in this area. Not only was he evasive with their questions, but he even denied knowing anything about what the pair was planning.

Tomi sat in the common area of the camp, reading Elba's official report.

> Survey Service scientists Julie Bogar and Judith Smiley interfered with the rangers' attempt to apprehend a gang of poachers on Abraxis, resulting in Bogar's death and Smiley's arrest.
>
> A subsequent investigation of their quarters showed that the pair was manufacturing false data and test results for the

sentience test for a fictitious species they claimed to be native to the planet Abraxis. Had their report been successfully published under the Federation accords for the treatment of sentient beings, the result would have been immediate cessation of all harvesting, extraction, and development on the above-named planet.

Bogar's body is being transported to her family. Smiley will be expelled from the expedition on Abraxis, and it is the strong recommendation of the Federation Rangers that she be banned from any future expeditions.

Considering the scientific fraud that Smiley and Bogar had tried to perpetuate, Tomi felt Smiley had gotten off easy. Normally in academic circles, falsifying results like that would get one not only terminated but declared *persona non grata* from any future jobs in their field of study. By some estimates, Smiley could look for work somewhere else as soon as she got back to Earth and continue on with her life as though nothing had happened, and that pissed Tomi off.

She wrinkled up the report and tossed it across the common room just as Healy walked in.

"Can't win 'em all, rookie," he told her. "Besides, tomorrow's another day."

The last four months seemed to fly by. As quickly as the base camp was set up, it was just as quickly broken down and shipped to the next survey area on the other side of the continent. Having finished their rotation, Tomi and her fellow rangers were due to head back on the *Bass Reeves* while the rest of the expedition returned to their respective institutions via the Survey Service ship.

After everyone took their group pictures and said their goodbyes, the rangers were the last to leave in order to ensure no one was left behind. With little left to do on a nearly abandoned planet, Tomi walked around the ghost camp where the buildings had been located just moments prior. The only clue that humans had ever been there were the holes from the foundation piers. If felt so surreal how quickly things could change; Goliath had been at its zenith when disassembly started and was now setting, its harsh glare giving way to David's soft red.

Her wrist comp chimed as Healy's voice came over the comm channel, pulling her back to reality.

"Hey Ryan, you done reminiscing? You missed Elba's departure and Captain Everly is here. It's time to move out."

"Coming," Tomi answered. She felt bad for not having said goodbye to Elba. Maybe she'd see him again sometime.

She jogged back to the landing area just as the dropship was on final approach. Seeing her delayed arrival when even Zimmerman had been there waiting, Watry couldn't help but give her some ribbing.

"Hurry up, rookie! I want to get off this mudball. Aren't you ready to get back to clean beds, hot showers, and flushable toilets? Or do you prefer to roll around in the dirt?"

"I'm here! I'm ready to go," she shouted.

Shouldering her gear, she didn't waste any more time getting on board, pushing past the other rangers. When they were all inside, the ramp closed and the dropship lifted off. Tomi checked an external camera view and watched as the distance between them and Abraxis opened.

"Goodbye, Abraxis," she said aloud.

9

NO GOOD DEED

General Warnock loved being a marine. So much so, he finished secondary school a year early and browbeat his parents into signing the consent papers to allow him to join while he was still sixteen. Despite his young age, he excelled in taking on more and more responsibility. After putting in two years of active duty, his CO recommended him for OCS.

At first, Warnock tried to turn it down. His ambition was to be a gunnery sergeant, to be one of the marines who "really ran the corps." When he told this to his commanding officer of the time, Colonel Ortiz answered with a definite, "Negative, marine!" and explained that Warnock was too smart, too talented to simply be enlisted personnel. The corps needed him where he could do the most for the Federation Marines. So, off Warnock went to officer candidate school, followed by battlesuit school for officers.

As it turned out, Colonel Ortiz was a good judge of character; Warnock quickly advanced through the ranks. Along with having a head for strategy and tactics, he proved to also have a good understanding of the more mundane tasks, such as administration and logistics. The real test, though, was when he made his way up to the command-level ranks. Warnock was not only able to network with others but also maneuver the labyrinth of Federation politics with ease and finesse.

To say the sky was the limit was an understatement. Before Warnock knew it, he was made commandant of the Federation Marine Corps, a crowning achievement for a stellar career. All he had left to do now was deal with various political headaches before retirement. The latest headache he had was with congressional representatives who wanted the marines to play entourage.

"Cocksucking whores!" Warnock swore in response to his aide's question.

Colonel Raines pressed the issue. "Sir, those congressmen keep calling, demanding they have marine protection while they travel to colony worlds. We've got to give them an answer."

"I heard you, Raines. The fucking gall of these lying sonsabitches. They cut our funding and then have the nerve to ask us for protection? How are we supposed to keep the space lanes safe if we're too busy babysitting politicians?"

Warnock slumped back in his chair and rubbed his face with his hands in a vain attempt to relieve the stress of the situation. Truth was he would rather say no to the politicians than tell his marines they had to stand around and listen to the blowhards blather on about whatever bullshit pet project they were pushing at the moment. But what really worried him was that in order to make the politicians happy, way too many marine units would have to be pulled off antipirate duty, leaving whole sectors unprotected. Though Raines tried to reassure Warnock that the patrol and rangers would step up to help cover the gaps, it was a risky gamble.

"Lemme guess, one of those dumbasses suggested that?" Warnock asked.

Raines had to admit one of the congressional staffers had suggested that the patrol would just have to pick up the slack. Warnock shook his head. The patrol was having the same problems as the corps: too much work and not enough people or money. All so the politicians could make whatever special interest they're sucking up to at the moment happy.

"Tell me, Raines, who do you think is going to be more pissed about this clusterfuck, our marines or the patrol?" Warnock asked.

"Sir, with all due respect, I'd say the patrol." When Warnock shot him a quizzical look, Raines added, "Those congressmen announced their little tour, including our marine-provided security on all of the hyperspace channels. Every pirate from Terra out to the frontier knows what's going on."

Warnock growled and shoved the papers off his desk. All he could was do was hope that some way, somehow those patrolmen and rangers made it through the inevitable shitstorm that was heading their way.

The freighter *Stella Warren* was completing its transit into open space, preparing to engage warp drive. The ship's navigator finished the final calculations for the ship's course to the border world of Olympus.

"Course plotted and entered into helm," Abelson reported. "She's all yours, skipper."

Captain Croft checked the helm controls. "Good, we're ready to go then. Engage warp drive in ten seconds."

The ship's computer, known as Mabel, started the countdown. Mabel stopped before reaching three, reporting, "An unknown ship has docked at number one airlock." This was quickly followed by, "Number one airlock cycling."

"Shit!" Croft swore as he activated the intruder alert. At the alarm, all crew and passengers should start moving toward their emergency stations.

"What is it?" Abelson asked.

"Send an SOS immediately! We're being hijacked by pirates."

Ranger Healy was right. It was nice to get back onto a nice, clean ship. With the marines being pulled from their pirate watch, the *Bass Reeves* had acquired a larger crew combining the rangers with a team from the Space Patrol and even a reporter. The patrolmen occasionally complained about the cramped quarters and the stale air. After spending months of walking, crawling, and rolling around in the dirt, mud, and everything else on planet Abraxis, Tomi new better. She understood it was a luxury to get out of a soft, warm bed in the morning and not have to put her boots on to use the head.

Being the only female on the ship, Tomi got to enjoy a rare treat for someone of her low pay grade—she had her own quarters. She still had to share the head with everyone else, but she could deal with that. Wrapped in a towel, she went to take a shower after a quick a pitstop. She plopped down on one of the toilets, relishing in the fact that she didn't have to squat and the toilet seat wasn't freezing.

The ship's computer announced the time. It had been fourteen hours since Tomi had gone to bed to take a "short nap." She didn't realize how tired she had been, which would also explain why her bladder was so full. She entered one of the shower stalls, took off her towel, and started soaking herself down, allowing the hot water to relax her muscles. She started soaping up her body, but just as she was about start on her hair, another announcement came over the speaker—this one with more alarm.

"Attention all hands! Attention all hands! All personnel are to report immediately to the ship's common area. Attendance is mandatory. That is all."

"Damn it!" she cursed. Tomi rinsed the dollop of shampoo off her hand, wishing she'd had time to get the grime and grease out of her hair first.

Tomi jogged back to her room through an empty passageway. With no one around to get a generous view of her naked ass, she started to dry herself off as she ran. She was half tempted to just put on a utility uniform, but decided against it, opting instead to pull on a fresh bra and pair of panties before putting on the rest of her uniform and pulling her wet and unwashed hair up into a messy bun. She made a mental note to chop it short so it would take less time to deal with.

Arriving late to the ship's common area, Tomi tried not to blush when everyone turned and looked at her.

"Finally decided to grace us with your presence, Ranger Ryan?" It was Captain Everly. "So sorry we interrupted your little spa day, but this meeting needed to commence ten minutes ago."

Tomi nodded and took her seat as Everly activated the holographic display. It showed the 3D image of an interstellar bulk freighter.

"This is the mission, so listen good. You're looking at the *Stella Warren*, a privately owned freighter homeported out of Eden. It carries a load of 50,000 tons when fully loaded, a standard crew of six or seven, and the possibility of passengers. Five minutes ago, an FTL distress call was received saying the ship had been hijacked by pirates.

"We do not know how many perpetrators there are or how they are equipped, but what we do know is that the pirates who have been operating in this sector are known to send anyone they find out the airlock or disable life support altogether to ensure zero witnesses. Since time is of the essence, I have already set course for the *Stella Warren*'s location at maximum warp. We should be there in less than twenty minutes.

"Since this is a joint effort, the Federation has ordered that the Space Patrol be put on point for such missions. Therefore, Sergeant Payne will be leading the boarding party and the rangers will be joining under his command. I will be offering my support from the air. Good luck."

Four rangers and four patrolmen were up against an unknown number of criminals. The journalist, Gerald Nash, insisted on tagging along, but that was quickly nixed by all present. Then Sergeant Payne stepped up to lay out the plan.

"We'll split into teams of two," he instructed. "Leopold and Maynard will secure the crew quarters and common area. Scotch is with me; we will take the bridge. Zimmerman and Watry will take the ship's loading bay, and Healy and Ryan will secure engineering."

Everyone nodded and prepared to gear up.

"One last thing," Payne added. "Be sure to set your omniblasters to stun and stun only. We aren't looking for a bloodbath here."

"You do realize there's a very good chance the perps will be wearing spacesuits?" Watry questioned. Before he could say that stun bolts wouldn't penetrate a spacesuit, Payne's pride got the better of him.

"Don't argue with me, ranger! I'm in charge here, and I want prisoners, not bodies. I'm not going to let you rangers turn this op into a frontier shootout for the fun of it."

Tomi was going to ask what equipment the rangers could bring, but a look from Healy told her it wouldn't be a good idea.

After the meeting concluded, the rangers went back to their quarters to gear up. In addition to their exosuits and sidearms, they opted to bring their auto grapples, plasma cutters, and portable defense screens. Like any good ranger, they each made sure to include their bush knife to complete their loadout.

Over the comm system, an announcement informed everyone that *Stella Warren* was within sensor range with an ETA of five minutes.

"Okay, you heard them," Healy said. "Get your butts to the airlock. We're jumping into this shit in five."

While engaged, one of the perks of using warp drive was the ship became quite literally untouchable. The creation of the warp bubble around the ship meant there was no real way to get to it from the outside. There were safeguards in place to make sure a ship didn't run out of control, but unless the problem got on board before the warp drive powered up, there was no problem.

Unfortunately for them, this often made starship crews a little complacent. They sometimes forgot that they were still vulnerable to attacks, hijacking attempts, and collisions. Once out in open space with no one else around, it was even easier to forget.

This lack of attention was exactly what George "Psycho" Knight and the rest of the Star Demon Syndicate depended on. With the right information and a little planning, such ships were easily caught flatfooted. It was in this exact manner on the other side of the sector that another pirate, known as Blowtorch, currently had his crew raiding the *Stella Warren*.

Meanwhile, Psycho took advantage of the understaffed and overloaded lawmen focusing on Blowtorch's attack. He ordered his crew to attack the nearby tramp freighter known as the *Serena Dawn*, quickly making it just another statistic. Normally, hijacking a ship would be a mad dash to cycle through the airlock to take control of the vital spaces like the bridge. Even when they accomplished this step, the ship's crew sometimes locked all of the controls with a security protocol so the would-be hijackers were stuck either towing the ship or beating the security codes out of the ship's captain.

Instead, this particular band of pirates had an edge in the form of military-grade electronic warfare override software. By linking to one of the freighter's antennae, the pirates easily downloaded a software spike into the mark's computer system to take full control. At that point, the pirate crew leader could control any and all of the ship's functions linked to the computer right from his personal controller. No more mad dash.

This was the first time Psycho had used the EW module on a

real-world mark. At the push of a button, his men were in. All pressure doors, security gates, defense screens, and security lockouts opened, allowing the pirates access to ransack the whole ship. Though in the process of testing his new toy, Psycho discovered that unlocking all the doors had one major drawback: all of the crew and passengers also had free range of the ship, giving them a chance of escaping.

Even with all of the pirates firing simultaneously at the passengers of the *Serena Dawn*, that's exactly what had happened. Some of them managed to make it to a lifeboat and flee from the attack with their lives. Psycho wasn't too thrilled about there being witnesses. Next time, he'd have to remember to leave all of the stateroom doors locked.

Psycho made a mental note of the direction of the lifeboat and smirked. *Perfect.* They were heading for Yardang, the location of Psycho's secret hideout.

With the rest of the ship secured, it was time to get work. The Star Demon had given him a long list of supplies and equipment to rustle up. After they were gathered, Psycho would make sure all of the evidence was disposed of, including those on the lifeboat. No evidence, no crime. No crime, no hassle.

10

PUNISH THE INNOCENT

Tomi found the aftermath of the hostage rescue on the *Stella Warren* a bit disappointing. She expected congratulations, promises to receive a commendation, a pat on the back, something. Instead, she got to hear Payne scream his head off about what a disaster the op was. The most ridiculous part about the whole thing was that the pirates *he* tried to apprehend were the ones who got away.

Looking at her fellow rangers she could see the recognition on their faces too—Payne was trying to cover up his own failure. Even his fellow patrolmen were not happy. They seemed embarrassed not only by their shortcoming but also by their sergeant's behavior. Though, Payne wasn't the only one being unrealistic.

While Tomi and the others were rescuing the crew of the *Stella Warren*, another call had come in from the other side of the sector, informing them of the attack Psycho had conducted on the *Serena Dawn*. By the time any lawmen ships arrived, it was no longer there and its current whereabouts were now unknown. Other patrol ships were looking for her, but they weren't holding out much hope.

Nash, the reporter, filled the lawmen in on the politics of the situation.

"They'll likely blame the marines for being spread so thin, and you all for not protecting the *Serena Dawn*," he said, almost sounding as if he were hoping to rile them up.

Healy turned to his rookie rangers, Tomi and Zimmerman. "What'd I tell you? This is definitely a thankless job." He looked back at Nash. "You could change the narrative, you know."

"How do you mean?" Nash said, intrigued.

Watching his body language, Tomi could swear he only seemed interested if there was something in it for him—the seedy little bastard.

Healy said, "Do your job honestly by informing the public that it was the politicians who cut the budgets and insisted on playing around with the marines' assignments."

Nash acted taken aback. "As a journalist, I do not take sides. My job isn't to push an agenda, but rather to simply report the facts." The trouble for Nash was nobody on board the *Bass Reeves* believed he didn't have an agenda of his own.

When all was said and done, they finally let Nash on board the *Stella Warren*. He lost all interest in the passengers once he found out that the pirates had all been spacer parahumans. Since only the dead ones were available to examine, he started peppering Tomi and the others with questions about the pirates. It seemed Tomi's initial assessment of the reporter was accurate, and her patience was wearing thin.

Despite the fact that they didn't have any live pirates for Nash to interrogate, the lifeless bodies still spoke volumes about who they were and where they came from. Tomi and Zimmerman took notes as the more experienced rangers and the patrolmen examined the bodies and equipment of each pirate.

One thing stood out right away: their spacesuits. Along with the fact that they were modified with gloves instead of boots, Maynard noticed that these suits were standard issue for the dock workers at the planet Eden's main spaceport. Even with the Velcro patches removed, he could see the distinctive features the manufacturer had added to the design. While Nash was going on about how these poor, downtrodden parahumans had to resort to crimes in order to survive, the reality was these pirates were gainfully employed, plus benefits.

"With the added perk of having access to the shipping information for every ship coming and going from that port," Maynard concluded. "No wonder they were able to hijack these ships so easily."

"Especially once everyone everywhere heard the public announcement of the marines' mass excision from pirate watch," Everly added.

With this newfound lead to the ports of Eden, Captain Everly reported back to HQ to put out a BOLO for these pirates' coworkers. Nash still insinuated that the spacers lived in such poverty that they had been forced into a life of crime, no matter that it earned him warning looks from every ranger and patrolman present.

Healy grabbed Nash by the front of his jumpsuit and shoved him into the nearest bulkhead. "I've had enough of your bullshit, you fucking vulture. These impoverished parahumans you keep crying over easily make more than the average Federation enlistee, and that's without overtime. The only thing they have keeping them down is their greedy natures. They choose to steal some of the cargo they handle, but they wouldn't want to jeopardize their cushy jobs, so they blow the whole innocent crew out the airlock, sans spacesuits. Where's your sympathy for those lives?"

Nash started to open his mouth, but Healy pushed him even harder into the wall and continued his tirade. "They wreck so many lives just to make some extra scratch. But then, being a journalist, you would understand that quite well, wouldn't you?"

Finally, Watry came up and separated them, although

reluctantly. Everyone had been enjoying Nash's well-deserved scolding. "Come on, Healy. Go cool off."

Nash started to thank Watry for saving his life, but Watry put his hand up to stop him. "Just...shut the fuck up," he warned the reporter.

In the awkward silence that followed, Tomi couldn't help but blurt out, "So, what are we going to do next?"

"That's easy, Ranger Ryan. We're going to look for the *Serena Dawn*," Everly answered.

When Tomi wondered aloud how that was possible or where they'd even begin, the skipper smiled and said, "This ship's namesake was able to track down and apprehend over 3,000 fugitives despite the fact there was no electronic communications back then *and* he was illiterate."

Seeing Tomi's dumb look, he continued, "There's only so many places those pirates can go, and only so many places they could hide that ship. We just need to find the right people to ask questions."

To kill two birds with one stone, the *Bass Reeves* would escort the *Stella Warren* back to port, and while there, the lawmen would find out which social circles the deceased pirates used to run in. That was something Tomi remembered from criminology class—even crooks liked to get together to swap stories and trade information. If one pirate captain had information on more than one juicy mark and didn't have time to go after them all, he would sell one for a finder's fee. Better to make a little money, rather than none at all.

By the time the *Bass Reeves* and the *Stella Warren* pulled into port, Tomi had received an extensive education on how space pirates operated. It turned out, the valuable cargo the *Stella Warren* was carrying was...fertilizer. Not precious metals, gems, radioactive elements, or exotic biologicals, but 50,000 tons of high-quality fertilizer. It seemed like an odd score to Tomi, but Maynard did the math aloud.

"The fertilizer is worth 400 credits per ton on the open market. Multiply that by 50,000 and you have twenty million credits. All you have to do is find someone who would buy it at half price, no questions asked, and the pirates net a nice little profit of ten million."

Tomi guessed beauty must really be in the eye of the beholder.

Once in port, each patrolman paired up with a ranger to investigate and interrogate to ensure that whatever information was found, there was representation of each branch present to testify to it. While Zimmerman, Scotch, Healy, and Leopold scoured the town for the pirates' social circles, Tomi, Maynard, Payne, and Watry chased down the pirates' place of employment.

Tomi and Maynard found the port superintendent, who was evasive at first and kept trying to answer a question with a question. Maynard wouldn't have any of it.

"This is an official Federation Space Patrol investigation. Stonewall me one more time and you will be arrested for interfering with it," he warned.

The sup held up his hands in surrender, allowing Maynard to look at the manifest data.

"Look at this!" he exclaimed, motioning for Tomi to come look. "I just identified all of our corpses back on the *Stella Warren*, and it looks like we now know who got away. Not only were these twelve employees not working the day of the hijacking, but the four who escaped have since reported back to work."

Maynard hopped on the comm channel. "Payne, this is Maynard. I'm sending you the data on the four pirates who got away. You won't believe it—the dumbasses came back to work! The schedule says they should be here right now."

While Tomi and Maynard made sure the port superintendent stayed seated in the corner of his office and made no attempts to contact anyone, Patrolman Payne and Ranger Watry arrived on scene. They were going to see if the pirates did indeed report to work today.

They found the pirates in question going about their duties as dock workers as though the incident on the *Stella Warren* never happened. They were smart enough to try to get away when they saw the lawmen approaching, but the good guys were faster with their blasters than the bad guys were with their feet. While one managed to get away, two of the pirates were dropped by stun blasts, and the fourth decided he couldn't outrun them and surrendered on the spot.

As the three pirates were taken into custody, Watry told Tomi, "Told ya these crooks are morons. They hijack a ship, were seconds away from committing a half a dozen counts of capital murder, lose eight of their own in a firefight, and then they go back to work the next day like nothing happened."

"Idiots," Maynard agreed, shaking his head and laughing.

"But one got away," Tomi pointed out. "What about him?"

"A bird in the hand, rookie." Healy shrugged and added, "He got lucky. If he's smart, he'll find a new job elsewhere."

"So, what happens to these ones?" Tomi asked, motioning to the three they had.

"Since they didn't succeed at actually killing anyone, the judge will just send these losers to everyone's favorite penal colony here in the Federation, affectionately known as the hive."

Once everyone had reunited aboard the *Bass Reeves*, the captured pirates put up the tough guy act at first, but slowly, realization that they were getting shipped to the Federation penal colony for the rest of their natural lives started to sink in. Only the fear of reprisal from the Star Demon himself would be worse. That same fear caused the pirates to hold their tongues rather than barter for reduced sentences in exchange for insider information.

But then the investigators had a stroke of luck. One of them kept a ledger—a little black book recording all of his business transactions. Likely a bargaining chip in case he was to ever to go down, but he was clearly too afraid to use it. Since the patrol found it on their own, they didn't owe the pirate a damn thing. While they heard the him swear in multiple languages at his lack of luck, Maynard flipped through to the last entry in the ledger and read it aloud.

"'Psycho, 1,000 credits for info on SD.' This entry was from just a few days ago."

"SD..." Healy said, making the connection. "Psycho must be the pirate he sold the details of the *Serena Dawn* to."

Checking their records system, George "Psycho" Knight was a known associate of the Star Demon Syndicate with numerous warrants for piracy, larceny, kidnapping, murder, and unauthorized smoking, among other crimes. Leopold perked up at the name.

"Contact Patrolman Curtis on the *Michael Healy*. He's been chasing those guys for the better part of a year. He might even know where they possibly ditched the *Serena Dawn*."

The tip paid off. A little more than a week later, Patrolman Curtis was able to track down what was left of the *Serena Dawn* at one of the Star Demon's favorite dumping grounds. There were many planets in the sector; some habitable but none explored, which made for a quiet place to dump trash after the riches were salvaged.

Unfortunately, the ship was discovered spinning, stuck tumbling forever through space on its final trajectory before it lost power. It was way off course by now and Curtis didn't have time to wait around for a tug to come stabilize it. Antsy to follow Psycho's trail while it was still hot, he sent a ship to pick up Patrolman Payne and his crew so they could join him on his hunt for Psycho and back him up if he was lucky enough to find him.

Since the *Serena Dawn* still needed to be dealt with, Curtis requested Everly and his rangers to report to the recently located hulk of a passenger liner do an investigation in his stead. Tomi was grateful when Nash decided to follow the patrolmen, assuming they'd have a more exciting story to report than the rangers. He assumed incorrectly.

By the time the rangers arrived, the *Serena Dawn* had been stabilized by a deep-space tug. Accessing the ship would require everyone to suit up with full life support and free-fall equipment. A salvage crew was clearing the ship out, and as the rangers worked their way through the darkness of space toward the *Serena Dawn*, one of the workers gave them a fair warning in passing.

"Hope you haven't eaten yet," he said through his speaker.

Tomi and Zimmerman eyed each other. Was this their life now? Really though, Tomi didn't mind. At least the lack of predictability kept the boredom at bay. Hell, she'd already been a ranger for more than half a year now and she hadn't had very many uneventful days since her mistaken assignment on the mining colony.

She muttered to herself, "Improvise, adapt, overcome," and set foot on the ramp of the *Serena Dawn*.

Inside, the ship looked like a set for a grade-B horror movie. Flashing red emergency lights were the only ones on. With the artificial gravity off, there was a whole assortment of objects floating in the ship's passageways. Among the debris were the remains of passengers and crew—some whole, while others had obviously been attacked with high-energy weapons.

As the rangers searched the ship using their grip boots, there was little hope that there would be any survivors left on board; the life support had been inactive for far too long by this point. The only good news was that the lifeboat was missing. The rangers could only hope that meant a few of them had managed to escape.

The cargo hold had clearly been searched. Several containers had been removed from their stored positions. A manifest check revealed the missing items included generators and drilling equipment. It seemed strange that the pirates were getting into the petroleum business, but anything profitable seemed to be fair game these days.

Tomi entered another room and discovered it was the hibernation bay. She walked over to get a closer look at the rows and columns of pods and was taken aback when so many of them were still occupied by passengers. She found it disturbing to see several hibernating men and women floating naked in a solution, tubes coming out of their arms and noses, completely unaware of the fate of their ship.

It was eerie, these people stuck in a state of limbo, neither alive nor dead. *Could they still be alive?* Tomi checked individual pods and was surprised to learn they were still operating; the occupants were, in fact, alive.

"Healy," she called through her wrist comp. "Come look at this."

He appeared through the doorway and she explained what she'd found. Healy looked them over and showed her that the pods still had enough backup power to last a couple of months, even without the ship's power.

"Did you run a bioscan?" he asked.

"Not yet, but I will now." Her bioscanner detected something outside of the pods: blood drops on the floor and walls. "Whose blood is this?"

"Is there any evidence that one of the hibernating passengers was removed?"

"No, all of the pods in this compartment are still occupied."

Healy started his own scanner and then turned around to one of the computer panels. He tapped it, powering it up. After inputting some commands, a video recording started to play.

Tomi watched as a holograph of a man, neither passenger nor crew, was trying to decant one of the female passengers. Another holographic man, probably his superior, came over and looked angry.

"What are you doing, Valk? We don't have time to decant any of these people."

"Ah come on, Psycho. Why can't I get me a piece of ass?"

"Pick from the ones who are awake, you idiot!"

"But they're all dogs!"

The superior had heard enough and started pistol whipping the one called Valk. The recording ended as the two pirates left the compartment.

"He was going to take her," Tomi said, peering into the pod from the recording. The young woman, not a day over twenty, no doubt was attractive. Her long brown hair was tied up in a top knot as per safety regulations. Approximately five and half feet tall, she was quite beautiful with curved hips, a thin waist, and large breasts. She had shaved before going into hibernation; her only hair was on her head. It was clear why Valk had wanted her.

"She'll never know how lucky she was," Healy agreed. "If that idiot didn't kill her with a botched decantation, the rough ride back to their base certainly would have."

After calling for the *Comfort*, a mobile aerospace hospital ship, to come decant the remaining crewmembers and safely ease them into the reality of what had happened, Everly called a meeting. The rangers discussed their observations and they all agreed that what happened on the *Serena Dawn* was no accident. The ship was obviously hijacked by more pirates. The blood left behind was identified as belonging to a Ferris K. Valk from Earth, which made sense from the recording. It seemed likely he started freighter jumping in order to outrun the various debt collectors and loan sharks after him. Definitely pirate material.

All of the food and booze were taken from the galley, an autofac was missing, and all of the hydrogen fuel from the reactor as well. These items weren't as likely to be sold on the black market. It seemed more likely that the pirates were on a supply run, and once finished, they'd set the ship on a collision course with the system's star.

But the most disturbing find was the use of military-grade hacking software to disable the ship. It was becoming more and more critical to find these pirates and their supplier. Tomi was grateful Patrolman Curtis and his team were already in pursuit of Psycho and his bastard crew. She just hoped he was successful.

On the day the *Serena Dawn* was attacked by pirates, Jared Salinger felt like they'd had such a narrow escape in the lifeboat. The pirates should have easily been able to chase after and destroy them, but all was oddly quiet. What Salinger didn't know was that Psycho and his crew had momentarily gone quiet to throw off the rangers and patrolmen who'd already managed to track down Blowtorch's crew at the docks.

Salinger looked anxiously at the other passengers. Isabelle, Lenny, Buddy, and himself were all that remained of the *Serena Dawn's* unfortunate crew. Regardless of their small number, it took Salinger an hour to convince them to get into their hibernation tubes.

"According to the onboard computer, the nearest habitable planet is almost a week away and there aren't enough supplies to last us that long," he pointed out. "Besides, we'll need those supplies once we land."

Isabelle, Lenny, and Buddy still looked apprehensive to comply.

"The computer will wake us before we start reentry," Salinger added. "Look, we don't really have any options here. If we want to survive this, our best bet is to enter hibernation until we land."

When the lifeboat's onboard computer woke them up about a week later, everyone was too weak to be scared. It was a bumpy ride on the way down, even with all of the stability the lifeboat's designers had put in. Plummeting through an atmosphere was very stressful on humans and equipment alike, but the lifeboat managed to survive reentry and activated its braking system.

With that accomplished, a ram-air parachute deployed to slow the craft down even further. Finally, as the altimeter ticked toward zero, airbags inflated on the craft's exterior surface so when the ship hit the ground, the airbags would take the brunt of the impact. It still wasn't enough to make for a smooth landing, but at least they had landed.

When he regained his senses, Salinger checked himself for injuries. He was grateful when he found none—so far, so good. Releasing his safety harness, he looked back at the other passengers. While they all had stunned looks on their faces, none of them showed any signs of injury.

"What's next?" Isabelle asked.

It was not lost on Salinger that she had directed her question at him specifically. They all seemed to be leaning on Salinger as their impromptu leader. Taking his new role in stride, he checked the computer's atmospheric analysis.

Pressure: .99 atm
Temperature: 20°F
Humidity: 35%

Composition: 78% nitrogen, 20% oxygen, 1% argon

It was cold outside, but otherwise okay. Salinger opened the hatch, feeling the rush of cold air. All he could see outside was a black abyss. Grabbing a flashlight, he illuminated the ground as he went out to look at the area around the lifeboat. Sand and rock—very dry sand and rock. He concluded they had landed in a desert, far from an ideal survival situation. Good thing they had used the hibernation tubes and reserved their supplies, because they were going to need them.

Climbing back aboard, Salinger informed the others of their situation. "Looks like we're stranded in the middle of a desert. It's below freezing right now, but during the day, it'll likely rise to high temps. We'll need to be cautious about staying hydrated."

"So, what's the plan, chief?" Lenny asked him.

"We need to inventory what we have, putting a priority on water. Let's hope help gets here soon."

11

THE SHELTERING SKY

Departing from the *Serena Dawn*'s remains, the rangers' first priority were the passengers who had managed to evacuate. Since all lifeboats and escape pods were programmed to head toward the nearest habitable planet within range, it seemed this crew would likely be headed to Yardang, the only planet inside the biozone of Hickenlooper's Star.

As the *Bass Reeves* approached the planet, sensor sweeps showed nothing in orbit. The world appeared to be uninhabited, yet there was a warning that came up mentioning an interstellar treaty with an alien species known as Anar-phuts that stated humans would not set foot on the planet. But treaties didn't apply in the case of rescue missions.

After entering low orbit, sensors located the lifeboat. Everly ordered Watry and Tomi to investigate.

"Okay, rookie, we're going to use orbital insertion to reach the surface," Watry said.

"Is that necessary?" Tomi asked, knowing it would be a rough ride.

Healy looked her in the eye and replied, "It's faster, quieter, cheaper, and more ecologically sound than a shuttle. No more chatter, rookie. Gear up!"

As she glanced toward the flitters, Tomi remembered her sudden need to pee during the intense rescue of the *Stella Warren*. She promptly excused herself to use the ship's washroom before departing. Tomi knew the other rangers would give her plenty of ribbing for it, but she still felt it was better than taking a dump down the leg of her exosuit in her moment of glory.

Tomi and Watry's orbital insertion went quite well, no mishaps or problems. Normally, coasting through space was pretty boring—one too many shuttle flights would do that to a person—but it was the anticipation of meeting atmosphere with just some ionized plasma protecting a fragile human being from a burning inferno that truly caused one's pulse to quicken.

As if that wasn't enough, once reentry was completed successfully, the change in gravity caused the two rangers to find themselves in free fall on their flitters. Tomi panicked at first, but she noticed Watry had remained calm and collected, using his own weight to steer toward the lifeboat. She kept quiet and followed his lead as they plummeted downward, trying her best to ignore the fact that her palms were sweating under her tight grip on the handlebars.

At 10,000 feet, Watry finally throttled the engine to his flitter, adjusting to the planet's gravity and slowing his descent. Tomi plunged several yards past him before she managed to do the same. To her relief, they continued to glide easily toward their target at a much more controllable speed after that.

Both Tomi and Watry touched down smoothly and glided to a stop. She killed the engine to her flitter, dismounted, and quickly pulled her repulsor rifle from its soft case. Using the scope, Tomi pretended the journey hadn't fazed her at all and

THE SHELTERING SKY

began scanning the horizon to see if anyone or anything was watching them.

"Don't worry, rook. If there was anyone out there, we would have seen them on the way down," Watry said.

He had time to scan the area on the way down? Tomi's heart had been pounding so hard the whole way, all she could remember was everything flying past her at high speed. Then again, this was only her first time using the flitter in such a manner. Hopefully with more practice, her perception under stress would be as sharp as her fellow ranger.

"Come on, Ryan," Watry said, snapping her out of her reverie. "Get your head in the game!"

Many miles away, an odd-looking aircraft fluttered along, quite literally flapping its wings. The only thing even odder than the ship was the pilot who had wings of his own. The Anar-phut known as Seeker-of-Many-Different-Living-Things had been sent out to perform a biological and zoological survey. But in the middle of a dry, burning desert there wasn't much movement, especially during the day.

Seeker leaned lazily on the window of his ornithopter, boredom practically oozing out of him. His survey leader, Teacher-of-Many-Ancient-Myths-and-Legends, was obviously punishing him for being so thorough in questioning the specimen cataloging procedures. Now here he was, looking for living things in a place where living things were not meant to live.

He jumped when his ornithopter's comm system crackled to life and began emitting a shrill squeal like a hungry newborn. He checked the display; the system had just detected a complex pulsating signal. Seeker fluted verbal commands in his native tongue, telling the system to display more information and sounding more like a poor attempt at playing an instrument. The wave form appeared to be too complex to be caused by any natural phenomena. It would require intelligence to make this.

What worried Seeker the most was the fact the system couldn't identify or even understand any of the data it was conveying. How was he to know what he was about to face without the proper information to prepare him? Seeker sighed. He would have to write another complaint to Teacher—this comm system's database was in desperate need of an upgrade.

Looking in the direction of the signal's origin, Seeker became progressively more concerned. No member of his survey team was supposed to be out here—except for him, of course. On top of that, only members of his species were allowed access to the planet Yardang. Since there were no native species on the planet with the technology to broadcast such a signal, the most likely explanation would be another starfaring race conducting operations on Yardang in violation of the interstellar treaty.

Seeker puffed out his chest at this intrusion. He would certainly be making a complaint about this when he returned to base camp.

Then he saw it. The ship wasn't too big. In fact, it wasn't big enough for any significant operation to get around in—enough room to carry a few of individuals, but not much else. The human species had a reputation for eccentric behavior such as journeying to far-off places in order to do something they called recreation. Though Seeker couldn't understand it, he wondered if that was what was happening here.

Problem was the treaty clearly stated humans weren't supposed to be here. There was no denying that these particular humans were in clear violation, but in order to file a grievance with the humans' government, Seeker would need more evidence. With the matter decided, he guided his ornithopter toward the human landing site.

Approaching from the opposite direction of the Federation Rangers' landing site, none of the humans saw the ornithopter's approach, and since it was powered by He3 fusion batteries driving polymer fiber bundles, the humans didn't hear anything either. Setting down on its tripod landing gear, Seeker shut his transport down and climbed out to get a closer look. Retrieving his field pack with his tail, he moved forward with camera in hand and observed Yardang's latest invaders.

The castaways were taking shelter from the early morning sun in the shade of the lifeboat's starboard wing. Some of them were beginning to grow restless. Salinger was eager for rescue as well, but what else could they do except wait?

"I don't understand why we're just sitting here," Isabelle complained for the *n*th time. "Why don't we at least try to find civilization?"

Salinger was tired of the negative comments from the others who weren't offering any real solutions. He stood and turned to face her, his muscles tensed angrily.

"Look around you," he practically shouted. "Do you see any signs of civilization? It's too cold during the night and too hot during the day. If we leave this lifeboat, we'll get lost before the day is out and then we'll have nothing to shelter us." Salinger was making a lot of big hand gestures as he spoke, his frustration apparent. "We wouldn't survive, Isabelle! Our best hope is to stay nearby where we're most likely to be spotted by a rescue mission."

Agitated, Isabelle was about to say more when she noticed two people fall out of the sky. She jumped up, bouncing over and over on her feet. Pointing in their direction, she cried out, "We're saved!"

Everyone stood excitedly and looked. When Salinger saw nothing besides some slight shimmering, he huffed, figuring she was either messing with him or hallucinating.

"It's just the desert playing tricks on you, Isabelle. The heat waves can make you think you're seeing something that isn't really there."

Disappointed, everyone else sat down again, but Isabelle was adamant there were people out there and they were coming this way to rescue them. Some of the passengers started to tell her to be quiet when they heard someone speak, startling them all back up to their feet.

"Federation Rangers! Don't move!"

All of the survivors frantically looked in the direction of the voice, throwing their arms in the air in surrender, but could see no one.

Lenny begged, "Don't shoot! We escaped a freighter by the name of the *Serena Dawn*. We were attacked by pirates, and we're all that remain."

More suspicious than the others, Salinger demanded of the ghost, "If you're really here to rescue us, let us see you."

Confirming that none of the people present were pirates, Tomi whipped the hood of her chameleon cloak back and opened the front. Several members of the group cheered, ran forward, and hugged Tomi, much to her dismay. A moment later, Watry popped out of his cloak while his partner was being smothered by the grateful crew.

Laughing at her wrinkled nose, he said, "Okay, rookie, you do the health assessments and I'll do the interviews."

Tomi grabbed her medical pack and paused when she heard something on her audio pickups, a buzzing sort of noise. "Hey, Watry! Do you hear that?"

Watry was about to ask what she was talking about when he heard it to. Concern rising, he ordered, "Everyone to cover! Ryan, with me."

Tomi wondered why Watry was so jumpy. "Maybe it's another ranger rescue crew?"

"Negative. We're the only rangers assigned to this area and we didn't call for any support." A moment later, he added, "That sounds like a multirotor VTOL. Our flitters use ducted fans, so whoever is coming represents someone else—possibly the pirates coming to finish the job."

Isabelle let out a scream of sheer terror at this suggestion.

"But it's been a couple of weeks already," Tomi said. "Wouldn't they have taken out the lifeboat long before it landed?"

"Normally, yes. Unless they were laying low because they heard what happened to Blowtorch's crew," Watry answered. "Just keep your eyes open."

Tomi nodded as an aircraft flew over and went into a pylon turn, obviously surveying the crash site. The pilot appeared to have found what he was looking for because he immediately opened fire with a laser cannon.

Seeker had hidden behind a rock pinnacle close to the humans, trying to assess exactly what they were up to. Just as he lifted his camera to capture some images, a VTOL whipped overhead. He ducked back behind the hoodoo as bullets began to rain down all around him.

The shot burned thru the thrusters in the back of the lifeboat, causing the reaction mass tanks to burst in a loud explosion.

"Get away from the lifeboat!" Watry yelled.

He didn't have to say it twice—everyone scattered as quickly as they could just as a missile streaked and hit the front of the lifeboat. The VTOL adjusted and fired its laser again, and two more explosions followed.

"Motherfucking son of a bitch! They took out our flitters," Watry cursed. He watched as the VTOL altered course again, pulsing its laser at some unknown target. "What the hell is it doing?"

Tomi wondered what could be over there that they didn't know about. Watry had been certain they were the only ones out here. Even so, there was a bright flash, an explosion of blue sparks and a loud crack like a fusion battery rupturing. Something had clearly been there, but it wasn't anymore.

The VTOL swung back to take another pass at the lifeboat. Tomi readied her long rifle, looking through the scope and aiming at the enemy ship. The ballistics computer blinked, indicating it had a firing solution on the VTOL. Depressing the trigger and moving the reticle to the target, her weapon fired. With a loud crack, the projectile flew and tore through the machine's center of mass, but still it stayed airborne.

Tomi flipped the selector to full auto and squeezed the trigger again. The VTOL tried to take evasive action. Regardless, it caught a stream of bullets, stitching it from one end to the other. Every vital system was hit, fusion batteries caught fire, and the aircraft plunged straight into the desert floor.

In half a second, Watry was on his feet yelling, "Ryan, secure the perimeter!"

Tomi jumped to her feet, switching her scanner on while sweeping the area through her scope. As she ran around what was left of the lifeboat, she caught sight of the smoke coming from her flitter. *Shit, now we'll have to do this the hard way.* Meeting back up with Watry on the other side, they both reported their sectors were clear.

"Good shooting, Ryan, but we have a new problem. Whoever sent that flier now knows we're dirtside, and you can bet they'll be sending a follow-up."

Tomi noted that Watry was almost shouting; he was just as jacked up on adrenaline as she was. It seems no matter how seasoned the ranger, the excitement never faded.

"We need to check on the survivors," he said.

Tomi had momentarily forgotten about them. The rangers hustled over to where the passengers were last seen and Tomi stopped dead in her tracks at the sight. Salinger was kneeling over one of the others, pressing a wadded-up shirt to the supine man's abdomen. It was saturated with red liquid—not good.

"Come on, Lenny," Salinger kept saying. "Hang in there, man. Lenny, don't you die on me!"

"Stand back," Tomi ordered as she jogged over to the moaning man.

Following procedure, she started running her scanner in medical mode, beginning at Lenny's feet and working her way up. When she passed her scanner glove over his abdomen, Tomi stopped. Lifting the soggy shirt, she could see Lenny had been struck with a piece of debris the size of a tea saucer, causing extensive damage to his liver, right kidney, and intestines. What was still intact was hanging out. This guy didn't have much of a chance.

Still, she was a ranger, and she had taken an oath to do whatever she could to protect the lives of others. This man would need a fully equipped hospital to live through this, but with her emergency life-support unit, she could at least keep him from dying long enough to get him to one. Tomi stood and was about to retrieve her ELSU, but quickly remembered it was on her now-burning flitter. All she had on her was her medkit, and it wouldn't be enough to save Lenny.

Noticing she had stopped working on his crewmate, Salinger stood angrily to shout at her. "What are you waiting for? Save him!"

Tomi shook her head and cast her gaze toward the ground. "I'm sorry. Your friend can't be saved. There's just too much damage and the equipment I need to have any chance has been lost in the attack." Tomi motioned toward the flitters still awash in flames.

Salinger didn't even turn his head to look. He wasn't having any of it. "Do something, you cunt! Help him! Help him!"

Still conscious, Lenny tried to speak. Kneeling down and

putting her ear next to his mouth, Tomi struggled to listen. It took Lenny a couple of tries to say it, but finally, she was able to make out the word pain.

She sat up straighter and said, "He's in pain. At this point, the only thing that can be done for him is to make him comfortable."

"You fucking bitch!" Salinger yelled.

Tomi's muscles tensed in defense of his unreasonable anger, but when Salinger started crying, her own rage subsided. Over the last several months of being a ranger, she had found she could handle seeing blood and guts and even shooting another human being. But crying was something else entirely, especially when it was a man.

Seeing a man cry stabbed her in the heart. She had always admired manly men who were strong and dauntless, even though she knew that was bullshit. She had seen her brother cry, her father, and others as well. Still, every time she saw a man break down under the weight of his emotions, she wanted to go and hide somewhere and shed a few tears herself. That wasn't an option right now.

Now, she was the one who had to be strong and dauntless because she couldn't run and hide from the situation at hand. Even so, she couldn't stop her eyes from betraying her sensitivity. With tears streaming down her face, Tomi used the hypo-injector to give Lenny a strong dose of neuroine, and he died an hour later.

Watry tried to contact the *Bass Reeves* to no avail. Judging from the static he was hearing, there weren't any problems with his comm gear. More likely, someone was jamming his communications. Tomi had just called through to tell him the enemy pilot was dead, so it worked well enough for nearby recipients at least, but he'd have to figure all of that out later. Right now, they needed to assess the situation for emergency protocol.

He surveyed the carnage left behind, noting that the situation looked dire. The explosions and resulting fire had gutted the lifeboat, leaving nothing salvageable—no food, water, or medical supplies besides what they had on their person. With it went the emergency locater beacon, which meant the *Bass Reeves* would have a difficult time locating their exact position. Worse, the rangers' vehicles were completely destroyed, so goodbye to all of that gear too. Watry even went and looked at the VTOL wreck in hopes he might find something that could be useful, but it was mangled on impact and the discharge from the He_3 batteries had incinerated what was left.

Tomi waited with the remaining survivors, now only numbering three, plus the two rangers. Knowing whatever came next would require a lot of physical effort, she eyed one of the survivors in particular. Salinger was obnoxious and prideful, but he was young and strong. Isabelle was also young and fit and seemed okay for the most part, although she did strike Tomi as the damsel-in-distress sort. But the one she was most concerned about was the one named Buddy. He was older and didn't look like he worked out regularly. He would have trouble keeping up if anything went wrong. She just hoped it wouldn't be long before they were all rescued.

The group watched as Watry returned, noticing that he didn't look very hopeful. He pulled Tomi aside for a private update before speaking with the rest of the group.

"There's nothing left and I can't get ahold of the *BR*—I think someone is jamming the communication system."

Tomi raised her eyebrows. "So, what do we do?"

"We'll need to take inventory of the supplies the crew managed to get off the lifeboat before the attack, but more worrisome is whether we can find potable water."

Having been through desert survival school, Tomi was handling this news better than the passengers might once they found out. If her instructors had taught her anything, it was how a positive attitude could carry you through. Those who just curled up and cried were the most certain to die.

As she and Watry were discussing which direction to go, Isabelle started shouting, "Oh my Deus! There's a monster coming!" She certainly was an observant one.

Tomi saw the creature next. "What the fuck?" It looked like something out of a horror story from the pits of hell. The creature was mostly red, darkening to black along the edges of its wings and down its back. Its silhouette reminded Tomi of a wyvern from the mythological roleplaying games she played back in school: bat-like wings, one pair of legs, and a long serpentine body with a wicked-looking spike on the end. "Wait a minute, isn't that a—"

Before she could finish her sentence, the creature bounded up to them. Tomi pulled her sidearm and the creature reared up, coiling its tail underneath and holding its feet, which looked more like hands, in a gesture of surrender. It obviously knew what Tomi's sidearm could do as it made frantic noises like some out-of-tune trumpet. Understanding that it meant no harm, Tomi kept her finger off the trigger.

"Ryan, turn your translator on," Watry said out of the corner of his mouth.

The wyvern was making sounds that were progressively higher pitched; it had gone from a trumpet to a flute to a piccolo and its tempo was getting more rapid and urgent. Switching on her translator, she heard the creature saying, "Don't shoot, you hairless ape! I'm harmless, mostly."

With all of the stress she'd had to deal with over the last few hours, hearing the creature's absurd statement was the funniest thing Tomi had heard all day. She dropped her omniblaster to the low-ready position and started laughing. Seeing her lower her guard, the creature also relaxed, dropping back down to its feet, lifting its tail, and scratching its head with the spiked tip. Rather than scratching an itch, it looked more like it was thinking.

Tomi holstered her weapon and introduced herself. "Hi, my name is Tomi Ryan and I am with the Federation Rangers."

The creature widened its eyes and used its tail to point at Tomi aggressively. "I knew it! The Federation is invading Yardang! This is a blatant violation of our treaty. I'll have to report you."

Watry interjected, "Now, hold on there. The treaty allows for emergencies, and this is a rescue mission."

"Then why did you obliterate my ornithopter? All of my field work was in it. Weeks of work, heartlessly incinerated." The creature picked a handful (or footful?) of sand and threw it into the wind.

"That wasn't us," Tomi said.

The creature was agitated, thrashing its tail around like an angry house cat. "And how am I supposed to believe you? All of you humans look alike. And besides, no one else is here." It looked around at the vacant desert to emphasize its point.

Tomi wanted to tell this thing off. "I told you my name. Now tell me yours."

The creature reared up on its tail again, folded its legs (or arms?), looked her in the eye with its strange multicolored eyes, and said, "My name is Seeker-of-Many-Different-Living-Things, and I am an Anar-phut." When it noticed Tomi staring blankly, it added, "You may call me Seeker."

Remembering what she had read about the Anar-phut, their coloration revealed their gender. The females had the opposite color pattern of the males who were mostly red, so Seeker must be a male. As Tomi examined him up and down like some science experiment, Seeker grew uncomfortable and impatient.

"Who destroyed my ornithopter?" he demanded again.

"I don't know, sorry." She motioned toward the fallen VTOL. "He was firing on us. I think you just happened to be in the way."

Seeker looked toward the burning VTOL for a moment, realizing what she said did make sense. After all, all of their vehicles were obliterated also. Dropping down onto his feet, Seeker turned and walked to a high spot where he could see the column of smoke marking the remains of his own vehicle. He'd lost weeks of research, no longer had a vehicle or supplies, and was now stranded in this Deus-forsaken desert with these *humans*. Letting the situation fully sink in, Seeker screamed in frustration, which to the humans sounded like a half a dozen conch shells being blown simultaneously.

Tomi honestly felt sorry for the alien, but there was nothing she could do. They were in a dire situation of their own. She turned to her partner who was messing with his wrist comp again.

"Any luck?" she asked him. Watry shook his head. Tomi turned to the others. "Well, everyone, looks like we're on our own."

"What do you mean?" Buddy asked. "Where's the rest of your team?"

"Someone is jamming the comm system. Help is not on the way," Watry said.

Looked like Tomi was right in her assessment of Isabelle—she was crying now. She was pretty good at judging character, she'd discovered lately.

"So, Watry, what's the plan? Spell out SOS with rocks and hope the *Bass Reeves* sees our signal?" Tomi said sarcastically, attempting to lighten the darkened mood.

"In Survival 101 class, that would be a good answer, but in this case, we've just been kicked all the way up to grad school," Watry shot back with equal sarcasm. "We've got two problems: first, our water is only going to last two days, maybe three, and that's factoring in our vapor canteens. Second, somebody is actively hunting us and that VTOL is just round one. I'm certain they will try again, and soon."

"Question is who are they?" Tomi asked.

"I couldn't get a solid ID since the pilot and his VTOL are now a pile of ashes, but my best guess is the Star Demon Syndicate is trying to clean up the mess left behind from the *Serena Dawn*. Either way, we need to get moving to get out of the line of fire and to find water. If it is those pirates, they aren't ones to give up very easily."

At this, Isabelle cried harder and Salinger gave the rangers a harsh look.

Watry simply shrugged and said, "It's either that, or lay down and die. Your call. But I'm heading out in five with or without you."

Tomi pointed toward the horizon. "Sunset is approaching and it's starting to cool down. We should try get to the next outcropping while we still have daylight."

Watry gave her an approving look. "Have you done this before?"

At first, Tomi thought he was criticizing her attempt at leadership, but then she realized he was actually complimenting her in a subtle way. It was the best option under the circumstances.

"What else you got, Ryan?" Watry prodded.

"Well, sitting in the same spot we've already been attacked in isn't going to serve our survival purposes. For one, there isn't anything left to salvage, and for another thing, our attacker knows about this location," Tomi said. Watry nodded, encouraging her to continue. "In addition, traveling during the day would consume the most water, and between the below-freezing temps and the blinding darkness on an alien planet, traveling at night is almost as dangerous."

The rangers' optics were equipped with night vision, but Tomi knew the passengers didn't have anything like that. If one of them got separated from the group, they would certainly die on their own. She also knew when they settled in somewhere for the night, they would need to huddle together to conserve heat. By traveling at dawn and dusk, the temperature would be more tolerable and there would be enough light to see by. It was the best plan they had.

"Well done, Ryan. Sounds like our plan is settled then." Watry turned to the three crewmembers of the *Serena Dawn*. "We're leaving in five. Gather whatever you can and be ready for a hike."

Seeker, who had remained at a distance since their

conversation, now walked back the group. "You are leaving? Searching for water and shelter?"

Tomi nodded. "It wouldn't be worthwhile or safe to linger here."

Seeker looked a bit bashful as he asked, "Can I join you?"

"What made you come around, Seeker?" Watry asked, having assumed the Anar-phut was not planning on befriending them.

"While it was certainly not my first choice, I don't seem to have any others."

As he looked back toward the plume of smoke that used to be his ship, Tomi had to hold in another burst of laughter. She wondered if all Anar-phuts weren't ones to mince words, or just this one in particular. She thought it would be quite entertaining to have him along on their journey.

Seeker continued, "And besides, they are in violation of an interstellar treaty."

The rangers nodded and Watry said, "You're more than welcome to join us."

As though he didn't hear the invitation, Seeker tried to prove his value. "I assure you I would be an asset and not a hindrance. I have in my possession mapping data showing stone structures we could use for shelter, as well as oases to obtain water, and—"

"Ah, even from a distance you were keeping an eye on us," Tomi said, unable to hide her amusement.

Seeker nodded his head. "Of course. You humans have a reputation for being fickle, unpredictable even, so I thought it would be prudent to act like I was ignoring you while not ignoring you."

Suddenly serious, Watry scolded, "Shut up!"

Tomi and Seeker both jumped and then noticed his tensed muscles as he listened intently to something in the distance. Just over the sound of the windblown sand, there was a buzzing sound. Bringing her rifle up, Tomi scanned through her helmet optics, sweeping her sector. Nothing.

Watry called out, "Multiple bogeys coming in from the north. Everybody, take cover!"

The others scattered, hiding by rock pinnacles and hoping the shadows from the sunset would hide them well enough. Tomi stayed where she was, wrapping her cloak around herself and letting its metamaterial properties bend the light around it to make her virtually disappear from sight.

The VTOLs came in fast, flying over the outcropping where the survivors had been sheltering. Not seeing anyone, they came in for a landing near the destroyed lifeboat for a closer look. Armed humans started jumping out, some forming a perimeter around their aircrafts, and others running toward the various wreckage sites. Tomi noticed the symbol painted on the sides of the three VTOLs—these guys definitely belonged to the Star Demon Syndicate.

"Check it out, Watry," she whispered into her wrist comp. "We're in luck. The pirates have decided to come to us."

On the other end of the outcropping, Watry cautioned, "Right now, they're just looking for survivors from the *Serena Dawn*. If they have brains in their heads, they'll realize from the remainder of the flitters that there are rangers dirtside as well."

Watry was right to worry. While the pirates found Lenny's cold body, Tomi could see from the body language of the lead pirate that he wasn't satisfied. He ordered for the perimeter to be searched. Tomi moved slowly and took cover behind a large boulder; she was going to need it when the inevitable shooting started.

The pirates spread out in a search pattern, scanning the ground for any signs of human activity. One of them was moving toward the three survivors' position when he spotted what looked like tracks. Tomi cursed herself. She should have obliterated any tracks leading away from the lifeboat. It was too late now.

Watry whispered over their comm channel, "Here we go. Get ready." He brought his rifle up, and Tomi followed suit.

"Hey, I think I found something," the pirate called out to his comrades as he continued following the tracks. He came to the top of the rise where he could see the survivors clear as day. Waving his right arm to get the attention of his buddies, he yelled, "Over here! I found—"

He was cut short by a loud crack. A large cloud of pink mist erupted from his chest. With a stunned look, the pirate fell flat on his face and his shipmates stood frozen. The rangers didn't wait for an invitation. Better to launch their attack before the pirates came out of shock.

Tomi focused on the pirates on the left while Watry concentrated his fire on the right, allowing their zones of fire to interlock. Tomi moved from target to target, squeezing off a single shot each time. By the time the marauders got their wits back, six of them were already on the ground. Some dove for cover, while others tried to run back to their transports. Even while they were moving, the rangers' ballistic computers were able to lead each target and pick them off.

From behind cover, the pirate officer was shouting at the top of his lungs, "Get the gunships up! Get the fucking gunships up now!"

The fusion air ram engines of the VTOLs spun up, creating a maelstrom of wind and sand. Out of the pirates still on the ground, none moved as the gunships started to lift off. Over the din, Tomi could barely hear Watry on her wrist comp.

"Shoot the cockpits! If those gunships get airborne, they'll run us down."

Watry aimed and fired his rifle on full auto, stitching the windscreen of the VTOL in his zone of fire. It had already lifted off when the rounds hit, but with the energy of 12mm cannon shells, Watry's bullets tore through the transparent aluminum like paper. One shot took off the copilot's left arm and another decapitated the pilot. Both let go of the controls and their ship wobbled in the air before slamming into the desert floor.

Tomi tried to do the same with her own target, but her VTOL

was facing away from her. *Think fast,* she thought to herself. *Improvise, adapt, overcome.* "That's it!" she said out loud, swinging her aimpoint over to the craft's port nacelle. She flipped her rifle's selector over to full auto and fired. The rounds hit low and made a trail traveling up the nacelle's exterior cowling, but the results weren't what she was hoping for.

The VTOL didn't even shudder, and instead yawed, bringing its guns to bear on Tomi. *This is it,* she thought. *I'm going to die on this Deus-forsaken planet.* But before the pirate gunner could shoot, the engine Tomi had hit suddenly spewed pieces of itself out the exhaust and started to sputter. Through her scope, she could see the pilots' frantic attempts to land the craft safely, but they failed. As its port engine experienced catastrophic failure, the starboard engine lifted the VTOL and flipped it, sending it cartwheeling into the lifeboat. The VTOL must have been loaded for bear as it made a spectacular explosion. It was so intense, Tomi had to take cover behind the boulder to avoid getting hit with debris.

Staying there, she raised her rifle and used her HUD to survey the damage. The pirates had had enough. The ones who remained breathing jumped into the third VTOL and flew away. As the ship flew over the survivors, it ejected a single piece of paper. Tomi grabbed at it as it fluttered toward her. On one side was the symbol of the Star Demon Syndicate, and on the other in hasty handwriting, it said, "We no who u r. We will hunt u down. U r going 2 die." She tossed the card and went to check on the others.

As Tomi searched for survivors in the aftermath, she called out. Isabelle responded and appeared unharmed. Seeker stood up and shook off a powdering of sand.

"Have the hostilities ceased?" Seeker asked. "I do not hear any more explosions."

Tomi nodded but her eyes were drawn toward Salinger. He was shaking Buddy who was screaming for it to stop. Buddy was in shock, but he was also in one piece. Tomi breathed a sigh of relief—

that was good enough in her book. Then she noticed Watry still in position, sprawled on the ground.

"Watry!" she yelled, running over to him.

Switching on her bioscanner, she shook him and yelled in his face, waiting for it to boot up. He stirred but didn't say anything intelligible. Tomi breathed a sigh of relief. Watry was still breathing. The bioscanner started its med scan, taking his pulse, blood pressure, and respiration—all good.

"Is he alive?"

Tomi jumped slightly, noticing suddenly that Seeker had followed her over to her fellow ranger. "Looks like Watry is just stunned," she answered. "His exosuit is damaged and his collarbone is fractured. He isn't getting out of this caper unscathed, but he'll survive."

Pulling out her medical kit, she found the portable autodoc. Placing it over Watry's broken bone, Tomi activated the device and it went to work on the fracture, first injecting Watry with no-shock and pain killers so he wouldn't struggle. Tomi and Seeker watched as both ends of the break were treated with skeletal adhesive and joined together. With the repairs completed, Tomi left the autodoc in place to continue monitoring the ranger's vital signs.

She stood and assessed the rest of their situation. Seeker had finally wandered off and given her some space, but Salinger was now staring at her from not too far away.

"Is he going to be okay?" he asked.

"Yes," Tomi answered, but before she could ask for everyone's attention, Salinger got in her face, his own turning beet red.

"Then why couldn't do that for Lenny, you cunt? Your buddy's life is worth saving, but Lenny's wasn't worth a flying fuck? Answer me, you bitch!" His rage boiling over, Salinger shoved Tomi, which was a big mistake.

She felt bad for the guy, losing his crewmate. She really did. But once he laid hands on her, it was game over. She grabbed Salinger's left arm and pulled the man off balance. Slamming her right knee into his crotch, he doubled over. Salinger wasn't in the mood for a fight anymore, too busy rolling around and groaning. Tomi felt justified, but she could still hear instructor berating her for using such a predictable technique. *Whatever,* she thought. *It worked, didn't it?*

12

PASSAGE FROM PERDITION TO PARADISE

Seeing the commotion, Seeker came loping back over to Tomi. She had never seen an Anar-phut run before and she found it interesting; Seeker was using his wings like front legs to launch himself forward in concert with his only pair of legs. It was like watching a vampire bat run, just scaled way up. Stopping in front of Salinger's crumpled form, Seeker lifted his tail up like a scorpion, ready to strike.

"Wait!" Tomi yelled, surprised Seeker had come to her aid. *Guess he wasn't so anti-human after all,* she thought. *Just anti-some-humans.* "It's okay, Seeker. We just had a little misunderstanding. You can put your stinger away."

Seeker looked at his stinger and then used it to scratch his head almost like he was pretending his intensions were never meant to be hostile. Lifting his wings off the ground, he followed Tomi back over to the rest of the group.

"Your friend is injured; will this alter your plans?" Seeker asked her.

"No. Our problems are still the same. We need water in a very serious way, which means we have to get moving." It was that simple. There were no other options. She knew Watry would have told her the same thing if he could. She just hoped he regained consciousness soon so they didn't have to wait too long to get out of there.

"What's with him?" Watry asked, motioning with his head toward a still-pouting Salinger. Watry had rejoined the land of the living a few minutes prior and the rangers sat together while he gathered his bearings.

"Oh, him? Nothing. He just needed to be taught a lesson is all." Tomi feigned seriousness, but ended up giving her partner a smirk.

Watry laughed and slapped Tomi on the shoulder. "Atta girl." He laughed again and then stood to address their small motley crew.

"Okay, everyone, we've lost enough time. We need to get moving."

"You sure you're ready for a hike?" Tomi questioned.

"No choice, rookie. Improvise, adapt, overcome," he reminded her.

Tomi nodded as Watry urged the others to their feet to begin the trek north toward the nearest rest point.

They arrived just as darkness fell, the temperature dropping fast. Tomi noticed that Buddy, as the oldest present, seemed to be the most tired of them all. She wasn't sure he would make it if the situation intensified. Why hadn't anybody come looking for them yet?

"Okay, this is camp for the night. Make yourselves comfortable," Watry announced.

Tomi and Watry set their survival watches to wake them just

after sunrise, and they all huddled together to conserve heat. The rangers took the outside of the group since their exosuits helped maintain their normal body temperatures. Those who had never been in a desert would be surprised, for as hot as the temperature could be during the day, conversely it could be very cold at night. Even huddled together and covered with emergency blankets, the humans and the Anar-phut found their rest a little chilly.

Tomi woke, eyes still closed, and thought how nice it was nice to rest after walking for hours, but she knew that couldn't last forever. As if on cue, the alarms on the rangers' survival watches went off. Watry stirred, still smarting from his collarbone injury. He groaned as he stretched, working his arm carefully so he didn't reinjure it. The bone adhesive was holding, but he didn't want to push his luck. Shouldering his pack and rifle on his good arm, he started waking up the survivors.

"Wakey, wakey, no eggs and bakey," he announced.

Salinger and Isabelle groaned and worked themselves awake. Buddy sat up, looking weak, but not making a single complaint. Seeker was proving to be a real trooper too, Tomi had noticed.

"Sorry, no eggs or bacon, but we do have survival rations," she said. "Eat every crumb because you're going to need every calorie to get through this day."

"Good advice, Ranger Ryan. We'll be walking for several hours to get to the next rock formation," said Watry. "Ryan, take point."

When at last everyone was finished eating their rations, they got moving. They needed to get as far as possible before the sun made it too hot. Seeker followed behind Tomi just in case she couldn't read his map. Tomi would have thought Seeker was being condescending, but when she looked at the Anar-phut's map, she saw a near-empty sketch of the surrounding territory, vacant and bare. There were no routes marked and she was confused for a minute before she remembered Seeker's species could see in infrared and ultraviolet. There were likely lines on the map the humans couldn't see without assistance.

"Seeker, is there some way you could adjust the display's spectrum?" she asked.

Seeker moved alongside Tomi, using the tip of his tail to adjust the picture's color. Tomi thanked him, found the marking of a water source, and looked up to get her bearing. She paused when she saw what looked like people standing side by side off in the distance.

"Who...what the hell is that?" Tomi asked.

Following her gaze, Seeker saw them too. "The Ur-not. I was hoping to avoid them," he answered.

"Are they dangerous or just annoying?"

"They can be territorial, but if you keep your distance, they will not attack. The problem is they burrow under the sand for shelter, so one can literally and unknowingly trip over one of them and—"

"And you get attacked before you know what happened," Tomi finished.

Seeker nodded. "It gets worse. The social organization of the Ur-not appears to be a hive mind. What is done to one is done to the rest of the group. It is best to simply fly over them."

Too bad we humans don't have wings, Tomi thought to herself. Better inform Watry of the potential threat. She pointed them out and told him how Seeker had advised they avoid the Ur-not as much as possible. If they went around the ones they could see, hopefully they wouldn't have any unpleasant surprises.

"Can we alter course completely?" Watry asked her, thinking complete avoidance might be best considering their circumstances.

Tomi shook her head solemnly. "They're between us and the nearest water source. As it is, it could take us another day or two to reach this one."

Watry pursed his lips and shook his half-empty canteen. "We'd better hustle then. If we have to make any detours, it'll cost us time and we don't want to get caught out in the midday sun."

Tomi nodded and moved back up to the front. Looking at where she had seen the Ur-not just minutes earlier, she was alarmed to see they were now nowhere in sight.

"Did you see where they went?" she asked Seeker.

"They withdrew behind the rise. They can be skittish but do not become complacent, their territory is not clearly delineated. I have not determined how they mark their territory nor how they navigate. All I have ascertained is that if one gets within three meters an Ur-not, it will rear up and display threatening gestures. If that happens, it is best to back away, otherwise it will attack," Seeker counseled.

The group made it to the next outcropping without incident where the rangers announced that they would wait in the shade until dusk. Despite their success, neither the rangers nor the Anar-phut biologist were breathing a sigh of relief just yet. Seeing them still tensed, Salinger approached the rangers.

"What's the matter?" he asked. "We managed to steer clear of the Ur-whatever. Aren't we in the clear now?"

"The Ur-not are found all over this desert region and the area we are heading into is much more rugged," Seeker answered. "Assuming we detect any Ur-not in time, it will become progressively more difficult to go around them. We all must remain vigilant."

George "Psycho" Knight was royally pissed off. He'd sent out over two dozen well-armed men and most of the stupid fuckers had gotten themselves killed, not to mention the loss of three of their VTOLs. The ones who returned faced a blistering ass chewing and the promise of certain death if they failed a second time. They offered to try again and even promised to bring back the right ear of each of their victims.

"You've had your chance," Psycho said with a snarl. After a pause, he said, "When you last saw them, you said they were heading north?"

They all nodded in agreement, swallowing back their fear. Calling up a holomap of the area, the pirate lieutenant realized something.

"The dumb bastards are heading straight into Ur-not territory," he announced, smirking. Turning to his men, he ordered, "Send out an attack VTOL, but don't attack them directly. Strafe the area around them. That should really piss of those sand monsters and then the desert will swallow up our friends for sure."

Relieved to hear their officer laugh for once, the pirates leaped into action without another word.

With the sun heading toward the horizon, it was time for the ragtag group of survivors to get moving again. Though still on alert, Tomi thought they had been pretty lucky so far; they'd so far managed to steer clear of any physical altercations with the Ur-not, though they were definitely being watched.

Every so often on their trek across the desert, a few Ur-nots would pop their heads up for a brief moment and look right at them before disappearing below ground again. Even now as they gathered their meager supplies to get moving again, Tomi could see them well off into the distance, silently watching.

Keeping an eye on them, she consulted with Watry and Seeker. "The terrain ahead doesn't look great—less dunes and more rock. The topography will limit where we can trek, which in turn will make it more difficult to avoid the Ur-nots."

Watry nodded. "The only upside is that the terrain change will provide more cover from pirate attacks."

"I can fly ahead and scout a path for us," Seeker offered.

"That would be helpful," Watry agreed.

From the air, Seeker was able to spot any blind alleys, preventing the group from having to backtrack if they took a wrong turn. They really didn't have the time to spare for such errors. This method did work well for a while, but on his latest jaunt, Seeker suddenly dove back down and out of sight.

"What the hell?" Tomi started to say when they heard why the Anar-phut had taken cover—the whine of a VTOL's engines was growing nearer.

"Take cover! The pirates are coming back," Tomi shouted.

The VTOL barreled in at top speed, opening up with a Gauss machine gun. The hypersonic projectiles stitched across a nearby rockface, showering everyone with pulverized stone. Tomi was starting to lose her patience with these marauders, but she thought their actions seemed odd.

"They're just praying and spraying," she said.

"No," Watry countered, shaking his head. "They're using our friends to their benefit."

Tomi knew he was referring to the Ur-nots. The pirates were trying to stir them up so they would attack on their behalf. Taking up her shooting position, she knew the ravine they were in would force the VTOL to approach from one of two directions. A fifty-fifty chance, Tomi decided since he'd attacked from the north the first time, she would face south.

Making sure her rifle was set to full auto, Tomi kept both eyes open. She chose correctly; the VTOL came in from the south to perform another strafing run. The machine gun started up again and the gunner walked his burst toward Buddy's hiding position in front of Tomi.

Blending in with the rock she was using as a rest, the VTOL pilot didn't even realize Tomi was there until her own burst from her long rifle ripped apart the right side of the cockpit. The pilot was unscathed and the right seat unoccupied, but if someone had been sitting there, they would have been torn to pieces just like the seat had been.

Pulling up, the pilot decided that firing over 500 rounds was enough. He didn't care how much Pyscho chewed his ass later, he wasn't taking the chance that the invisible attacker might correct her aim and take his head off. With warning lights going off from the damage Tomi had inflicted, it was time to return to base. Let the aliens do the rest of the hard work.

The pilot landed safely a few minutes later, killing the engine to the VTOL and climbing out of the severely damaged cockpit. It wasn't long before his boss interrogated him.

"Well?" Psycho demanded.

As the VTOL bugged out, Tomi let out a sigh of relief. Her solace didn't last long.

"Ryan, behind you!" Watry called out.

Tomi turned in time to see the Ur-not standing a few feet from her. It was huge—easily over 500 pounds—with a hide that was indistinguishable from the surrounding rock. Swinging its arms out in sweeping movements, it made not a sound, a detail which Tomi found eerie. Seeker would later tell her that all Ur-nots were mutes.

She tried to call out to Watry, "Don't shoot!"

But he had already double-tapped the hulking creature with his long rifle. Tomi could hear the sharp cracks as the two projectiles streaked past her. Both bullets tore through the Ur-not's upper torso, erupting in a creamy green mist behind it. Despite the force of impact, the Ur-not lurched forward and fell on Tomi, pinning her down.

"Holy shit! Tomi, are you hurt?" Watry yelled. When he got no answer, he yelled at the others instead. "Help me!" he said, urging everyone to help roll the creature off his fellow ranger. "Get on one side and push."

It took them a few tries, but Tomi was finally free of the creature's bulk. The force of the Ur-not falling on top of her had knocked the wind out of her. Struggling to get air back into her lungs, Tomi rolled onto her side facing away from everyone and heaved a few deep breaths.

"Ryan, you good?" Watry asked again.

Tomi nodded, still catching her breath. A few seconds later, she rose to a kneeling position. Why was everyone staring at her? Sure, she'd just been attacked by a 500-pound mute beast, but it's not like her face had been rearranged to resemble a Picasso painting.

Isabelle cleared her throat. "Uh, your..." She motioned her hand toward her own chest and then pointed at Tomi's.

Tomi followed the woman's gaze and glanced downward, expecting to see blood or anything other than what she actually discovered. It seemed in the process of falling on her, one of the creature's digging claws had grazed her chest and torn through both the nanoweave mesh of her exosuit and her bra, leaving Tomi's right breast hanging out. She would have been embarrassed, but she was too busy being annoyed by the shameless gaping coming from Salinger and Buddy. *Are these guys virgins?* At least her fellow ranger and Seeker had the common courtesy of keeping their eyes on her face.

Maintaining her professionalism, Tomi didn't feel any pain but checked for blood anyway. There was none. She pulled the tear in her suit shut and rose to her feet. As everyone regained their composure, Seeker turned to Watry and scolded him.

"Why did you do shoot it? Now all the Ur-nots will start attacking us!"

"I had to. It would have killed Ryan if I didn't!" Watry retorted.

"Seeker, it's not his fault," Tomi intervened. "I never told him what you shared with me about Ur-not behavior." She turned to

Watry to catch him up. "The Ur-not was just doing a threatening display in an attempt to scare us off. It wouldn't have attacked unless we made the first move. If I backed away, it would have backed down," Tomi explained.

Watry let out a breath, absorbing this information.

"The Ur-nots have a hive mind," Seeker added. "Now that we have killed one of their own, the others will attack without warning." He pointed at the surrounding cliffs and said, "Look." Already other Ur-nots were gathering, and more joined with each passing second.

"Best get moving," Tomi said.

Everyone immediately gathered their things, moving as fast as they could to get away from the slowly converging horde.

The rocky barrens were starting to thin out, giving way to vegetated savanna, but the Ur-nots were still in pursuit. Slow though it was, the creatures' efforts showed an extreme level of coordination. Their hive mind kept them effortlessly synchronized. The fact that the Ur-nots moved slower than the humans could provided a little comfort, but they were still worried. Eventually, they would need to stop and rest, giving the Ur-nots a chance to catch up.

"Seeker," Watry asked quietly, "just how smart are these creatures? Could they extrapolate our direction of travel and cut us off?"

To the rangers' dismay, Seeker nodded. "It is very possible."

Sure enough, as the group rounded the last ridge, there they were: a whole line of Ur-nots barring the way north into the grasslands. Without hesitation, the creatures started to advance.

"Oh Deus! Oh Deus! What are we going to do?" Isabelle immediately began panicking, her voice trembling with fear.

In all honesty, Tomi felt just as scared and could tell everyone else was ready to load their pants too. But she was a ranger. She didn't have time to allow her fears to overcome her. She needed to be ready for anything.

"Improvise, adapt, overcome," Tomi said to herself as she loaded her spare magazine into her rifle.

"You're starting to sound like a seasoned ranger, Ryan," Watry said. Tomi couldn't help but smile at his subtle praise. After a brief pause, Watry instructed, "Switch to semi-auto and make every shot count."

"Why don't you give us your pistols?" Salinger asked. "I'm a fair shot. How hard can it be?"

"No good. Our pistols have grip recognition. They wouldn't work for you," Watry replied. "Just stay behind us."

The Ur-nots were advancing from behind. If they were going to be able to rest at nightfall, they'd have to take action to secure their safety now.

Tomi got into position and started shooting first with Watry a close second behind her. Each shot left a small hole in the front of each creature's torso and erupted out the back into a hole the size of a man's head. Firing in rapid succession, the two rangers shot twenty-one Ur-nots in eleven seconds, filling the air with green mist and the metallic smell of blood.

Salinger, Buddy, and Isabelle were stunned by the sheer number of Ur-not carcasses lying in front of them. Salinger loathed the idea of killing anything, but he also recognized that they were running out of options. For once, he kept his mouth shut.

With enough of them cleared, Watry screamed, "Go! Go! Go! The others will be on our asses any second."

Tomi was already grabbing Isabelle by the arm and forcing her to run, but Salinger didn't have to be asked twice. Seeker had started loping forward in his awkward-looking gait, easily keeping pace with the humans. The trouble was Buddy. Just as Tomi had suspected, when shit hit the fan, he wasn't able to keep up.

"Hey, Buddy, you need to run faster," Salinger yelled back to him.

Watry noticed as well and urged the man to hurry. Buddy had been looking progressively worse on this journey, though Tomi had to admire how he'd tried to tough it out without complaining, but fact of the matter was he wasn't a young man and the exercise he'd skipped over the years was taking its toll in his greatest moment of need. Tomi could hear Buddy wheezing and saw his movements becoming clumsier. Then, he stumbled.

She wanted to run back and help him, but Watry yelled at her to keep running. In the ranger pipeline, the instructors stressed how it was a ranger's duty to rescue those in distress, though they tempered this attitude with the reality that not everyone could be saved. Tomi could see that cold truth in this very moment. If any of them had gone back to help, the Ur-nots would have killed them too. Though it was a difficult pill to swallow, their best bet for saving the majority present was to sacrifice the one.

Watry did try firing at the creatures, dropping two of them, but all it did was slow the inevitable. The remainder of the horde converged up on Buddy as he lay on the ground clutching his left arm, a sign that he was suffering a heart attack. One of the Ur-nots landed a blow with its digging claw and Buddy was thrown over twenty feet, his body bent in two. Upon hitting the ground with a hard thud, he was motionless. There was nothing anyone could do for him.

Isabelle was a total wreck, but there was no time to mourn. With Buddy ceasing to be a threat, the Ur-nots continued past his body without a second look. The survivors continued running, adrenaline pushing them onward with the last of the barren outcroppings now behind them. At last, they were running through a sparsely vegetated grassland. Grass meant there was water somewhere nearby; even in their haste, they had maintained their direction.

What's more, the Ur-nots were slowing to a stop where the sand met the grass.

"They're stopping. What's the matter, they don't like grass?" Tomi asked.

"The Ur-nots are at home in the desert, but outside of that, they are not as comfortable," Seeker answered.

"Does that mean we can stop?" Isabelle gasped, bending over and resting her hands on her knees. "I think I'm going to die."

"We should at least keep walking to gain a safe distance," Seeker suggested. "It's the excess moisture that the Ur-nots do not like. It promotes the growth of mold and bacteria in their skin, making them rot. We should be safe where the grass gets thicker over there in the distance." He pointed to a well-grown area with his tail spike.

Now down to two remaining survivors, they barely made it to the edge of the tall grass before Isabelle and Salinger collapsed and fell asleep. Tomi thanked herself and everyone who'd ever encouraged her to exercise. It had made their impromptu run and walking the extra distance that much easier for her.

"How soon should we get moving again?" Tomi asked Watry.

"Let 'em sleep; they'll need their strength. We're not done yet."

13

LOST CITY OF LOST SOULS

"Our comms still don't work," Watry said, grumbling. "The power needed to jam such a wide area means they've got to be using something a lot bigger than a portable unit."

"Those bastards must have a whole base nearby," Tomi agreed.

Between the pirate hardware they had already seen and now the strength of these electronic countermeasures, they must have one serious operation here on Yardang. Tomi, Watry, and Seeker looked at the map. Several possibilities presented themselves, but Isabelle was the one to offer the best one.

Stepping forward and peering over their shoulders, she pointed to a spot on the map. "What does that symbol mean?" she asked. "The one next to where we are."

"That is the site of some ancient ruins that Teacher, my superior, is investigating," Seeker stated.

Everyone perked up and Tomi asked, "Then why don't we go there? I'm sure they'd have supplies and a way for us to contact the *Bass Reeves*."

"Mmm..." Seeker looked down at his feet and shook his head. "Teacher and I do not get along. She would be rather upset if I returned so soon," he answered.

"Seeker, this is an emergency situation. I would hope she'd understand why you came back," Watry exclaimed.

Seeker shook his head even more intently this time. "Oh, no! If I return with four humans, Teacher would *definitely* be livid—"

This time, all of the humans shouted in unison, "Seeker!"

Outnumbered, the Anar-phut relented and started leading the way to the Lost City.

In a series of chambers located deep inside the main structure of the Lost City known as the Step Pyramid, an Anar-phut was flipping through her catalog of languages, trying to find a particular symbol. She rustled her wings in frustration and voiced several curses, which to human ears would have sounded like a chaotic rendition of revile. Tossing her tablet aside, she started pacing back and forth trying to think of something she'd missed, but to no avail.

As she continued to pace, one of the junior members of the expedition, known as Runner-of-the-Drones, came loping into the chamber.

"Teacher-of-Many-Ancient-Myths-and-Legends, come quick!"

Teacher was annoyed. Runner had turned out to be the very excitable type. Every discovery was the find of a lifetime. Every problem, a major crisis.

"Calm down and speak slowly, Runner. What is going on?" she asked bluntly and without emotion.

"Seeker has returned—"

"That ingrate!" Teacher cut him off in a rage. "I told him to spend two weeks studying the mating habits of the Ur-nots. It's only been four days! Why is he back so soon?" Teacher lamented.

"Do I have to do everything around here? Must I endure all of you simpletons with no respite?"

"You do not understand. Seeker has walked back to base...and he has brought *aliens* with him!" Runner finished, feeling proud of himself for having such important information to offer. He knew Teacher would not be happy with Seeker for letting the outsiders infiltrate their base, but if Runner was hoping for a reward or even a little praise, he would be waiting a very long time.

"Aliens?" Teacher said in disbelief. She folded her wings over her head, the Anar-phut equivalent of burying one's head in their hands. Wondering which spirits she'd offended to deserve this curse called Seeker-of-Many-Different-Living-Things, she demanded, "Where is Seeker now?"

"He and the aliens are waiting up at the main entrance to the Step Pyramid and—"

Without another word, Teacher rushed out of the chamber, ready to unleash her righteous fury on her subordinate. Runner didn't have time to tell Teacher the rest.

All of the members of the Anar-phut expedition had stopped what they were doing to meet the new curiosities Seeker had unlawfully brought with him—the humans. Being based on Yardang where humans were not allowed, none of these Anar-phuts had ever met one before, and being scientists, they were very curious to learn more.

One of the other Anar-phut biologists, Collector-of-Many-Rare-and-Beautiful-Things, approached Tomi and Isabelle. From the reverse color scheme, mostly black with red edging, Tomi could tell that this was a female.

"What is this? You must be female." Unapologetically staring at their breasts, Collector said, "I have only seen pictures of human mammary glands. What are they like?" The Anar-phut rested on her tail and reached for Tomi's right breast, which was barely covered from her torn exosuit.

"Stop! Hands off the merchandise!" Tomi barked as she slapped the Anar-phut's extended manipulator away.

"Merchandise?" Collector questioned. "Are you saying I must offer you something of value before I can proceed?"

Tomi pulled out her omniblaster. "No, I'm saying if you touch me again, I'll stun your ass. No touching—ever!" Tomi said emphatically.

Isabelle had hidden behind Tomi when Collector had first approached. She was even less inclined to be groped by an alien, especially one that looked like a giant bat from the abyss. Watry stepped between Collector and Tomi in an attempt to keep the peace between the two groups.

Softly pushing her omniblaster into a lowered position, Watry smiled at the Anar-phut before whispering to Tomi, "Play nice, desperado. Remember, we're here to ask for their help."

Tomi sighed, but acquiesced right as the expedition leader emerged from the entrance of the Step Pyramid.

Looking down from her vantage point, Teacher could see the aliens Seeker had brought with him—*humans*. Teacher was no longer irritated with Seeker; she was absolutely livid. She spread her wings and glided from the top of the steps toward them. Being only the second time they had seen an Anar-phut in flight and the fact that Teacher, being female, was bigger than Seeker, the humans were quite impressed by her wingspan and graceful movement. With her black colorization, the humans could see exactly how these creatures had gotten the nickname demon bat.

Teacher landed so close to the survivors their hair visibly fluttered from the gust of air from her sizable wings. Teacher started right in to chastising Seeker, even before she had addressed their unwelcomed guests or folded her wings.

"There is no possible way that you finished that survey already. And where did these humans come from? And where is the ornithopter you checked out? Answer me!"

Teacher was talking so fast, the rangers' translators were having trouble keeping up. Throughout all of this, she pointed her tail spike right at Seeker's face, a very threatening gesture among the Anar-phut. Seeker held his manipulators up and tried to explain the situation, but Teacher would have none of it and continued her rant.

Tomi had enough and stepped in between the two, getting in Teacher's face. "Will you shut up and let us talk?"

Tomi's voice echoed throughout the Lost City and Teacher looked at her stunned. No one had ever dared to talk to her in such a manner. The members of her expedition certainly knew well enough not to challenge her. This human had some nerve.

Seeing she had the leader's attention, Tomi continued, "There are human criminals on the way who will kill all of us, and they don't care if they're violating a treaty!"

Teacher narrowed her eyes. "What do you mean there are other humans on Yardang? The agreement was that this planet be left to the Anar-phuts and humans would stay away. Are you telling me that you have dared to break our interstellar treaty?"

"They're criminals! They break the law. That's how they do a lot of things," Tomi pointed out, exasperated.

Teacher was ready to lay into this human when she remembered something. Her eyes widened and she looked around the gathered crowd. "Runner! Get over here," she called as the young Anar-phut loped over. "Didn't you say for some inexplicable reason, we keep losing drones in the hills north of here?"

"Yes, Teacher. Three drones were lost and I made sure to run diagnostics on each one before it was sent out," Runner replied.

Teacher turned back to Tomi. "Do you know how many of these criminals are here on Yardang?" she asked.

Tomi shook her head. "My partner and I managed to kill several of them the first time they attacked us, but we still don't know how many there are in total. From what we gather, it's a large operation—large enough to have a base somewhere on this planet. Thanks for the clue though; that explains why the follow-up attacks came more frequently as we traveled north."

"Hey, everyone," Salinger said irritably, "I'm glad to see the progress we've made in our interspecies dialogue, but you do realize those pirates might be dropping by to see what happened to us any minute?"

"Shut up, Salinger!" Watry said. Rolling his eyes, he admitted to Teacher, "He's annoying, but he does have a point."

"And how do you propose we get these criminals off Yardang?" she asked. "Our communications have been nonfunctional; can you call for assistance?"

"Negative," Watry said. "Our communications have been jammed as well. It's got something to do with our pirate friends."

"They are your friends?" Collector cut in, confused. "Then you can just tell them to leave Yardang due to the interstellar treaty and—"

Watry shook his head. "No, it's a turn of phrase." When the Anar-phuts all looked confused, Watry looked at Teacher, hoping maybe she would get what he meant. "An expression? An idiom, a—"

The Anar-phuts all widened their eyes and gasped. Runner pointed his tail spike at Watry and said, "Now see here, you puny human, no one insults Teacher like that!"

"Wait!" Seeker interjected as tensions rose, which made the rangers even more grateful to have met this Anar-phut. "I think we are getting lost in translation here. I have been traveling with the humans for the last couple of days and I do not think any of those here wish us harm or think poorly of us."

Teacher continued to glare at Watry, but she said, "Very well. Runner, withdraw your tail spike."

Tomi sighed, putting a hand on Watry's shoulder. "We'll have to travel to the pirate base," she said. "That has to be the location of their electronic warfare gear. They would need a large power source to run something powerful enough to affect an entire region."

"Uh, hey guys, I think the pirates are back again," Isabelle said, pointing up at the sky toward an incoming VTOL.

Teacher ordered the humans to go into the Step Pyramid, and Runner to retrieve the fléchette guns from their storage locker. She told the other expedition members to act like they were simply going about their usual duties in an attempt to throw the pirates off.

Everyone did as told while Teacher remained stoic and turned to face the approaching VTOL as it came in for a landing. Several male humans disembarked and walked over to her. The one in front, whom Teacher assumed was the leader, fumbled with a translator and started to speak.

"Salutations. My name is George," he said. Psycho figured his "good name" might appear less threatening and cause the Anar-phut to be more inclined to assist them. "Sorry to intrude upon your camp here, but I'm looking for—"

"Under Federation treaty, this planet called Yardang is to be left exclusively to the Anar-phuts. Who authorized you to be here? They will be held responsible for a major treaty violation," Teacher snapped at the human leader.

The other humans displayed peculiar body language and, instead of acting disciplined like the patrol or the marines, these individuals made *ohhh* and *ahhh* sounds, seemingly amused by Teacher's directness. She also noticed some of them moving slowly from behind George in an attempt to move around her flanks. Although her specialty was xenoarcheology, Teacher had studied enough about humans to know that these ones were obviously up to no good.

By now, there was a human to each side, and both of them lunged for her. She buffeted one with her wing, while the other grabbed her around her waist. Teacher didn't panic. Knowing humans were vertebrates with a centralized nervous system, she brought her tail around and rammed its spike into the back of the attacking human's neck. He let out a yelp and fell to the ground.

"Damn it, kill the freak before it stabs someone else!" Psycho shouted, pulling out his laser pistol.

The other pirates pulled their weapons and started to surround Teacher when they all heard a loud crack. One of the pirates had worked his way to Teacher's left and had been about to shoot her with an electro stunner, but instead, he was the one who got stunned.

There was another crack, and then another. The rangers had come to Teacher's aid when they heard things going south. *Maybe not all humans are dreadful mouth-breathers after all,* she thought.

With the rangers in their chameleon cloaks, the pirates couldn't see who was firing at them.

"Fuck! We're under attack," Psycho shouted and dove for cover. He started firing his pistol in the direction the shots were coming from, hoping just one pulse would land. "Kill the motherfuckers! Fucking kill them now!"

Four of his men were down with the remainder running every which way. The alien he had been talking to had already run for cover using that strange-looking loping gait with its wings. Psycho could see the situation was screwed, so he continued to fire his pistol as he ran in a serpentine pattern back to the VTOL.

He boarded the ship in a hurry and ordered the pilot, "Get us the fuck out of here now!" Psycho was not interested in waiting for anyone else.

Stun bolts cracked against the VTOL's cockpit as its engines powered up and lifted off. *Whoever these survivors are, they're really starting to piss me off,* Psycho thought to himself.

As the aircraft's engines faded into the distance, Anar-phut and human alike emerged from their hiding places. Teacher was the first to check on the human pirates who were left behind in their leader's haste to escape.

"Prisoners?" she said poking one of the stunned pirates. "Speak! Speak now or I will do vile things to your tender parts," she threatened.

"He can't talk right now," Tomi informed her. "I stunned him, but he should be ready in another thirty minutes."

"Good, because I will be skewering these ingrates myself for this latest violation," Teacher ranted.

"Do you guys have any transports we could use?" Watry asked. "It's probably going to be a long trip to the pirates' base and we'd better get moving if they're just going to keep sending attacks our way."

Teacher spun around to face the ranger, her anger at the situation coming out toward him for daring to speak. "And do tell how you plan to locate this base? Did you locate it from orbit or divine its location by looking in a spirit pool?" Teacher's sarcasm was as obvious as her contempt. Though they had just saved her, others like them were the reason the saving was needed in the first place. Humans were nothing but trouble in her eyes.

Watry rightly ignored her anger and answered simply and honestly. "Finding them won't be a problem. We'll just use one of your comm units and follow their jamming signal back to its point of origin, which will be at their base."

Hearing Watry's plan, Tomi remembered in comm class how the thing with transmitting any signal was that you were essentially announcing your exact location to the entire universe. When she saw Teacher about to raise an objection, Tomi backed up her partner.

"Or would you rather we all sit here until they return to kill us? And I mean *all* of us." Tomi raised her eyebrows and she could see Teacher waver. After all, what Teacher really wanted was to get all of these deviant humans off Yardang.

Teacher sighed. "What can we do to help?"

14

GOING IN COUNTRY

Looking at the ornithopter, Tomi was taken aback. She had trained on some strange aircraft before, but this was new to her. The machine's name summed it up—it literally flapped its wings in order to fly. It had ducted fans to give it an extra boost, but otherwise flew like a bird.

Since neither she nor Watry had ever trained on such a machine, Seeker and Runner offered to act as their pilots. The plan was simple: get to altitude, spread far enough apart to search a wider area, use geometry to their benefit, and switch on their respective aircraft's comm system. Once a signal direction was detected, it would be a simple matter of triangulation to figure out where the jamming signal was coming from.

Simple. Hopefully, it was simple enough. Even though Murphy's Law was coined many centuries ago, it still rang true even in the New World. It only took one thing to go wrong and the whole operation would be in jeopardy. While Tomi expressed this reservation, Watry pointed out another saying from the past: "Who dares wins."

"Yeah, yeah. Nothing ventured, nothing gained. No risk, no

reward," Tomi said, rolling her eyes. "I've heard all the motivational speeches. I'm just pissed because we were caught flatfooted by a bunch of lowlife scumbags. I just wish I had been more prepared. Then so many people wouldn't have died."

"Hey, cut yourself some slack, kid," Watry said. "You're young and you still have a lot to learn, but most important of all, you've got to remember that your mistakes are what teach you the most. So, here's another old quote to remember: 'If you're no longer making mistakes, you're no longer on the frontier.' Believe me, you'll be making plenty more mistakes. Besides, what's the ranger motto?"

Dutifully, Tomi shouted, "Improvise! Adapt! Overcome!"

Watry nodded approvingly. "Now, saddle up! Let's get these birds in the air."

Ending the conversation, he climbed into Runner's ornithopter, and Tomi in Seeker's.

Taking off in an ornithopter was not like any other aircraft. Unlike those with rotors, ducted fans, or jets, there was no beating, buzzing, or roaring. Instead, the ornithopter used a power cell to provide electricity to the polymer muscles that moved the wings, so there was no engine noise, and unlike the silent repulsor lift or gravity drive of other aircrafts, the ornithopter simply stirred the air, just like when a bird took flight.

When Seeker powered up the ship, the polymer muscles in the wings contracted in sequence, causing the wings to unfold and start flapping. Tomi could feel the craft start to lift off. Throttling up, the ornithopter leaped into the sky, and once airborne, Seeker throttled the fans back down. Tomi found it strange—as the craft glided through the sky, all she could feel was the beating of its wings.

"Are you in position yet?" Watry's voice came over the craft's comm system.

"Almost. I've just finished making the adjustments to the unit to start signal finding," Tomi responded.

Her unit immediately flashed data on the screen. Looking through her HUD, her translator indicated north-northeast. She sent a visual to Watry who was over forty miles away.

"Have received your data and got them!" he called out.

Seeker tapped a command into the comm display and a map appeared with the combined data from the two ornithopters.

"Now that we have the origin of their jamming signal, what's next?" Seeker asked.

"Easy, we sneak in and disable the pirates' EW transmitter, and then call for help from the *Bass Reeves*," Tomi replied.

She wished it was as easy as it sounded. The truth was their orbital data showed both savanna and forest between them and the pirate base. Worse, they would certainly be shot at if they got too close to it. They were in for a long trek through the forest, but she would keep that part to herself for now. She didn't dare ruin morale before they'd even gotten started.

Returning to the Anar-phut camp, they informed Teacher of the jamming signal's location.

"Ryan and I will handle this. No need for any Anar-phut lives to be put at risk," Watry said.

Seeker had other plans. "I disagree, human. These criminals are our problem as well. I will help."

"I volunteer too," Runner fluted enthusiastically.

Watry tried to convey the risks they would be taking. "Don't get me wrong, I appreciate any help we can get. But you have to realize these are not nice people. It's a known fact that every last one of them has committed at least one homicide, which means any one of them would have no qualms killing you."

"We are aware of that," Runner acknowledged as Seeker

nodded enthusiastically. "We didn't join the Explorer Corps to be safe. The Anar-phuts evolved from predators just like you humans. Besides, you will need Seeker and myself to pilot the ornithopters."

Teacher nodded solemnly, agreeing with her subordinates. "If these males are willing to fly into the jaws of death, they must be prepared." She motioned to others and they brought over Gauss fléchette rifles and laser pistols. "There is not enough room for the rest of us to ride in the ornithopters, so we will have to follow under our own power."

Tomi was impressed—these guys were no fools, but they had guts.

At last, Psycho arrived back at the pirate outpost after a bit of a joy ride to ease his tension. It didn't work. He was absolutely pissed. For the first time in his life, he found himself with a problem he couldn't seem to overcome. He'd lost a combat drone, three transports, and over a dozen men all because of two measly Federation Rangers. Or at least, he thought there were only two—he never actually saw them, so his assumption was based upon the angles of the shots fired at him. Either way, they sure could put up one hell of a fight.

One thing was for sure: Psycho would never live this down, which was really tarnishing his reputation. The Star Demon had chosen Psycho because he's smart, ruthless, and above all, he got results. The rangers, the passengers, and those aliens they'd partnered with all needed to be shot, or better yet, vaporized so nothing was left of them but a bad dream.

"Get everyone ready. We're going back out and we're going to kill all of those motherfuckers!" he said as soon as he walked into the main building.

Without turning away from his console, the pirate on watch said, "Hey, Psycho, you might want to rethink that. About a half hour ago, I detected two aircraft flying around to the south, and then they disappeared..." He trailed off, unsure how Psycho would react to this first half of the news.

Psycho paused his steps, balled his fists, and shook his head as he said, "And?"

"They're up again...and they're heading this way."

"Fuckin' A! Those crazy fuckers must have balls made of titanium alloy. They're going to fight us on our own turf?" Psycho gave a wicked grin. "Tell everyone to get ready."

The two ornithopters lifted off for the second time that day, this time with a half a dozen Anar-phuts flying alongside them. The remainder had stayed behind to guard the pirate prisoners, and Isabelle and Salinger had also opted to stay at the camp. Tomi was grateful Salinger didn't try to force his way into the mission like some daring vigilante. They already had enough to worry about without having to babysit his overinflated ego.

Seeker entered the signal location and pointed straight at it. As they continued toward their destination, Tomi was taking in the sights. She liked flying, especially on a clear day. While others would only see mile after mile of grassland, she could pick out different trees and had even spotted an unmapped ruin. She pointed it out to Seeker and he marked it on the navigation display.

"Hopefully we will survive the coming hostilities so we can go see it," Seeker said. "The Anar-phuts might even name the sight in your honor."

"Yeah, right, Seeker." Tomi rolled her eyes. "I don't think Teacher would go for that."

"True," he admitted. "But you never know. Teacher shows gratitude sometimes."

Tomi couldn't help but laugh. This Anar-phut was funny without trying to be. She liked him.

Thick forest appeared on the horizon. Tomi signaled at Watry in the other ornithopter. He returned the signal and motioned at the trailing Anar-phuts. Teacher signaled that she could see the approaching woodlands as well. According to their combined data, the pirate outpost wasn't much further. It was time to prepare for their infiltration.

Tomi started double-checking her gear when Seeker sounded alarmed.

"There is an unknown craft in the air and it is heading right toward us."

She quickly looked up and set her HUD to maximum magnification. "Son of a bitch," she cursed. "Turn and burn, Seeker!"

Seeker had never heard such a term, but was quite certain she meant evasive action. His theory was confirmed when Tomi used her wrist comp to alert everyone else.

"They know we're coming!" she yelled. "Everyone take evasive action!"

Psycho watched the live feed on console at their base, seeing the enemy scatter and dive toward the trees below.

The pilot he'd sent after them gave a rebel yell over their private channel and announced, "The miserable pukes are running away!"

"Moron!" Psycho scolded him. "If they run, it will take longer to kill them all. You're not to come back here until every last one of them ceases to breathe! You hear me? Now, attack!"

Trying to appease his superior, the pilot picked one of the big ones and went after it.

"Son of a bitch!" Tomi cursed again. "He's chasing us!"

As Seeker pulled the ornithopter into a tight turn, the pirate VTOL fired its Gauss machine gun. The trail it left sheared off branches from the trees below, but missed them entirely.

"Shit, that was close!" Tomi exclaimed. She looked around the craft's interior, wishing there was some way to shoot at their pursuer. Then she noticed an observation blister. Crawling up to it, she tried to open it but it wouldn't budge. It appeared to be bolted in place. Fortunately, becoming a ranger had taught Tomi to be quick on her feet and she came up with an idea.

"Seeker, I'm apologizing in advance," she said.

"Apologizing? For what?" Seeker asked.

Without a word, Tomi took aim with her omniblaster.

"Wait!" Seeker pleaded, but it was too late.

Tomi fired, blowing the aluminum oxynitride blister off the back of the ornithopter. Holstering her sidearm, she brought her rifle to bear.

"Sorry, Seeker, but now you have a tail gunner!" Tomi offered. Trying to line up a shot, she marked the VTOL as her target.

In the VTOL's cockpit, the pilot could hear the tone indicating he has a missile lock.

"This one's going right up the old poop chute," he said, smirking as he pressed the button on his control stick.

There was a loud crack and a star-shaped fracture appeared in his windscreen. The excruciating pain the pirate felt was momentary and he quickly passed out, eviscerated by a hypervelocity projectile. The pilot's hands went slack and the VTOL plunged into the trees below in a magnificent explosion.

"Yes! We got 'em!" Tomi cheered, stopping short when she noticed the missile heading toward them. "Shit, we're screwed!" she exclaimed.

Seeker didn't pause to ask for details. He banked the ornithopter so hard that it literally pinwheeled in midair. The g-forces slammed Tomi into the interior wall, stunning her. The missile turned to follow, but not fast enough. It detonated too far away to be a kill, merely wounding the Anar-phut craft, but it was enough to force their hand into landing.

"We have taken damage. The left wing is losing lift and there is a 30% reduction in the pectoral fiber bundles. We have to land immediately," Seeker called out.

Shaking the cobwebs out of her head, Tomi managed to respond, "Damn! I was hoping to fly just a little further in."

"Apologies, it cannot be helped. The only other choice is crashing, which I do not recommend," Seeker replied.

Tomi was growing used to his unintentional humorous way with words and she nodded in acknowledgment. "Let's land this thing."

The ornithopter kept sliding to the left due to the structural damage, but even so, it managed to come in slowly enough that it was almost hovering. Seeker wished he had better managed to line up his landing with the tree line on his right, but there was no time to circle around and try again. Instead of a normally graceful landing, the craft dropped hard with a sickening crunch.

Seeker hit the emergency release and the ornithopter's side door popped off. He climbed out first, followed by Tomi. She checked herself and Seeker for injuries, and then the ornithopter.

"At least it didn't catch fire. If that had happened, we would have been totally fucked," Tomi commented.

"Yes, the photonic cell's housing held. If it had ruptured, the whole craft could have been instantly vaporized, including us. The landing gear has been crushed, but did its job absorbing the brunt of the impact."

As they pulled their gear from the wrecked ornithopter, the other Anar-phuts arrived. Running in their characteristic loping gait, each one came up to ensure Seeker and his human companion were uninjured.

"Don't worry, we made it down in one piece," Tomi assured her winged benefactors. From what Tomi could tell, they were genuinely concerned for her well-being as much as for Seeker's. So much for comparing them to hell's spawn.

Runner's ornithopter was the last to arrive. Watry jumped out before Runner could bring it to a full stop.

"Holy shit, Ryan!" Watry yelled as he ran up and hugged her.

"Watry, you're squishing me. Let me go!" Tomi complained. When he let her go, she laughed. "I'm glad to see you too."

"Runner and I were sure you bought the farm when we saw that missile launch. I'd call you one lucky son of a bitch, but—"

Tomi held up a hand. "That's okay, I'll take it as a compliment."

Tomi and Watry smiled at each other in relief. Every day, another close call—it certainly made you grateful for each survival and closer with your partners.

"It's a relief to get that pirate VTOL off our backs, but now what?" she asked.

"Improvise, adapt, overcome," Watry replied with a smile. "The ornithopter may be screwed, but it got us close enough that we should be able to hoof it from here."

He turned to Teacher. "Ryan and I will travel by foot. You should travel by air. Since the pirates are expecting an air attack from you guys, they'll be too busy looking up. We'll be in touch." Teacher nodded, and Watry concluded, "When you get near the outpost, be on the lookout for their air defenses. I can guarantee they will shoot first."

"Runner, get your ornithopter in the air," Teacher ordered. Bidding the humans well, she said, "May your deity of choice smile upon you, humans. I am certain you will need it."

"Good luck to you and your people as well, Teacher. I think we will all need it," Tomi replied.

Teacher reared up on her tail and beat her chest with her right wing—a sign of respect among their kind. The Anar-phuts followed Teacher's lead and took to the air, all except for Seeker.

"What about you, Seeker? Aren't you going to fly there too?" Tomi asked.

"I am one who studies living things, a biologist, as you humans call it. How can I pass up an opportunity to study a species I have never met before? While it is preferred to study any creature under less stressful circumstances, there is still much insight to be gained to see how one reacts to stress," Seeker pointed out.

"Now I feel like I'm under pressure. What if I wet myself?" Tomi asked, only half joking.

Seeker expressed puzzlement with the expression, so Watry chimed in. "Don't worry, Ryan, your exosuit will contain any 'accidents' you might have. Now let's hurry up. According to this bioscan, there's a trail of some kind leading to their hideout. I don't want to keep Teacher waiting too long."

The three packed their gear and traveled together along the boundary between the grass and the tree line. Seeker had brought along a machete and Watry was able to convert his memory metal tool into a chopping blade, so it didn't take them too long to find the trail. Tomi made another mental note to get her hands on one of those memory tools someday.

From the looks of it, the trail had been cleared by machinery rather than animal activity.

"Keep your scanners sweeping," Watry instructed. "I don't think they would booby trap this trail, but they'll at least be monitoring it."

15

COPS IN THE WOODS

Crabs was hiking along the trail from the pirate base into the woods. "Get it done," Psycho had said to him, ordering Crabs to take some of the boys to go out and check the front door, all fucking three miles of trail included. *Fucking bastard.*

When Crabs had suggested he use the security robots, Psycho about lost it, insisting the robots needed to remain at the outpost because they were "too valuable." *What a joke!* This was exactly the sort of task those tin cans were designed for. If Psycho would just send them out, they could sweep the whole area with their sensors in less than half an hour.

But no, Crabs's life wasn't as valuable as those robots, so he was the lucky one to get sent out. He muttered some curse words to himself. It was clear Psycho just wanted to cover his own ass and fuck everybody else. What an asshole, but what else was new?

"What the fuck was that?" exclaimed Rodent, one of the younger pirates with Crabs. He swung his laser rifle to and fro, trying to catch sight of the source of a strange animal call.

"Damn it, Rodent! Watch where you point that thing. You're

gonna toast someone's skull, you fucking idiot!" Crabs yelled at the novice buccaneer.

That was the worst part of this whole mission. When Crabs insisted on taking some men along on this task, Psycho had given him all of the new guys they just "recruited" off the last freighter they snatched. Not only were they unseasoned, if it weren't for their mountains of debt or fear of being murdered, they wouldn't have ever signed up to be here in the first place. These guys had never even fired a weapon in their lives. Crabs heaved a sigh. This little outing was going to take all day.

He urged his charges on, but it seemed more like prodding. When he was their age, he was full of so much piss and vinegar that he couldn't wait to get into the shit. These fucking new guys were so jittery he was certain they would shit their pants the moment something actually happened, if not sooner. After leaving their base through the back door, they'd been jittery and jumping at every sound made by the forest.

"At least you stupid fuckers are alert, unlike the last bunch I had to work with," Crabs admitted. "Still, you're all fucking pathetic!" Crabs spat on the ground to emphasize his point.

Rodent spun to face Crabs, ears red with rage. Crabs shot the newbie a withering glare that seemed to say, *Just try it, kid, and we'll see how long you last on this crew.* Reading between the lines, Rodent smartly turned his attention back to the trail ahead of them.

Then there was a sound even Crabs had never heard before, at least not from an animal. It sounded like somebody was playing a trumpet, but although the notes were complex, they didn't match any music he had ever heard before. In a moment of clarity, Crabs remembered what species communicated like that.

"Shit! It's those damn demon bats. Eyes open, guns up!" Crabs yelled.

The pirates all aimed in the direction that the notes were coming from without covering their rear.

"Damn it! Cover your six, you fucking—" Crabs tried to yell before he was hit by a stun bolt from behind.

He fell to the ground convulsing, while the other four marauders started firing blindly into the forest in front of them. One after another, a loud crack was heard and another pirate dropped. As the last remaining on his feet, Rodent turned just in time to see a floating hand aiming an omniblaster right at him. There was one more loud crack as a stun bolt hit him square in the chest and Rodent fell flat on his face.

Emerging from cover, Tomi and Watry doffed their chameleon cloaks and holstered their omniblasters.

"Area secured, Seeker. Well done. You can come out now," Tomi called.

The Anar-phut emerged from the treetops, descending to the forest floor. "Are all humans this unintelligent?"

"Their real problem is they're inexperienced," Watry observed. "Did you see how much they were shaking?"

"Yeah, you could smell their lack of experience too," Tomi added, pinching her nose. "I think some of them crapped their pants,"

Taking the pirates' weapons and tying them up, the rangers pulled their prisoners off the trail and hid them in the underbrush. In their stunned state, the pirates couldn't be questioned, though Watry was still able to find something useful.

"A key fob," he said, holding the object up for the others to see. "Looks like we have the keys to their kingdom."

"Perfect!" Tomi smiled. "When we get there, we'll need to signal to Teacher to distract the pirates so we can sneak in and disable their EW system."

"One right answer, Ranger Ryan. Now let's get this show on the road," Watry said.

To ensure the pirates couldn't use anything if they got loose, the rangers broke the equipment they couldn't take with them. After marking their location on their wrist comps so they could later send out patrolmen to secure these five prisoners, Tomi, Watry, and Seeker continued down the path toward the outpost. From what they could hear over Crab's comm device, these five pirates were the only patrol sent out on the ground. They were definitely expecting an air attack.

Before the trio could see the entrance, the rangers' scanners detected the outpost's perimeter wall—a twelve-foot-high electrified plasma field. It was designed more to keep wildlife out than sentient beings, though it was still quite effective on both fronts. Depending on the intensity of its setting, whatever touched it could get anything from a nasty shock to cardiac arrest.

"Yup, the only way in is through the front gate," Watry said. "Okay, call Teacher and let her know we're ready anytime."

Seeker nodded and notified her of their arrival.

"You rangers certainly took long enough," Teacher responded, her impatience palpable through the comm interface.

"Yes, we're doing just fine, thanks for asking," Watry said sarcastically. "Is your merry little band ready?"

"Most definitely. I have worked out various scenarios for our attack. What do you need from us?"

"Easy, focus your attacks on the side of the outpost, opposite the front gate," Watry responded. "Keep doing that until we get in, and then clear a path to the transmitter. It's that building with the antenna sticking out the top."

"As you wish, human. Good luck," Teacher said.

"Has that lice-infested bastard reported in yet?" Psycho asked for the seventh time.

Bong, the pirates' resident wirehead, was getting annoyed. "For the last time, I'll let you know when Crabs calls in. So far, it's been nothing but crickets."

Bong didn't like it when anyone looked over his shoulder, and Psycho had been hovering ever since Crabs and his crew had left that morning. If it had been anyone else pestering him, Bong would have yelled and chased their sorry ass out of the comm room, but Psycho was different. George Knight was smart and tough and he'd earned the name Psycho because he didn't care who he had to kill to get the job done. So, although Bong was beyond annoyed with Psycho, he didn't dare get in a duel with him.

Psycho kept playing with one of his many knives, something he often did when he was pissed or antsy. This whole situation was going to hell, and none of his efforts had gotten him the results he wanted: all of the human survivors dead. He couldn't even manage to kill any of the demonic-looking aliens who were dirtside. Had the world flipped on its head? What was going on that he couldn't manage a single kill that counted for anything?

"Fucking Federation treaty, my ass. Bunch of dumbass scientists," he muttered aloud.

Bong was smart enough to not say anything in response to his boss's rant, even as Psycho wandered back to look over his shoulder again. Psycho checked the status display for the perimeter fence. Everything was still working perfectly. Looking at the other systems, the EW suite appeared to be working as well, so at least the rangers couldn't call for help. Even so, his skin began to crawl.

"They're planning something, I know it. Get everyone—" The security alarm went off, interrupting his thoughts.

Just outside the shack, someone was shouting, "We're under attack! We're under attack! Demon bats—at least a half a dozen of them. They're attacking the north perimeter!"

"Son of a bitch!" Psycho swore and ran outside.

In the distance, he could hear cracking sounds. Gunfire? No, laser rifles. Anything more would be unusual for a scientific expedition. Their defense batteries started firing. Psycho could see the demon bats pinwheeling this way and that, trying to dodge the defense lasers. Then, just as quickly as they appeared, they dispersed.

"Pathetic," Psycho said.

"Hey, Psycho," Bong called over the comm channel, "Crabs just got back."

"Where has he been? Tell him to report to me immediately!" Psycho snapped.

"He's not answering his communicator, so I can't tell him anything," Bong replied. "Maybe it broke while they were out checking everything. That would explain why he hasn't responded this whole time."

Psycho smacked his forehead. "If you haven't spoken with him, then how do you know he's back?"

"The front gate was opened less than a minute ago with Crab's key fob," Bong explained.

Now Psycho was really confused. Crabs was competent enough to know to report in immediately upon his arrival, especially if his communicator had been busted. It shouldn't take him that long to reach the main building from the front gate. Adrenaline spiked Psycho's heart rate as realization dawned on him.

"Get to the front door now! We've been breached," he shouted over the comm channel, but he was too late. Several cracks were heard and then the main generator exploded in a shower of sparks, taking everything down including the comm jammer. "Motherfucking son of a bitch!" he cursed.

As he ran toward the generator, he noticed some blurred movement. Pulling his laser pistol, he aimed and fired. As his laser pulses cracked, blaster bolts came right back at him.

"Fucking rangers!" he said under his breath. "Shit! Shit! Shit!"

The rangers have a well-deserved reputation for being invisible, so he knew he had a difficult task ahead of him if he was to succeed in taking this one down. Not only that but he needed to do the deed quickly, or else he would call down an orbital bombardment from his ship. If that happened, the pirates wouldn't stand a chance.

Taking cover behind some crates, Psycho tried to think of what to do next. The power was down, which meant the security fence was down too. It was probable that the rangers' unlikely ally, those oversized bats, would be joining them soon. It was clear now that their air assault had merely been a distraction. Psycho had to hand it to them, it was a smart tactic.

Rather than chase a ghost, Psycho decided it would be better to get the hell out of dodge. "Plan B," he yelled out to anyone within range. He sprayed laser shots in the general direction of his invisible enemy to cover himself and made a run for it.

Watry easily weathered the pirate's barrage of laser fire from behind the building he used as cover. Since it was a pulse laser, all of the shots created a surface explosion against the side of the building instead of penetrating the way a beamer would. Peeking out, he was startled when something ran past him. It wasn't until he heard Tomi speak that he realized who it was. Was he down on his game, or was she just becoming a skilled ranger?

"Watry, what are you waiting for?" she scolded. "I've already sent the distress call to the *Bass Reeves*; help is on the way, but we're not in the clear yet. The pirates are all running to the east side of the compound. We've got to go after them!"

"Son of a bitch! No wonder that pirate ran into a dead end. They must have some escape route!" Watry responded.

He followed Tomi's lead in pursuit of the pirate leader. Along the way, the rangers encountered a few lingering pirates fleeing in the same direction from other parts of the compound. The result was a running gun battle as neither side dared slow down long enough to take cover.

As shots were exchanged, the rangers proved more accurate,

their stun bolts connecting with and dropping several pirates. Those they didn't hit kept running; even the possibility of being shot wouldn't stop them from their attempted escape plan. Tomi and Watry kept after them until they noticed an unlucky pirate just ahead of them who was lagging way behind the others.

He shouted between breaths, "Wait for me, you bastards! Don't leave me behind!"

Just then, an explosion boomed across the compound, powerful enough to make both the pirate and the rangers stumble as it rocked the very ground they stood on.

"Son of a bitch," he shouted at the backs of his fellow pirates who didn't seem to care enough to help him. "You cocksuckers! If I'm going down, you're coming with me!" He stopped running and took aim at one of them, but it was that same moment that Tomi ran up behind him.

"Federation Rangers! Don't move!" she shouted.

The pirate looked to be only a few years older than her, but she saw now why he was not very quick on his feet. His left leg had been burned by a stray laser shot, slowing his escape considerably. He limped around to face her, throwing his arms in the air and dropping his blaster.

"I surrender! Don't shoot, damn it! I surrender," the pirate yelled.

Watry ran over, searched the pirate, and then bound his hands together. "Tell us where you were going in such a hurry," Watry demanded.

"Fuck off!" the pirate said defiantly. "I may have surrendered, but it doesn't mean we're friends, copper."

The pirate spit toward Watry, so the ranger stuck his finger into the pirate's leg wound with a nauseating squishing sound, causing him to fall to his knees screaming.

"Okay, okay!" he yelled, begging Watry to ease up on him. Through his tightly clenched teeth, he managed to say, "It's over there, you fucking cocksucking pig! You can't miss it."

"Good boy," Watry said, patting the pirate's head in a demeaning manner.

Watry wiped his bloody fingers on the marauder's shoulder, and then forced him to his feet. The rangers walked him in the direction everyone else had been heading. Rounding a large tree, they saw what looked like a tunnel heading into the side of the hill. As they got closer, they noticed it was sealed by a cave-in—that would explain the explosion.

"Clever bastards," Tomi commented.

Seeing the body of one of the fleeing pirates buried in the collapse, Watry added, "And ruthless."

The engines of an approaching dropship rose from the deafening post-explosion silence. Looking up, Tomi could see a familiar sight; the *Bass Reeves* was heading for one of the vacant landing pads. A second ship also arrived with the Space Patrol emblem on the side. With so many of the VTOLs lost in action, there was plenty of space for them both to land.

Seeker loped toward the rangers across the now-empty pirate base, reminding Watry to hop on the comm and inform their partners to not hurt their new allies. Next, he called Teacher to let her know the cavalry had arrived.

"What's next?" Tomi asked as Seeker reached them.

"Well, we still have to get the rest of these pirates off Yardang, as per Federation treaty. Am I right, Seeker?" Watry said.

"Yes, I checked the treaty. If there is an incursion by any humans, the Federation is obligated to remove them," Seeker answered.

"And what if they're Imperial citizens?" Tomi countered.

"The treaty specifically says humans. It does not make any distinction on citizenship," the Anar-phut said.

"In other words, all humans are the same," Watry concluded.

"Correct," Seeker nodded emphatically.

"Well then," Tomi said, "we'll need more firepower than our 'thunder and lightning.' What do we have aboard the *Bass Reeves*?"

"Let's go find out. Who knows? The skipper might have some ideas of his own on how to handle this little infestation."

As Seeker loped off to meet up with his people, the ramp of the Space Patrol's dropship had already extended, disgorging several men under Patrolman Curtis's orders. They quickly gathered the stunned pirates into custody, securing each of them into one-man cages on board their dropship.

When they relieved Tomi and Watry of their personal prisoner, Curtis asked for a sitrep while Healy and Zimmerman approached and listened in.

"Several escaped into a tunnel," Tomi admitted. "We were unable to follow due to an intentional cave-in."

"Their leader, Psycho, was among the first to enter it. We aren't sure where it leads," Watry added.

Though Curtis seemed disappointed that his target had escaped yet again, he maintained professionalism. "Good work, rangers. We're not done here. I hear there is another base on Yardang? As for Psycho, we'll get him sooner or later."

"It's possible the tunnel led the escaped pirates to that other base," Tomi offered. "We might find him yet."

When Curtis walked away, Healy said, "You two had us worried! First, comms went down, and when we took a look at the lifeboat's crash site, everything was blown to hell. We must have counted at least six destroyed vehicles during our search for you, including your flitters."

"We didn't know what to think," Zimmerman added. "The fires had all died out long before we realized what had happened, and we didn't see you two anywhere."

"Yeah, well, I guess these pirates really wanted to keep their hideout a secret," Tomi said. "They tried more than once to kill us, and some of the passengers didn't make it." She looked down at her feet for a moment. "We're down to just two survivors who are taking shelter at the nearby Anar-phut expedition camp."

"So, you really did get to meet the Anar-phuts?" Zimmerman asked. Did Tomi detect a hint of jealousy?

"Yes," she answered. "Some are actually okay, just watch out for their expedition leader, Teacher." She and Watry exchanged a look and a laugh.

"Yeah, she's a fiery one," Watry added.

As if on cue, the Anar-phuts all flew down to a vacant landing pad. Seeker waved, looking worried as Teacher stormed up to them. *What now?* Tomi wondered.

Without bothering with introductions, Teacher immediately started talking to Healy in a demanding tone. "The pirates are not gone yet!" she complained. "Our expedition cartographer informed me there is another larger facility set up just north of this location. What are you humans going to do about that?" She was pointing her tail spike at Healy, but more so in a frustrated way than a directly threatening way.

"Ah, Teacher, you never disappoint," Watry said. "We were about to get to that topic."

"Thank you for assisting my rangers," Healy said to Teacher. "We will handle the remaining pirates and remove them from Yardang. You may return to your work, and we will send Curtis to come pick up Isabelle, Salinger, and the other prisoners from your camp once they return."

Teacher looked at the patrol ship whose engine was whirring back to life for liftoff. With a ship full of prisoners, the Space Patrol needed to get them to the hive before coming back to collect the rest.

Turning back to Healy, Teacher asked, "Just the four of you?"

"Aw, Teacher, you're sweet to show concern like that," Healy said with a hint of sarcasm. Everyone knew she more concerned about whether they'd be able to successfully rid the pirate infestation with such small numbers. Healy laughed. "Don't worry. We have another ranger with specialty equipment who should be arriving shortly."

Teacher nodded, returning to her people to announce that they could return to the Lost City. From afar, Seeker turned to look at Tomi after listening to Teacher's update. He reared up on his tail and used his limb to wave another goodbye, looking grateful and perhaps a little sad. Tomi had to admit that she felt a little pang of sadness too. He was growing on her.

"So, how are we going to take down the pirate base? Do we have any surveillance?" Watry asked.

"Here," Healy said and projected a hologram of the latest sensor sweeps. A large map appeared showing the base's relative position to theirs. Healy then zoomed in to show a more detailed layout of the terrain. "A river feeding into a large lake," he pointed out. "Makes sense: plenty of water to run a facility and support others, but..." Healy faded to silence.

"But what?" Tomi asked.

"Water is usually considered a barrier as well as a resource," he finished.

"We rangers aren't afraid of a little water, are we, Ranger Ryan?" Watry finished.

She pursed her lips and nodded, understanding what he was implying, though she wasn't thrilled about it. "Some of us will be doing a water infiltration."

Healy laughed. "Ding, ding, ding! Right answer, Ryan," he said. "Now let's take a look at the details of this pirate compound, shall we?"

Psycho and his fellow pirates had been caught unprepared for spelunking—the idiot who was supposed to place the necessary gear *before* an emergency like this came up hadn't done so. It was a miracle they hadn't gotten lost or broken their necks without any sort of light source. As it was, several had bumps, bruises, cuts, and scrapes from falling or hitting their heads. The one upside was the explosives had been placed, and with them, Psycho had managed to seal the escape entrance and prevent pursuit by anyone, but that seemed to be the only upside.

Emerging from the other end of the cave, Psycho was cold, filthy, tired, and royally pissed off, and without any comm devices, they were on their own in the wilderness. There was no choice but to start trekking toward their main base. He just hoped he got there before any of the rangers did.

16

JUSTICE FOR THE SERENA DAWN

The main pirate base was situated along a river that flowed out of a nearby lake—an excellent choice if one needed plenty of water. Judging from orbital scans of the compound, the pirates maintained several large storage tanks of water, far more than the average water needs for the number of people they had there. Tomi found this puzzling, but then remembered that, among other things, the *Serena Dawn* was missing mining equipment. Could it be that along with piracy, these marauders were also claim jumpers?

It seemed an odd play for pirates. Mining of any kind was a long-term investment, and pirates were typically more the grab-and-dash types. Tomi pointed this out to the others to see if they had any thoughts on the matter.

"Who knows?" Healy answered as their backup flew overhead and came in for a landing. "Maybe the Star Demon Syndicate is branching out. It's not the first time criminals have done it."

In a way, it made sense to Tomi. A pirate's life tended to be short, or else they were forced into early retirement if they lost too many body parts or were otherwise no longer useful. Some would try to squirrel away enough money while they could in order survive. Maybe others decided they could go into mining and sell some valuable metals, gemstones, and the like. She shrugged it off as the rangers began discussing their plan of attack.

"We'll be performing a pincer maneuver on the pirate base from both land and water," Healy announced to them. "The four of us will be doing the water infiltration, and our backup will handle the land infiltration."

"Hey, Zim," she exclaimed, slapping his shoulder, "with us going in by water, you'll get to put those water adaptions to good use finally. This should be a walk in the park for you."

"Think again," Healy cut in. "Never underestimate a mission. That's what gets you in trouble." He eyed Tomi sternly to ensure his message sunk in. "Zim, you'll be leading the swim portion of the mission. Underwater navigation will be left to you, and just like in training, you surface, you fail," he said. "Only here, failure can mean death."

"No room for fuck ups, Zim," Watry added.

"Yeah, no pressure," Zimmerman said, rolling his eyes. "So, what's the load out? I can breathe just fine, but what about you guys?"

Healy pointed over to the gear bags he and Zimmerman had brought down with them. "We have combat swimmer kits."

Tomi remembered using these in the swim portion of their training: nanotech suits with artificial gills and built-in sonar as well as plasma, repulsor, and EMP grenades. She noticed there were even plasma limpet mines on these ones.

"What are we going to blow up with those?" she asked.

"The pirates have their vehicles, main power generator, and water purification plant all located near the water. Our job is to plant those mines to neutralize them. That way, their main defenses will go down and they won't be able to run," Healy answered.

As he said this, a fully armored exoskeleton walked off the newly arrived dropship and headed toward them. Tomi admired the Hostile Environment eXploration suit, or HEX for short. Just as magnificent as the photos she'd seen in the pipeline, it was yet another piece of gear on her wish list and she was excited to see it in action. She'd heard they could do some serious damage.

Though it was similar to the battlesuit that the Federation Marines used when dirtside, there were also several differences. The more obvious was the flight system. Where the marine version was designed for short hops, the HEX suit had sustained flights over 30,000 feet, thanks to the repulsor jets and antigravity panels. The propulsion system also worked underwater, giving the suit an all-environment capability. The other noticeable difference were the sensors. It had a tactical sensor array, a multi-function scanner, and sonar all built into the suit's head.

What was less obvious was the fact that the suit's armor, though still present, was thinner than military-grade suits to allow for greater speed and mobility. To compensate for the lack of protection, the suit's stealth systems could meet and even exceed the ranger's chameleon cloaks with active multispectral camouflage and sound cancellation. The suit could essentially make you invisible.

Tomi dreamed of the day she got to try one on, but was snapped back to reality when the person in the HEX suit stopped in front of her team. Towering over them in stature, the HEX suit's chest unsealed, revealing the head of a woman in her late twenties.

"Ranger Emily Brooks reporting. I hear you guys are doing the water infiltration?" she asked.

"I thought you said another team was joining us?" Zimmerman asked Healy. "Where's the rest of the team?"

"Do you see her suit?" Healy asked, motioning toward Brooks. "She'll be fine. Besides, she was supposed to be on vacation right now, but Brooks can't pass up a good pirate battle, can you, Brooks?"

Brooks laughed and as Healy acknowledged her original question, Tomi took the opportunity to look closer at the HEX suit, figuring out where the ranger fit inside the oversized shell. Her legs went inside the thighs and her head in the chest. To fit the operator's arms into the suit's arms would require breaking them in several places. Instead, the arms extended out from the mid-torso, contained within limblets. While impressive, Tomi noticed something lacking and she couldn't help but ask.

"No weapons?" Tomi queried.

Brooks laughed. "No worries, kid. I can load at least two heavy weapons on the arms. I'll have no problem dealing with whatever heavy artillery the pirates picked up on the black market."

Tomi was glad the ranger was so confident in her machine; from what she'd seen so far of these pirates, she would be needing it, even with a HEX suit in her arsenal.

Tomi's nanotech cybersuit wasn't quite a HEX suit, but she still found it to be amazing. She had used the different technologies separately, but never before experienced them being integrated into one seamless system. The suit's controls were fused into the liner. With a mere impulse from the operator, the desired system would switch on or off.

Normally a diver couldn't see through river water—being an erosive force, it was always cloudy. Even in the best conditions Tomi had experienced when diving in open water, she still couldn't see her own feet, and sometimes she couldn't even see her dive light in front of her face. Because of this, Tomi's instructors insisted on teaching them how to navigate blindly in the water, but also admitted that when every second counts, they should use whatever tech they had available. Thankfully, the nanotech cybersuit's dive mask contained a HUD that displayed all sorts of useful information including views using the suit's sonar and lidar. With the sensors, she would be able to make out details underwater almost as clear as day.

One of the less glamorous but vital components of the suit was the distance counter and mission clock. With both, Tomi and the others could keep track of their progress. For this particular mission, knowing that information was particularly important. They needed to coordinate their attack with Brooks's attack from the land.

Entering the water, Tomi noticed the river's current was slow, but swimming against it would be exhausting for even the most well-adapted water dwellers, which was why the rangers were grateful for the underwater propulsion units on their suits. While not huge, the river was big enough the rangers could completely submerge and remain totally unseen. With Zim in the lead, they moved up river.

If they had come across one of the larger river predators or a territorial herbivore, they might have to scrub the mission. Fortunately, the only obstacles they encountered were boulders that they had to maneuver around and the occasional wildlife swimming in the river, but nothing too big so far. *Good to be skilled, better to be lucky,* Tomi thought to herself.

The fact that the water's turbidity was so high was both a blessing and a curse. While they were blind visually, their sonar worked perfectly through the murky water. Unless the pirates were also using sonar, they wouldn't see the rangers until it was too late.

After several nerve-racking minutes, according to their navigation, they had arrived. Tomi only dated guys, but Luck be a lady, and today she smiled on them. Rather than stick their heads out of the water, Healy used one of their recon drones to take a look. It was early morning and still dark outside. The multispectral sensors showed no activity or active sensors.

Swimming around the bend, they could see the pirate base. Lights were on, but nobody was near the water. Just as expected, the marauders were so busy guarding the front door, they forgot to guard the rear entrance. Once Healy was satisfied there were no roving patrols, he signaled to everyone to proceed.

Tomi was tasked with attaching her limpet mine to the main power generator. She silently exited the water under cover of darkness, placing her mine on the main power distributor and arming it. When detonated, all power to the base would be cut. Successful, Tomi made her way back to the rally point.

Everyone maintained noise discipline by using hand signals. With everyone flashing the okay signal for each of their missions having been completed, the next step was to move into position and wait for zero hour. Looking at her mission clock, Tomi could see that it was mere minutes away. The hardest part was the waiting.

When the moment of truth arrived, Healy detonated the limpet mines. Four miniature suns illuminated the compound for a brief instant with blinding light followed by thunderous explosions. In the same instant, all of the pirate base's lights were extinguished. Tomi was relieved she had done her part correctly, but there was no time to celebrate; they needed to get moving.

Valk was up in the high-hide, but he wasn't manning the 10mm Gauss machine gun nor standing watch, for that matter. He was doing what everyone else wished they were doing. Quite simply, he was screwing off. And what better place to hide from his lieutenant than here?

It was such a pain in the ass to climb up to this position, nobody would ever look here. But while it was too not worth the effort for most, it had been more than worth it for Valk. Doing so had secured him a private moment to do absolutely nothing with no one around to tell him otherwise. It was hot and humid up here, but at least there was a roof to catch the rain.

Content with himself, Valk lay down and fell asleep, oblivious to the Federation Rangers who were closing in on their second base.

Upon reaching the base, Tomi and Watry were sent ahead to clear some buildings. They entered through an open door and found themselves interrupting preparations for the pirates' breakfast. The cook, a very big and fat man called Crispy, looked up from some less-than-appetizing food he was in the middle of overcooking. It was clear how he'd earned his nickname.

Accompanying Crispy were five general-purpose androids working as his assistants. When Crispy sensed a presence nearing him, he naturally assumed it was one of the robots. That is, until he looked up to see two heavy blaster pistols hovering in midair and aimed at his face.

"What the fuck?" he said, just in time for Watry to fire. The stun bolt struck Crispy in the solar plexus and he fell to the floor, but it didn't knock him completely out of commission. "What are you waiting for? Kill them!" he yelled at the robots.

The AI's moved forward with their weaponless hands reaching out. They were not programmed for battle, so this should be fairly easy for the rangers. Tomi raised her Gauss rifle and started firing short bursts over Watry's shoulder. The hypervelocity projectiles ripped through the leading AI's torso like paper, pulverizing its power cell, and then continued on through to the android directly behind it. The rounds perforated the second robot's power distributor with just as much ease.

The third AI continued forward toward Watry. With no time to change weapons, he switched his pistol to kill and fired. The shot hit the android dead center with an explosion of sparks. As it fell to the floor, Watry noticed Crispy had gotten back to his feet. His extra bulk must have allowed him to absorb the stun better than most would. Watry fired at him again, realizing too late that his pistol was still set on kill and watched Crispy get knocked out of his boots.

"Whoops," Watry said, unconcerned.

No time to see what Watry was talking about, Tomi engaged the fourth AI. A short burst sheared its head off, and with one final burst, she cut the last android in half. This one collapsed to the floor, still twitching.

To Watry's surprise, Crispy stood up again, though still trembling from the harder jolt he'd taken the second time. Watry shrugged and dialed his weapon up to disintegrate. Firing his gun, the particle stream blasted a fist-sized hole through Crispy's chest. The cook stopped his forward movement, showing only a brief look of shock before falling to the floor, knocking pots and pans off the counter with a crash. There was no way he'd be getting up a third time.

Watry switched his sidearm to stun and motioned toward the door on the opposite side of the kitchen, but before the rangers could go through it, another pirate walked in to see what the commotion was all about. With their chameleon cloaks still on, this newcomer didn't notice their presence. He approached the supine cook and gave him a kick.

"Hey, Crispy, get your fat ass—" He stopped when he noticed the look of surprise lingering on Crispy's face and the hole through his chest. A second later, Watry stunned him.

The pirate fell on his side convulsing. At least this time, the stun setting had worked like it was supposed to. Watry put cuff tape on this pirate's wrists and ankles—he would have to wait to be processed. With him secured, the rangers proceeded into the dining area, although mess hall was definitely a more accurate description. Since it was an open room with no hiding places, they quickly cleared it and moved on.

As they were about to head back outside, a machine gun started firing. It sounded like the gunner was an amateur—he was firing full cyclic, slinging bullets everywhere without care. Tomi and Watry looked at each other. Had something gone wrong with Healy's plan? The two rangers steeled themselves and looked outside.

Just moments prior, Brooks had been camouflaged in her HEX suit in the forest. Her flares and decoys had worked. The combat robots guarding the base were heading out into the forest to investigate, right past Brooks's HEX suit.

Ranger Brooks swung around to face their backs and opened fire on the largest combat robot with her particle cannon, burning a hole clean through it. She put down each robot in rapid succession, alternating between her Gauss machine gun and particle cannon to keep both weapons from overheating. Catching the robots from behind worked like a charm. By the time they realized where Brooks was attacking from, they were already smoldering scrap metal.

Mission accomplished, she headed through the main entrance of the pirate base.

This was about the time Valk woke up from his peaceful slumber. It had taken several explosions to do so and he finally noticed the base was under attack. He got to his feet and peered out over the compound. He could hear the sound of blaster fire and gunshots over by the main entrance. Several of the pirates' toughest robots were exploding, but he couldn't see who or what was doing the shooting.

Following the beam shots to their origin, Valk pinpointed Brooks's location even without seeing her. Proud of his extrapolation, he energized the Gauss machine gun, aimed, and pulled the trigger. The Gauss machine gun sounded like a buzz saw, but hit like an autocannon. Brush, branches, and even whole tree trunks turned into toothpicks as the 10mm projectiles streamed out of the gun's muzzle.

"Holy shit!" Valk exclaimed.

He traversed the gun, trying to find the hidden enemy as he literally mowed down the forest like a field of wheat in the process. Without knowing whether he'd hit his unseen target, he continued peppering the entire area. It was a good thing the manufacturer of the machine gun included a heat sink to help cool the weapon, because it was generating so much heat Crispy could have fried an egg on top of it.

Once outside, Tomi and Watry noticed the weapons fire sounds were coming from above. They looked up and saw a pirate in the high-hide about thirty feet above them. It had appeared unmanned upon their initial arrival, but now the pirate was firing upon the forest in the exact location Brooks had been planning her part of the attack. They could see the combat bots on the ground, but couldn't get an eye on Brooks.

They also couldn't get a clear line of sight on the gunner, which meant their blaster's stun setting wouldn't work. Their sensors could see through the hide's walls, but all they could do would be to shoot toward the gunner with their repulsor rifles and hope it landed. Normally their rifles would certainly wound and even kill the occupant, it would all depend upon their aim being near perfect and successfully going through a barrier. Then Tomi had an idea.

"Get ready to take cover," she told Watry.

Tomi pulled out one of her repulsor grenades. Arming it, she threw the grenade up and into the hide.

Valk didn't notice Tomi's grenade landing next to his feet and activating, so he was surprised when its omnidirectional repulsor matrix powered up and forcefully pushed him outward. As Valk flew through the air, he felt like he had just been hit by a large truck and the hide itself looked the same as he felt. The walls were blown out, the roof flew off, and even the Gauss machine gun was thrown across the compound.

Conveniently, the pirate landed not too far from Tomi and Watry. It was obvious that many of his bones had been broken, but it was mostly from the grenade rather than his landing. Tomi approached the shocked pirate and checked his vital signs.

"He's still alive," she told Watry, rolling the pirate over.

"Lucky for him you got here before I did," they heard Brooks say. She continued moving past them to her next target.

Informing Valk that he was under arrest, Tomi bound his hands with cuff tape even though both his arms were fairly useless in their broken state, not to mention his legs that looked like rubber bent in unnatural directions. Still, nobody was going to accuse her of not following procedure.

Hondo, Merc, and Spaz had been in the portable toilet when the raid started. Luckily for these three pirates, the shitter was located on the opposite side of the ranger's entry point, which gave them time to make their way into the vehicle garage unnoticed. If they'd learned anything in their time as a pirate, it was every man for himself when the shit hit the fan. Their only goal at this point was escaping.

They started the six-wheeled ATV parked inside, and without bothering to open the garage door, the trio accelerated right through it.

Watry was covering Tomi while she finished securing Valk. The three pirates crashed through the garage door and Watry opened fire on the ATV, pulling the trigger three times. But with his blaster still set to stun, the bolts couldn't penetrate the ATV's windscreen.

The pirates accelerated, seeking to escape with their lives and freedom. Tomi stood upright to fire her Gauss rifle at the tires as it passed, realizing too late that they were solid rubber, rendering her bullets ineffective. Not stopping for any reason, the three pirates kept on going out into the rainforest. Nothing to be done about them right now, Tomi and Watry continued to move through the camp.

Off in the distance, they noticed Ranger Brooks engaging with two combat robots. She fired at them, destroying the first one, but its attack had taken off the left arm of her battlesuit including her Gauss gun. She fired at the second robot, taking its head clean off. It used its backup sensors and the processor located in its torso to take aim at Brooks, but Tomi and Watry were within range now.

Tomi pulled out a plasma grenade, set it to smart mode, armed it, and sent it on its way. The grenade followed a parabolic arc through the air and landed perfectly on top of the combat robot. On impact, the grenade erupted in a white-hot ball of plasma. The shock wave shattered the robot's upper torso armor and fused its exposed circuitry. It fell just a few yards from Brooks.

"Holy fuck!" she exclaimed. "That was too fucking close!"

Suddenly, they heard weapons fire from the other side of the base.

"Climb on," Brooks said, and the two rangers hitched a ride on the back of Brooks's battlesuit.

17

WOLF AMONGST THE SHEEP

Moving at a professional sprinter's pace to the far end of the pirate base, the rangers got there in no time flat with Brooks's help. The problem was immediately obvious: it was a hostage standoff between some pirates and their fellow rangers, Healy and Zimmerman. One pirate was using a hostage as a shield and another was taking cover just inside the doorway.

"This must be where they keep their hostages," Watry said as they joined the others.

"What do they do with them?" Zimmerman asked, aiming at the hostage taker as Healy stood nearby.

"They either use them as collateral for ransom or turn them into pirates. If all else fails, they kill them."

"Not today," Zim said.

He squeezed off a single shot, straight through the pirate's nose and out the back of his head. It was the ultimate kill shot; the projectile severed the pirate's brainstem and he went limp, releasing the terrified hostage and falling to the ground. Tomi was impressed since Zim hadn't seen nearly the action she had since they'd graduated.

The hostage dropped to his knees and threw his arms in the air. "Don't shoot! Please, don't shoot!"

Healy could estimate where the other pirate was standing behind the wall. Setting his pistol to disintegrate and narrowing the beam to armor-piercing, he aimed above the hostage's head and a tad to the right. Without a word, he fired off three shots. All three went through the wall and struck the pirate hiding behind it in the torso, who was killed instantly. His body fell out into the doorway with a thump.

Tomi was certain the puddle beneath the hostage wasn't there a moment before. *Poor guy,* she thought. *Oh well, better him than me.*

Healy rushed forward to secure the hostage while the rest of the rangers began clearing the building. As suspected, the holding pens for the hostages were inside. Simple rooms with mattresses on the ground for them to sleep on. Eleven hostages were present; three of them had been there almost a year, while the others had been kidnapped just over a month ago.

Upon hearing the rangers yell, "Federation Rangers," many of them instantly broke down. Their nightmare was finally over.

With the hostages safely secured, Brooks offered to stay outside and protect them until the patrol returned since her HEX suit was too big to enter the building anyway. The rest of the rangers moved on to clear the rooms inside the main building. Scans showed eight biosignatures spread throughout. When Watry burst into what turned out to be the computer room, he found Clarence Evans hiding under a table. No tattoos or piercings, this guy was more likely to have a different pocket protector for every day of the week than shoot a gun, but he wasn't locked up with the hostages either.

"Let me guess, you must be the pirates' IT guy," Watry said sarcastically.

"Please, don't kill me," Evans said, shaking and squeezing his eyes shut.

"Then you'd better listen up," Watry responded. "I need you to start downloading all of the files onto this." He held out a small device for Evans to take.

When he slowly opened his eyes to look at the ranger, he received a little encouragement from Watry's blaster. Evans jumped to his feet, bumping his head on the table. He took the device, sat down, and quickly got to work, his fingers flying over the keyboard.

Seeing that Watry had this guy secured, Tomi moved on down the hall into one of the last rooms, where she found four women wearing lingerie. She figured they must be Psycho's private harem. The room certainly looked like something out of a bordello: a large bed, mood lighting, and even red velvet curtains. Though the women looked well taken care of, they made it very clear they were happy to get out of there.

After escorting them outside to Brooks, Tomi checked her bioscanner again. It seemed Healy and Zimmerman had taken care of two others, but there was still one last biosignature. She headed back inside to investigate.

Entering what appeared to be Psycho's private office, Tomi found a woman wearing just a bra and panties hiding under the desk. She claimed to be one of his love slaves, and having just found the rest of the harem, Tomi didn't see any reason to doubt her at first. But as she escorted the woman to meet up with Brooks and the others, Tomi noticed more and more things out of place with this one.

Her hair was done up quickly and she wasn't wearing any makeup. It was obvious she hadn't shaved her legs or armpits in weeks and she even had tattoos. To top it all off, she wasn't wearing silky, lacey lingerie like the others were, but instead had on a simple sports bra and cotton briefs, contrasting quite sharply with the captain's other love slaves.

Tomi decided she'd play along for now, while warning Brooks to keep a close eye on this one until they could question her. Fortunately, the dropship carrying Patrolman Curtis and his Space Patrol investigators had returned with empty jail cells. They were just setting down on the base landing pad as Tomi and the woman exited the building.

Curtis emerged along with several patrolmen, one being fresh out of the academy. He ordered the other patrolmen to gather up the stunned and cuffed pirates while he and the rookie approached Tomi.

"No sign of Psycho?" Curtis asked.

She shook her head. "The hunt will have to continue."

Curtis sighed. "Very well. Jonas, take custody of this woman," he ordered his rookie, pointing to Tomi's charge.

As Curtis walked away, Tomi tried to warn Jonas about her latest rescue. "Might want to question that one."

Attempting to appear important and in control, the rookie brushed her off saying, "Thank you, that will be all."

That didn't sit well with Tomi. "Listen here, you little snot-nosed noob," she said, getting in his face, "I'm trying to warn you that something's not right. Look at her! She's different from the others."

The patrolman did not like his authority being challenged, rookie though he was. He got right back in Tomi's face and started yelling at her while poking a finger into her sternum. "No, you listen! The Space Patrol is in charge of this operation, ranger. While we appreciate your efforts up to this point, we are here now, which means you yield to me. Am I making myself clear?" He emphasized each word as he said, "Stand down, ranger."

Tomi snarled down at his finger, which was still jabbing her chest. Grabbing his hand in her own with a firm grip, she twisted it awkwardly until he fell to his knees in submission. Holding him in place, she said, "Oh, I'm very clear who has the authority here, rookie. I'm not here to be your doormat. I have done your dirty work when we were meant to be here working as a team, and as such, I expect your respect."

By this point, everyone within hearing range had taken notice of the rookie patrolman's humbling moment, and the lead investigator walked over to intervene.

"What is going on here?" Curtis asked, looking between them and raising his eyebrows.

Tomi's rage was broken by the interruption and she released the young patrolman, who started right into demanding that she be put on report. Patrolman Curtis put up a hand, silencing his subordinate. Turning to Tomi, he asked for her to fill him in instead.

Tomi pointed out the fifth sex slave, noting the drastic difference between her and the others. Looking the women up and down, Curtis walked over and questioned each of them. When asked if they recognized the plain-looking woman on the end, none of them said they knew her. Curtis scanned the woman in question and a criminal record appeared on his screen: Pricilla S. Anderton, numerous arrest warrants.

"It looks like you found one of the missing pirates," the lead investigator commented. Then he turned to his red-faced patrolman. "Patrolman Jonas, you need to be more observant. This one almost got away again because you didn't notice she was out of place and were too stubborn to listen to the advice of others."

Curtis turned to the rest of the group who had been watching the whole exchange. "In light of this new information, I want scans done on everyone. Make sure there are no other wolves in sheep's clothing among us."

Tomi observed the hostages and four sex slaves as they were evacuated to the *Bass Reeves* to be medically evaluated and have their identities verified. Now that the jamming signal was disabled, Zimmerman was able to contact each of their next of kin to notify them that they were safe and sound.

The surviving pirates were now enjoying the some of the same experiences they'd inflicted upon their hostages. Namely, having shock collars placed around their necks as well as being strip searched and having any cybernetics removed or deactivated. After they were secured in the jail cells on board the patrol ship, the patrol officers went around inspecting the bodies of the dead pirates before they were also taken back to the dropship.

"Tomi," Watry called. He was standing near a flitter. "Come on! We aren't done."

Looking on from the bushes, Psycho and the others who'd managed to escape from the first infiltration watched in utter horror as they saw the cleanup happening at the main base. They were too late.

"What do we do, boss?" Bong asked.

"Shut up, I'm thinking!" Psycho all but yelled at him, trying to stay hidden from the lawmen.

With both bases having now been taken over and several of their men being dead or captured, those remaining at large were officially out of options. Hearing the whine from an approaching vehicle, the pirates dropped down onto their bellies in the dirt. Shortly after, a flitter flew past their hiding spot, and the fugitives breathed a sigh of relief when the two rangers didn't notice them.

"I think it's time to lay low for a while, boys," Psycho admitted.

"This must have been one hell of a fight," lead investigator Curtis commented when they saw the carnage in the kitchen.

The other patrol officers were speechless upon seeing the giant pirate, Crispy, laid out on the floor, the smell of burned flesh still in the air. There were also several destroyed androids, shot full of holes and a couple missing heads or limbs. There was no repairing these units—they were off to the scrap pile.

"How many rangers did you say cleared this room?" a young patrolman finally asked.

"Just the two: Watry and Ryan. Wait till you see the high-hide and a combat robot they blew up using their grenades," Curtis commented with his eyebrows raised. "Aren't you glad they're on our side?"

"Well, it's back to the beach for me," Brooks said to Healy as the cleanup came to a close. "I've still got a couple days left before I'm due back on duty."

"We sure appreciate you coming to help us during your time off," Healy acknowledged. "Couldn't have done it without you."

"You know I can't say no to ridding the world of a few more pirates," she said, suddenly distracted by the passing gurney carrying Crispy's remains.

Healy followed her gaze. "Speaking of which," he said.

"That must be the 500 pounds of asshole Watry and Ryan bagged," Brooks commented, showing personal pride in her fellow female. "Most rookies would have shat their pants just looking at that tub of lard. For a hot chick, that Ryan certainly has balls."

Healy laughed and looked around, noticing both subjects of the conversation were missing. "Where are they anyway?" he asked.

The imprisoned pirates watched as their injured and dead comrades were carted past them on the patrol ship.

"Lucky bastards," one of the prisoners commented. "Who knows what hellhole the Federation will dump us into."

Overhearing him, a patrolman replied, "If you get yourselves a good lawyer and cooperate, you *might* be lucky enough to get thrown into a hellhole. Otherwise, you pack of losers will have a date with the executioner."

The pirate who'd spoken gulped audibly and others turned pale, suddenly realizing just how dire of a situation they were in. To emphasize the patrolman's point, the repulsor gurney carrying Crispy's body floated by.

"They killed Crispy!"

Hondo kept the accelerator to the floor until the rainforest thinned out and they were finally traveling through savanna. Instead of going due south, he decided to go southeast in hopes that the rangers wouldn't think of looking for them there. Merc was manning a pintle-mounted gatling laser on the top of the ATV, pointing it as he did a panoramic scan.

"The coast is clear. We're home free, fellas!" he said.

Spaz wasn't so sure. "Look!" he said, pointing at somebody plodding along in the distance.

Hondo slowed their speed a bit as they assessed the situation. Spaz was uneasy as usual, but Merc sat up straighter when he recognized who it was.

"Crabs!" he exclaimed.

Hondo accelerated to meet up with him and then stopped the ATV. "Where the hell have you been?" he asked Crabs. "The whole world's gone to shit!"

"You're telling me! Got jumped by aliens and the damn rangers," Crabs replied.

"No shit! The base is out of commission and we barely got away," said Spaz.

"Yeah, you got away, but where you gonna go?" Crabs queried. "Everything's back at the base."

Hondo shook his head. "Nothing's left at the base. Rangers and patrolmen raided the whole place."

"Where's the rest of your crew?" Merc asked, seeing Crabs was alone although he'd been sent out with several guys.

Crabs shrugged, "I left their useless asses behind. They can fend for themselves."

None of them seemed to care about the noobie pirates, who were likely imprisoned by now anyway. Instead, Hondo was focused on something else Crabs had said. Having missed the entire Anar-phut involvement in the ranger infiltration, he was interested to learn more.

"Wait, did you say the rangers partnered with some aliens?" When Crabs confirmed he'd heard correctly, Hondo said, "That gives me an idea. Hop on!"

As Watry flew the flitter, Tomi kept a lookout using a pair of digital binoculars. They didn't seem necessary since the fleeing pirates had left a pretty obvious trail once they'd cleared the rainforest. Those tires may be puncture proof, but they really tore up the ground as a result. The real concern now was ensuring they didn't alert the pirates to their arrival. So far, stealth had been the most effective weapon against the pirates, so they would stick with the same old plan of going in with their chameleon cloaks.

From the back of the flitter, Tomi called out to Watry, "Found them! It looks like they can't seem to stay out of trouble; they've taken the Anar-phut science team hostage."

Tomi watched the situation unfolding as Watry brought them in for a landing several hundred yards away in high grass. From what she could see, neither the pirates nor the aliens noticed their approach. Watry attached a shotgun microphone to Tomi's rifle.

"Their vehicle's still running," he noted.

Some vehicles used fusion cells or nuclear power, some used super conductor solid-state batteries, and still others used internal combustion engines. This particular vehicle was making so much noise the pirates might as well have shouted to the world where they were.

Using their chameleon cloaks for concealment, the rangers approached within fifty yards. Any closer and somebody might see a visual distortion. Crabs was talking to a very angry-looking Teacher while waving a laser pistol in her face. The other three pirates were still on the ATV—Merc on the gatling laser, Hondo in the driver's seat, and Spaz in the back training a plasma carbine on the Anar-phuts.

Outnumbered two to one, Tomi decided to do something really stupid. Without consulting with Watry, she stood and shouted "Federation Rangers! You're surrounded!" She followed up her bluff by firing several warning bursts from her rifle overhead.

The pirates immediately turned their attention from the aliens and started shooting in the direction the voice came from. Since they couldn't see anyone, Merc and Spaz fired blindly while Hondo hit the accelerator, speeding away and leaving Crabs behind.

"Get back here, assholes!" Crabs recognized the irony of them abandoning him, but he didn't like when the tables were turned on him like that.

The Anar-phuts started to converge upon their former captor now that he was vulnerable and Tomi shouted, "Surrender or die."

Crabs fired his weapon at the sound of her voice, but hit nothing. Then a blaster bolt hit him in the lower torso, dropping him to the ground. The rangers decloaked and approached Teacher, who actually smiled at their presence.

"Welcome, rangers. We are glad you are here," she said.

WOLF AMONGST THE SHEEP

Seeker loped over at the sight of Tomi. "Oh, I am so glad to see you are still alive, Tomi Ryan!"

Tomi laughed. "Yep, still got some air left in these lungs."

After checking that the aliens were unharmed, the rangers turned their attention to Crabs. He was moaning in agony from his belly wound, but still conscious.

Watry said, "Take it away, Ryan. You're definitely no rookie anymore."

She had to fight a smile as she looked down at her prisoner. "You are under arrest for piracy and kidnapping. If you resist, I'll shoot you in the head."

Watry admired Tomi's bluntness. He also felt compelled to ask the pirate, "How did you get the name Crabs?" Shaking his head, he added, "Then again, maybe I don't wanna know."

After hastily applying first aid and cuff tape to Crabs, the rangers left him under the temporary mercy of the Anar-phuts, beginning again in their pursuit of the other three pirates. Even as the sun started to head down toward the horizon, it was easy to track them. They were driving so fast it kicked up a dust cloud that was visible for miles.

Seeing them in the distance, Watry accelerated. The flitter could easily outrun the ATV. Catching up, he flew out in front of the fleeing pirates so Tomi could take aim with a clear shot. Looking through her rifle's hybrid scope, she drew a bead on the driver and squeezed the trigger.

With a loud crack, the projectile penetrated the ATV's windscreen and hit Hondo in the face. He went limp, his foot came off the accelerator, and the vehicle rolled to a stop. When Merc turned to Hondo to ask why he was slowing down, he could still see the cloud of pink mist behind his comrade. The metallic taste in the air confirmed what he was seeing—Hondo had just been shot dead.

Merc started firing the gatling laser, sweeping it in an arc and hoping to hit the rangers he knew were out there even though all he could see was the now-parked flitter. Before the laser could overheat, a Gauss projectile hit it in the power connection at the back, rendering it inoperative. He reached down and grabbed a laser rifle while yelling at Spaz to start shooting. Spaz jumped out of the back of the vehicle and started looking for the shooter.

He saw their blurs—there was just two of them! Both he and Merc started firing from the hip, but at 200 yards, plasma bolts and laser beams were hitting only ground and sky. Then there was another loud crack, a cloud of pink mist, and Merc fell over backward, dead. With the power cell on his plasma carbine drained, Spaz looked at Merc's body, dropped his weapon, and raised his hands. He was out of choices.

Tomi and Watry walked up to Spaz, uncloaking themselves and ordering him to turn around and get on his knees.

"What the fuck! I'm not surrendering to a bitch!" Spaz exclaimed.

Tomi fired her omniblaster set on stun into his left leg, adding, "Shut up and do as you're told, bitch."

Watry flipped him on his belly and locked a shock collar around his neck. "Who's the bitch now?" Nudging Spaz with the barrel of his gun, he added, "Get up and load your friends into the back of this vehicle." He motioned to the ATV. "It's hereby impounded by the authority of the Federation Rangers."

Tomi drew the short straw and had to drive the ATV back to rendezvous with the Anar-phuts and pick up Crabs. Instead of driving, Tomi tied Spaz to the blood splattered drivers' seat and held the muzzle of her Gauss rifle to the back of his head.

"Now, drive back to where you left your partner in crime. In the event you suffer another bout of stupidity, I'll evacuate your cranium. Do you understand, bitch?"

Spaz was beginning to regret becoming a pirate, the smell of Hondo's blood was making him sick, he had an irate chick ready to blow his head off if he made one wrong move, and he already knew he would be going to the hive for the rest of his life. He started the ATV, and for the first time in his life, listened very carefully to what a woman was saying to him.

Healy and Zim had gone at the Anar-phut base camp looking for Tomi and Watry. Teacher told them they would be returning for some not-so-precious cargo—namely, Crabs—so they opted to wait for their fellow rangers' return. They found Crabs barely conscious from bleeding out, so they used the comm to radio for the *Comfort* to come pick him up for emergency surgery, requesting the patrol send a babysitter with him—preferably, anyone but Jonas.

As the wounded pirate was boarded onto the *Comfort* under watch of a more seasoned patrolman, the patrol ship had chosen to wait for the other rangers in case they succeeded in obtaining more prisoners. Curtis was holding out hope that Psycho would be located, but no such luck.

The mobile aerospace hospital ship departed just as Watry pulled up on his flitter, followed by Tomi on the ATV with their prisoner and a couple bodies.

"Well, take a look at this," Healy said, proud of his teammates.

"Will you pigs hurry up and untie me?" Spaz complained.

Healy worked his way forward and punched Spaz in the mouth. "I'm sorry could you repeat that? I couldn't hear you."

Spaz tried to act tough, but knew better than to say another word.

Pretending he hadn't seen anything that broke protocol, Curtis thanked Tomi and Watry. "We appreciate your assistance in this matter. We'll take it from here." He motioned for Jonas and another patrolman to come get the three pirates and load them into their dropship.

As they did so, Curtis gave Healy a serious look. "I know you won't be thrilled with this, Healy, but Jonas needs some training in interdepartmental cooperation. I'd like him to accompany your team aboard the *Bass Reeves* for the next month. He'll be under your command. Hell, have him clean the head if you want."

Tomi tried to protest, but Healy stopped her. Looking at Curtis, he bargained, "Two weeks."

Curtis agreed and shortly after, all of the other patrolmen departed, leaving a fuming Jonas and the rangers alone with the Anar-phuts. Still amazed with the aliens, Zimmerman wandered off to chat with Seeker and Runner. Feeling lost, Jonas followed the parahuman. Healy turned to Tomi, his pride obvious in his eyes.

"Ryan, you've come a long way in these last several months. I've seen both your perseverance and your courage grow tenfold."

Watry nodded in agreement. "If the pirates had succeeded in taking the Anar-phuts hostage, they would have created a diplomatic crisis."

Teacher stepped forward and offered her gratitude as well. "We are grateful to all of you for your pest-control practices. Ranger Tomi Ryan, from what we have seen and what Seeker has told us, you are a credit to your species."

"Thanks, I think?" Tomi said.

"You don't have to thank us," Healy said. "This is why we do this job." He spoke louder then, ordering his team, "Gather up your gear. We need to get back to the *Bass Reeves* pronto."

"Something else happening?" Zimmerman asked.

"A ranger's work is never done," Watry answered.

18

THE BIG BLUE

They say absence makes the heart grow fonder. Tomi found this to be very true, and for many different reasons. She missed her family, her friends, and even her ex-boyfriend, Olin. Though she'd broken up with him to maintain focus on her career, they had been together so long, she found that she still needed him in her life. Even if just as a friend.

Even more, after being on Yardang for so long, she missed the simple pleasures the most. From the desert to the savanna to the rain forest, she had her fair share of dirt, grime, and Deus only knows what else embedded into every nook and cranny in her gear and on her body. Now she could finally enjoy a nice hot Hollywood shower on board the *Bass Reeves*.

Taking a huge sigh of happiness in the steamy room, Tomi toweled off and dressed in her PT clothes—might as well be comfortable. She walked back to her quarters and shut the door behind her, looking at her exosuit. It needed a few repairs after her encounter with the Ur-not. Examining the tear, she realized what a miracle it was the Ur-not's claw didn't eviscerate her. Luckily, the nanoweave layer of her exosuit had been tough enough to absorb the brunt of the blow.

Her stomach growled. *It can wait,* she thought to herself. *I'll take care of my suit after I take care of my stomach.*

Walking into the galley, Tomi had made it all the way to the food dispenser when she realized she was still wearing her PT gear. She saw Watry sitting at the mess deck's only table and took note that he was even more informally dressed than she in a tank top and shorts. If he could break the rules, so could she. Tomi gathered an MRE, a drink, and some utensils on a tray and took it over to the table.

"Hello, Watry. Mind some company?" she asked.

Watry looked up with a mouthful of food and motioned with his fork toward an empty seat. She sat down and started preparing her meal just as Patrolman Jonas walked in. Even though the punishment was intended for his overstuffed ego, Tomi wondered who was really being punished here, Jonas or the rangers?

Noticing Tomi and Watry dressed so casually, Jonas looked upon them with contempt and stiffly walked over. *Could the guy ever relax?* Tomi wondered, eyeing his appearance. As usual, his uniform looked immaculate: cleaned and pressed with military creases and absolutely spotless. His boots were so polished that they could be used as mirrors. Even his belt buckle and badge were polished to a high shine.

"All personnel are required to be in uniform while in the ship's common areas," the young patrolman stated.

Tomi gave him a look that said, "Don't you have anything better to do?" She glanced at Watry who never gave the patrolman the time of day and instead kept shoveling food into his mouth. She hunched over and began eating again as well, not unaware of the fact that Jonas was focused on her more than Watry. What had she done that was so bad that Deus would send such an idiot to torment her?

"All personnel are required to be in uniform while in the ship's common areas," he repeated, stepping forward. Tomi tried to ignore him, but he persisted. "Hey, Ryan! Are you deaf? You have to be in uniform to be here. Suit up or get out."

He made the mistake of putting hands on her, grabbing Tomi by the upper arm and trying to pull her out of her seat. She resisted, glaring at the hand gripping her arm.

"You only get one warning, rookie: let go of me," she said firmly.

He wouldn't let go, so Tomi allowed muscle memory to take over. *Time to teach this punk his second lesson in humility.* She twisted her arm toward the gap between his thumb and fingers, simultaneously striking the inside of his wrist with her free hand, and followed it all up by kicking him in the groin. Losing his grip and his balance, the patrolman fell on his ass.

Huffing from the scuffle, Jonas did his best to sound unfazed. "That's it! I'm putting you on report!"

By this time, Watry was also on his feet standing over Tomi's latest victim. He had been ready to help her, but it seemed she didn't need it. Still, he warned the rookie patrolman, "Mess with a ranger, you mess with all rangers. Remember whose ship your ass is on."

"You're both going on report for this!" Jonas said, staring up at them from the ground with his brows knit tightly together.

Both rangers stood their ground, daring him to say anything else. Finally, Jonas got to his feet and stormed off in a huff. Tomi and Watry returned to their seats to finish their meals as though nothing happened.

After a moment's silence, Tomi had to ask, "Do you think he'll follow through with his threat?"

Watry laughed through his full mouth. "A snot-nosed noob like him? I wouldn't be surprised if he did. What's the matter, Ryan? Can't you handle a little ass chewing?" he ribbed.

"Really, Jonas, you're coming to me with this?" Captain Everly did not take the interruption lightly. Having Patrolman Jonas on board the *Bass Reeves* was almost as bad as babysitting a Survey Service expedition. Over the last two weeks, it seemed like nearly every other day the guy had something to complain about. Thank Deus his assignment with them was nearing conclusion.

"Let me get this straight," Captain Everly queried, "Ryan stood up to you, knocked you on your ass for your lack of skills when it comes to minding your own business, and now you want to put her on report. Am I getting this right?"

Patrolman Jonas remained firm. "Yes, sir. She disregarded regulations, refused to follow orders, and then assaulted me and disrespected my authority. She must be punished for her actions."

"You didn't mention anything about regs or orders," Everly noted, afraid his hands might be tied if Tomi really had done something against protocol.

Seeing the captain's interest piqued, Jonas nodded enthusiastically. "Yes, sir. She and Watry were dressed down in the mess hall."

When he heard Jonas's answer, Everly had to hold back a laugh. He feigned shock, gasping dramatically. "Tell me more! Were they eating?"

Jonas hadn't caught Everly's sarcasm, or he pretended not to anyway. "Yes, sir, they were."

Everly gasped. "How dare they take a brief moment to relax after such a harrowing mission infiltrating a pirate base that was supposed to fall under *your* department's duties," Captain Everly said, widening his eyes and leaning back in his chair.

Growing serious again, Everly added, "I think I'm getting a clear picture now. In the two weeks you've spent with us, you have yet to learn your lesson. You tried to drag Ranger Ryan off the mess deck because she wasn't wearing the uniform of the day. Then she knocked you—I mean, assaulted you—and now, here we are."

Everly motioned around his office and paused, waiting for Jonas to acknowledge the absurdity.

Not knowing what else to do, Jonas kept his mouth shut, waiting for whatever came next, though he knew it wasn't going to be in his favor. He felt his face growing redder by the second.

Everly sighed. "Son, let me tell you something. The Space Patrol is an admirable branch, it is. But it doesn't even begin to compare to what we rangers do on the wild frontier. Someone like you wouldn't last one day out there. Why do you think we went in first?"

Jonas gulped back his frustration.

Every continued, "Ryan, on the other hand, has faced pirates—more than once I might add—and lived to tell the tale. She has grown out of her rookie status and into a seasoned, well-trained, and confident ranger, and I am proud to have her serve under my command. One day, she just may make captain herself." He eyed the patrolman, expecting a response this time.

"Yes, sir," Jonas said, "but—"

"You truly expect me to take this steaming pile of crap to the ranger's OIC, Patrolman Jonas?" Captain Everly raised his eyebrows again. "You're not dealing with some spaceport bum or drunk crewman; these are Federation Rangers, for Deus's sake. Tough, self-reliant, at home on hostile and untamed worlds—I'm sure you've read all of the literature."

Pointing at the door, Everly added, "Those rangers just got back from a rescue mission on Yardang—a mission that should have been handled by *your* team, seeing as Patrolman Curtis is the lead investigator on this case. Instead, my rangers performed orbital insertion, rescued stranded passengers, joined forces with aliens, took out not one, but two pirate bases, and you wonder why they were a little cranky?" Everly chastised, leaning forward on his desk.

"But, sir! You can't let them get away with—" Jonas pleaded.

"Kid, I should be writing *you* up for your boneheaded daftness, but since you're fresh out of the academy and the fact that I don't want any delays in being able to hand your ass back over to Curtis, I'll let it slide this time." Everly stood and walked around his desk, opening the door to let Jonas out. "You may be stupid, son, but don't abuse the privilege."

After the door closed, the comm display on Everly's desk chimed with a priority message from HQ. Glancing at it, he quickly called the rangers into his office for an emergency meeting, being sure to tell them not to alert Patrolman Jonas. The last thing he needed was to have him get involved again.

Glancing over the message a second time, Captain Everly shook his head in disbelief. Things were about to get very busy for his rangers. *It's just as Granny used to say,* he thought. *"Ain't no rest for the wicked, and the good don't need none."*

When Healy, Watry, Tomi, and Zimmerman arrived, he read the message aloud and in full.

"And here we were worrying about pirates," Healy said.

"Yes, you heard right," Lieutenant Elba told Everly and his rangers. "The new president wants Pacifica back under Federation control, and you're one of the lucky teams who get to help secure it."

Via secure hyperlink, the rangers saw Elba standing with Captain Guy of the Federation Marines. Though he brought bad news, Tomi was grateful to see Lieutenant Elba again. He truly was an inspiration to her.

Elba had sent them a 3D image of the planet of the Pacifica, a contested world on the border between the Federation and the Imperium. Highlighted were the locations of Imperial occupation forces that had stealthily moved onto the planet during the administration of the Federation's previous president, who didn't seem to care enough to notice. But the new man in charge didn't like his toys being taken from him, and decided it was time to push back.

Images of the various units popped up on the 3D map—heavy tanks, mecha, infantry units, and ground-based orbital defenses. But it was the Imperial mobile fortress on that water-based planet that really grabbed their attention. Tomi used her tablet to focus on the fortress. It was massive: over a million tons, most of which was composite/ablative armor up to twenty yards thick covering nearly the whole structure.

Most of its weapons were mounted topside, including railguns, missile bays, and even an orbital-range laser. Below was protected in a very simple way: water. When on station, the Constantinople-class mobile defense station would float in a sufficiently deep body of water. Coupled with the station's thick armor, the lower 80 percent seemed impregnable, or at least that's what the Imperium would like everyone to think.

"That's where you rangers come in," Captain Guy said. "The missile detection system is not one solid chunk of composite, despite what you might think. Its armor is designed to withstand large-scale assaults from orbital or surface vessels using big coil guns, beam cannons, and anti-ship missiles. But it still has to have openings for suction, discharge, maintenance, and whatever else. You'll be briefed on the details, but I can say up front, this is the linchpin of the operation."

Tomi started scrolling through the list of equipment they would be using: cyber dolphins, aquaform submersible, cybernetic commando suits, and the list just kept going. Then she got to the weapons and gasped. Command was very serious about taking out the MDS.

"What's the hurry, Captain? Doesn't strategy dictate to save the toughest targets for last? Bypass them until they weaken, and then take them down?" Healy asked.

"Normally you would be correct in your assessment, but with

this MDS, it's more than that. Not only is it a mobile fortress, but the Imperial planetary garrison the CO is using it as his HQ." Guy paused and everyone gasped. "That's right, this is the C_3I center for the planet's defenses. If we can knock it out, the rest of the planet garrison will be easy as cake."

Nab the chief to catch the bandits, Tomi thought. "But that means they will be doubling, or even tripling, their defenses around their HQ. Do you really think they will leave any avenue for us to get in?" she queried.

"Like the briefing notes say, that's what the Imps would like you to think," Elba said. "In a perfect world, they would clamp everything airtight like a Pacifica stone oyster: nothing in, nothing out. But that's the clincher, they need to bring water in as coolant and discharge it after use, not to mention in order to deploy any underwater forces, they would need to provide access hatches for them."

While Tomi made a mental note to always read the whole briefing before making assumptions, she marveled at the irony of the whole situation. In order to provide launch points for their defenders, the Imps had to leave a door open for attackers to invade their otherwise impregnable fortress.

Up close, it seemed stupid to be so cavalier toward larger attacks like missiles or torpedoes, but when viewed from a distance, putting a torpedo through an open hatch or port would be a very lucky shot. Any openings were recessed underneath the main armor plates for added protection, so to get a shot through would require one to be at just the right angle. It would look like the trick shot Odysseus performed at the end of the *Odyssey*: shooting an arrow through a dozen ax heads. The rangers were good, but they weren't that good.

"So, we're just going to waltz right on in and do what, exactly?" Healy questioned. "I'm pretty sure the Imps will be keeping someone around to guard the big red button."

"Oh good, you guys are thinking," Guy said. "No, it won't be that easy. The back door will have some protection, no doubt. If the thing has a self-destruct option, we can't find any info on it. That means all of you will be kitted out with weapons, and of course, ultra-level demolition equipment."

"Ultra-level demo equipment? Are you sending us in with nukes?" Watry asked.

"You're not rangers, you're damn brain surgeons," Elba said sarcastically, tired of the interruptions. "I knew we got the best and the brightest." He sighed and crossed his arms.

The plan sounded insane, yet in order to take out an enemy king this big, it would take something with at least a yield of a ton of TNT to ensure its critical systems were disabled. The Constantinople-class mobile defense station had been around for many years and used in action on several planets. In all that time, the Federation had gathered quite a bit of intelligence on it, including technical details.

"The intel geeks earned their pay. We know the layout of the power generation and distribution systems," Zim commented as he read the briefing.

"But where's the detail? What if we run into a dead end? We could be chasing up blind alleys for days," Tomi said.

"Check your load out, all of you will be carrying fusion cutters," Guy answered.

Tomi winced. Another mark against her for not reading the briefing.

"Whatcha worried about, Ryan? Improvise, adapt, overcome," Healy ribbed.

"Thanks for reminding me, but that aside, now that we have all of these new toys, do we have an actual plan?" she asked.

"Now that's what I want to hear!" Elba said, clapping his hands together. "Okay then, listen up."

They dropped Patrolman Jonas off with Curtis a day early, rolling their eyes at his instantaneous complaints about his time with them, the *Bass Reeves* crew journeyed meet up with Elba and Guy. Tomi used the time to read the entire briefing from front to back and top to bottom.

The name Pacifica was derived from a word meaning peaceful, but in the planet's case they would be referring to the fact its hydrographic coverage was up around 90 percent. According to the cultural download, the planet's nickname was "The Big Blue" for obvious reasons. It was one decent-sized continent with various island chains scattered over the rest of the surface.

"Good luck, rangers. Whatever happens out there, it's been my honor to be your captain aboard the *Bass Reeves*," Everly said when they landed.

Healy and Watry gave their captain a salute before walking down the ramp to the dock. Zimmerman followed them, but Tomi lingered.

"You're not joining us?" Tomi asked Everly.

"A captain never leaves his ship," Everly reminded her. "Besides, I'm too old for war."

The reality of what they were about to get themselves into struck her full force in that moment. Tomi pursed her lips and nodded, accepting all of it as it was. "Captain," she said and then turned to follow her fellow rangers off the *BR* for the last time.

In their makeshift meeting room, Elba and Guy filled them in on the latest updates. The space battle had already started with Imperial forces taking a pounding by the marines. A few ships had been destroyed, but most were just crippled enough they could no longer fight. The Federation fleet ground forces were now gearing up for the inevitable orbital assault. And the planned infiltration had already been worked out; it was just a matter of execution at this point.

"A stealth dropship? When did they start making those?" Zimmerman queried.

"They've been around for years, Zim," Tomi answered. "Some of the conspiracy enthusiasts found out about them when they staked out an isolated base on Eden. At night, they would look up and every once in a while, one would fly over."

"And they were right," Elba added. "A lot of compartmentalized programs are sent out to Eden because it's so far away from prying eyes. What they saw was the first training squadron getting ready for real-world operations. It wasn't too long after that these babies were declassified."

"Almost," Healy said. "Federation brass are no longer hiding them, but they're not exactly advertising them either."

"Yeah," Watry added, "even today, Federation officers will still say, 'I have no idea what you are talking about' if you dare to ask."

The rangers looked at Captain Guy for an answer.

"I have no idea what you are talking about," he said, sending the rangers into a fit of boisterous laughter.

"We can talk about this dropship that doesn't exist later. Gear up and saddle up," Elba ordered.

They walked up the boarding ramp, and once inside the cargo compartment, they saw for the first time what would be transporting them to the target site. Tomi ogled this strange-looking machine. It looked like a whale. Even the surface felt like skin rather than plastic or metal. As she ran her hand along the exterior of it, Elba urged them to pick up the pace and get ready for departure.

Already hooked to an overhead gantry crane, the dropship moved through the screenlock and into the vacuum side of the hangar bay. Once in vacuum, the flight crew powered up the dropship's engines, and then opened the throttles just enough to push the big ship out of the bay and clear of the orbital assault ship.

Tomi and her team were permitted access to the dropship's sensor systems. They were set to passive mode, but still presented a vivid panorama. The sensors picked up anything from ultraviolet all the way down to microwaves and everything in between. They swept in all directions so the pilots could avoid colliding with any of the numerous obstacles including active ships, derelicts, and debris. Some drifted lazily along, while others streaked past at high velocity.

Tomi noticed that they had a highly skilled pilot. He wove through the orbital shooting gallery so gracefully she didn't notice any acceleration. She forced her attention back to the mission; it was easy to get lost in the spectacle of all the burning ships tumbling through space. Looking toward their target planet, she could see their flight path taking them to their planned drop point.

Slow and steady was working like a charm. Between that and the dropship's stealth suite, no one—Imperial or Federation—noticed their approach. *This might actually work,* Tomi thought to herself, though she didn't dare say it out loud. She had no wood to knock on and she knew for certain the others would scold her for jinxing the mission, especially if anything actually went wrong.

The tactical display showed they were entering the vector for final decent. The dropship's pilot was using every trick in the book in order to sneak in undetected. Since even a slow decent would heat the dropship's exterior to at least 1,000 degrees—almost hot enough to melt aluminum—he instead matched his vector and velocity to the various debris reentering Pacifica's atmosphere.

Tomi was no expert when it came to sensors and scanners, but she thought it was a pretty cool trick to blend in with the rest of the garbage falling from orbit.

After it was over, they continued along with the debris, checking the various energy bands to see if anyone was looking with radar, lidar, or any other active sensors. When it was decided that they had waited long enough, the pilot fired the engines up and maneuvered toward the night side of the planet. Infiltrate at night—one more trick in the book. Tomi felt like she was learning a lot on this mission.

Now in a controlled decent, the dropship came in low and slow over open water. The cargo ramp lowered, and when the green light was given, the submersible was allowed to slide out tail first, just like a real whale giving birth. Tomi and the others jumped out soon after it.

Once in the water, they boarded the submersible and ran through their checklists. After each ranger called go, Captain Guy gave the thumbs up, sending to the dropship pilot on his way. Tomi volunteered to be the lookout while the others finished prepping. She didn't want to admit to the others, but she really wanted to do some sightseeing. It was too bad it was nighttime though, making her view everything through her visor's low-light mode.

She got some ribbing here and there as someone would occasionally call out, "Ranger Ryan, report!" She would reply, "I see water to the horizon in all directions." After which, they all laughed at her expense.

Though she really didn't mind. She was imagining being her much younger self on an ocean boat with her family. Tomi had always enjoyed the wind in her face, the smell of the salt water, and the peaceful vista. Of course, nighttime made being out in the open water a little scarier, but still, two out of three wasn't bad.

It wasn't too long before Watry energized the sub's propulsion system and Orca, as it was called, started moving. Tomi marveled at what she saw. The sub's tail was more than camouflaged and moved up and down, moving them along just like a whale's tail.

"Lookout below! Prepare to dive!" Guy ordered.

Getting one last whiff of fresh air, Tomi descended the ladder into Orca's belly, the main cabin. Inside was rather cramped with six of them on board along with all of their gear, leaving sparse free space.

"What? No food replicator? How am I supposed to get a cup of coffee?" Healy wisecracked.

"The techs had to toss it so Ryan could have her automated pedicure machine installed," Watry chimed in.

"Up yours, Watry. I can trim my own toenails, thank you very much," Tomi retorted. "Here's your coffee, Healy." She shoved a thermos at him.

"You made coffee?" Healy asked, taking it from her. "I thought you hated coffee?"

"I do. It's just that this minisub has no lavatory, so there you go," Tomi answered.

Healy quickly tossed it back to her as everyone started laughing, urging him to chug Ryan's special coffee blend.

Being the sole marine on board Orca, Captain Guy shook his head. These Federation Rangers could sure play things pretty loose. He was used to things being high and tight. Fortunately for him, things settled down after that. Since their ETA was yet hours away, the rangers tried to get as much sleep as they could.

19

NAB THE CHIEF TO CATCH THE BANDITS

Tomi managed to nab an hour of sleep before she was woken by the alarm on her wrist comp reminding her to take over the watch from Healy. Treading carefully not to step on a sleeping ranger in the tight confines of Orca's belly, she made her way to the cockpit in the front of the cabin.

"Mornin', sunshine," Healy said as Tomi approached.

"Go grab a nap while you still can," she whispered.

While he headed back to the vacant cot, Tomi turned to the controls she was now in charge of monitoring. The minisub was on autopilot, using inertial navigation and gravitic radar set to passive mode to find its way. Tomi had read that inertial guidance had advanced considerably since the early days of mechanical gyroscopes. Now with a heuristic algorithm working with the TIMU sensors, the room for error was much smaller. Coupled with the gravitic radar sensing the ocean floor, the sub's onboard computer knew its location to within a couple of yards at all times.

Orca had a vague resemblance to its mammalian namesake except it didn't have any white markings. Instead, it was all black to help with camouflage and its nose was blunt like a sperm whale. Instead of ballast, the minisub would use its dive planes to force Orca to submerge. The dive planes were actually stub wings creating negative lift that pulled down as opposed to pulling up like an airplane wing—pretty clever. Orca was normally slightly above neutral buoyancy so its top hatch was just above the waterline. Air bladders could also be inflated in an emergency.

Checking the main holographic display, Orca's sensors painted a vivid picture of what was going on outside. The ocean they were passing through was active with all sorts of wildlife from animals the size of frigates to ones so small Tomi didn't notice them until they were right next to the sensor. Checking the speed, she saw they were moving along at a good clip—nearly 25 mph. Then something appeared on Orca's scopes.

Both the passive sonar and gravitic radar detected it. It wasn't a surface contact, but submerged. Tomi tried not to panic, slowing Orca down to a nice lazy 10 mph, and then waited. As the contact drew closer, the computer was able to identify it as a Glaucus-class mini attack submarine. The profile database spat out all sorts of information about it and Tomi's eyes quickly scanned it.

At over 100-feet long and displacing 400 tons, it wasn't very big as far as ships go, but the Imperium stuffed it full of supercavitating torpedoes to ruin the day of any opponent. Its twin counter-rotating ducted propellers moved it at an impressive speed of over 30 mph. Power was provided by a sterling engine fueled with either hydrocarbon-based fuel or hydrogen and oxygen coupled with superconducting rechargeable power cells. The submarine was also equipped with a snorkel so it could burn regular fuel while submerged.

Tomi watched as it drew near, noticing that it changed neither heading nor speed. It was running at periscope depth, probably checking for surface contacts. She bid her time, reminding herself to breathe as the sub churned its way along. Once it passed without incident, she knew it was safe to speed back up again. Later, she would have to make a report to Lieutenant Elba and Captain Guy, but she didn't see any reason to wake them.

Ensign Hannibal Larsen struggled to stay awake. He'd made the mistake of staying up late and having an "invasion party" with the rest of the sub crews. It didn't help that the next morning an alert was sounded and all Imperial attack submarines were put to sea immediately. Larsen had to do the whole thing hungover, and he was still hurting when he found out he would be the last to go on watch. Normally this would be a good thing, but he had been too sick to sleep, so when he started his watch, he was sick and tired, literally.

Now that Larsen was sobered up, his splitting headache and dry throat were finally gone, but exhaustion was taking over. He tried every trick he could think of without embarrassing himself in front of his shipmate, CWO Alonzo. Larsen considered the man a bastard and an asshole, mainly because Alonzo didn't get hungover and it had been his idea to have more than one drinking contest at the party. Larsen, on the other hand, would always end up with a terrible hangover when he drank, but that was nothing compared to the humiliation and ostracization inflicted if one failed to participate in the first place. To show weakness in front of Alonzo now would negate all his efforts from the night prior.

Larsen got up again and walked around the cramped control room. To call it a room was being too generous, even for a submarine. Though he stood at five-foot-eight, even he had to be careful as he walked from one side of the compartment to the other lest he hit his head. Anyone six foot or taller could easily ring their bell if they forgot to stoop. Then again, maybe Larsen should crack his skull. The pain would either keep him awake or earn him some much-needed rest.

Walking back to his station, he took notice that the sonar and periscope were both clear of any contacts. The only significant reading was a biologic moving along a course perpendicular to his. Nothing out of the ordinary, just another specimen of another nameless species in the domain of the Great Emperor of the Imperium. It didn't strike Larsen as unusual. That is, until it sped up just after passing their Imperial sub.

Larsen wanted to investigate the contact, but decided against it when he looked at the gauge for the energy banks: 70 percent. *Shit,* he thought to himself. The lieutenant would be righteously angry if the batteries were not fully charged when he woke up, and if Larsen used up even more to chase a contact that turned out to be just another biologic, he would be in even deeper shit.

If the designers of this thing had just splurged for an MHD turbine, the energy banks would already be recharged. Then again, it was the lieutenant's idea to run silently and deep so as to avoid enemy detection. Larsen rolled his eyes. The commanding officer watched way too many old war videos.

Instead of giving chase, he marked the biologic's location on the navigation display, taking note of the contact's speed and direction. Hopefully he would be able to come back to it later. He did find it curious that it was heading toward the planet's main defense headquarters. *Probably just a coincidence,* he thought and went back to his other duties.

"Don't sweat that attack sub, Ryan," Captain Guy said after he'd roused from his nap. "As long as it doesn't bother us, who cares? They likely either didn't see us, or assumed Orca was just another whale. Stay focused on the mission."

Tomi nodded and allowed her worries to wash away.

Now that everyone was up and ready for action, Guy addressed the whole crew. "It's departure time, rangers. Get ready to lock out."

With the AI piloting Orca, the rangers used the time to put on their cyber armor. Unlike their exosuits, the cyber armor suit was designed to withstand pressure down to 1,000 feet underwater and even deflected both kinetic and electromagnetic attacks. Along with their new apparel, their weapons were made to work underwater too.

Healy, Guy, and Elba each carried 4mm repulsor coil spearguns, which were based on the ranger repulsor rifle. Its feed mechanism had been redesigned to use 4mm fléchettes designed to supercavitate through water and air alike. Each one came with an underslung gyro jet launcher with a rotary magazine loaded with a variety of ammunition.

Zim was given one of the special weapons known as a slicer. Derived from a portable circular saw, Tomi remembered the pirate she'd encountered on the *Stella Warren* who had wielded one of these. After seeing the equipment and bulkhead cut to ribbons by its salvos, she knew it would have been quite deadly if he'd managed to hit anyone with it. The pirate's version of the slicer was illegally modified on the black market with mismatched parts and obvious signs of welding and soldering. The one Zim held was sleeker and more refined: a matte black with subdued markings lending to its stealthy lines.

Watry swung his antiparticle rifle to the ready. These were similar to the blaster rifles the patrol liked to use, except this one fired antimatter particles at near light speed, resulting in a significant explosion. A defense screen tunnel allowed the antimatter beam to travel through an atmosphere or even underwater, although it did have a limited range. It seemed an odd choice for a mission that involved traveling underwater, but the brass wanted to try it out.

Tomi was issued an oscillating tractor/pressor beam projector, or gravity gun for short. It looked odd since it didn't have a barrel or accelerator assembly like other weapons she had seen before. Instead, it had a fat cylinder with no openings that merged with the front of a portable vacuum cleaner. The cylinder had fins folded along its side, and Tomi knew enough not to obstruct them since they would fold out when the weapon fired. The two things Tomi recognized were the separate fusion battery that powered it and the multispectral/T-wave scope mounted on it. With the scope, she would apparently be able to target through solid objects—something Tomi had to see to believe.

All of the rangers were issued GP3 4mm Gauss pistols rather than their standard omniblasters. While less versatile than the omniblaster, the GP3 could discharge in virtually any environment whether air, vacuum, or underwater. While its range was limited underwater, it could still hit targets at fifty yards if the shooter could somehow see the target at that range, which they could thanks to their sensor visors with both multiband electromagnetic spectrum vision and active/passive sonar. Even when set to passive mode, the sonar could image an average-sized human out to 300 feet.

Last but not least, they strapped on their bush knives. If Tomi had learned anything during her few months as an active-duty ranger, it was how vital their least-assuming weapon was, but Zim complained about having to drag such an obsolete relic around.

"Remind me to make you do 1,000 push-ups when we get back, Zimmerman. To diss such an important piece of gear like that is blasphemy! Someday, that little knife of yours could save your life," Elba replied.

"Yeah, Zim, you should have Ryan tell you her bush knife story sometime," Healy chimed in.

Zimmerman raised his eyebrows at his fellow rookie who had apparently already surpassed him in experience. "Is that true, Ryan? You actually got to us your knife in a real-world scenario?"

Tomi nodded. "Yep, it's true. On the *Stella Warren*, a pirate was trying to turn Healy into cutlets and I had lost my blaster, so I improvised. I made the pirate leak first. Maybe someday I can tell you the whole story."

Zimmerman gave her a look of admiration and then glanced at his knife, seeing it in a different light now.

When Guy announced that propulsion from Orca to their target infiltration point would be accomplished using a cyber dolphin, Tomi was relieved. She had thought their resident marine might be macho enough to suggest they swim the six miles to the mobile headquarters. The contraption looked like a one-man version of Orca with grips so the rider could hold on. It would certainly make the journey easier and quicker.

With all of their gear in place, the team took turns cycling through the airlock. Normally, there would be enough room for two humans at a time, even one as big as Ranger Elba, but with the cyber dolphin each ranger brought along, they had to go single file. Since Zim was best-adapted to a marine environment, he took point. Elba, being the ranger in charge, went next. Then Guy, Watry, and Healy. Being last, Tomi locked Healy out and was left alone with Orca's AI.

"See ya later, Orca," Tomi said. "Thanks for the ride and have a safe trip back." The airlock controls signaled ready, and Tomi stepped into the airlock with her dolphin when Orca surprised her by responding.

"Thank you, Ranger Ryan. Good luck," Orca said.

That's some crazy intelligent AI, she thought. *Is this the future of piloting all ships?*

As the airlock flooded, she wondered if this was what it was like for people going into hibernation—squeezed into a pod being filled with cold water. Fortunately, it didn't take too long before the pressure equalized and the outer hatch opened. Tomi eased her cyber dolphin out first, then herself.

Through her visor's sonar vision, she could see the others. It looked like Elba was counting everything to make sure nothing was forgotten. The rangers were trained in hand signals for situations such as this, but their cyber armor was equipped with underwater communicators, making this particular job easier.

"Okay, that's everyone," Elba concluded.

"Grab your dolphin and your buddy. Zim, lead the way," Captain Guy ordered.

Tomi powered up her dolphin, letting the bionic tail swish up and down. Even though she had trained with one of these, the amount of thrust it produced still surprised her. Luckily, no one could see her expression beneath her faceplate.

Healy pulled up alongside her. "Whoa, slow down, Ryan. I don't want to be late either, but we don't want give ourselves away."

Tomi backed off the throttle a bit and her cyber dolphin's tail slowed its tempo until she matched speed with Healy. Checking her speedometer, they were doing an easy 10 mph. In just thirty-six minutes, they would arrive at the target location, assuming nothing went wrong.

"The contact slowed down as we got close, and then sped up after we passed," Larsen reported to Lieutenant Everson. "Its heading would have taken it straight to the mobile command center."

"And it looked like a...whale?" Everson clarified.

"Yes, sir."

Everson sighed and Alonzo saw his chance to get in a good ribbing.

"Now, now. Larsen, my friend, I think you need to relax. All of this hard work is making you see things. It won't be too long before you'll be seeing mermaids." Warrant Officer Alonzo snuck a glance at Everson and laughed at Larsen's expense.

"Hold your tongue, Alonzo! I know what I saw," Larsen snapped.

"That is enough from both of you!" Everson chastised. "Every contact is important, until it is not. The whole point of putting the general's HQ underwater is so it cannot be attacked. As much as this seems a simple biologic, it would be rather self-defeating if we let some Fed rat sneak in from underneath because we didn't heed Larsen's warning."

It was Larsen's turn to look smugly at Alonzo, and he did not hesitate to take advantage.

"I thought you said this mysterious contact of yours came this way, Ensign Larsen. I'm not seeing anything," commented Lieutenant Everson. They'd been searching for a while now, but saw no sign of it.

"Yes, sir, I'm certain of it."

Everson was about to call off the search when the contact showed up. Everyone crowded around the sonar display; it showed the same signature Larsen had talked about and it was hardly making any noise. There was only one glaring difference this time.

"It's heading in the opposite direction now," commented Alonzo. "There's no way it reached the fortress from the time you said you last saw it."

Larsen hid his disappointment. Looked like it wasn't the threat he had thought. He was about to apologize to Everson, but the lieutenant spoke first.

"Biologics do not reverse course and head back in the opposite direction. If it was a whale, it would simply swim around the obstacle and continue on. Whatever it is, it's thinking like a human. Ping it. I want to get to the bottom of this," Everson ordered.

Even Alonzo was not so reckless as to argue with the CO. In the Imperium, obedience was a top priority. Orders flowed from the top down the chain of command to the lowliest enlisted man. Insubordination was not merely a crime like in other militaries. It was unthinkable for a member of the Imperium, sometimes earning you capital punishment.

Instead of arguing, Alonzo switched the sonar to active, sending out acoustic pulses.

PING!

"What the hell was that?" Tomi exclaimed.

"Shit! Someone is pinging us with their sonar," Healy replied.

"Are they crazy? They just gave away their position," said Zimmerman.

"They obviously don't give a shit. They—" Watry started to say.

PING!

"Damn it to hell, that's irritating!" Elba complained.

"I agree, but at least they're moving away from us," Tomi pointed out.

"Sounds like they're chasing after Orca, which means we'll need to find another exfil route," Guy said.

"Do you think they'll take Orca out?" Tomi asked.

"Don't know, but one way or another, Orca won't be coming back to pick us up," Healy concluded.

There was nothing else they could do except continue swimming toward their target.

"That Imp submarine must have the most paranoid, neurotic CO in the whole Imperium," Orca lamented. "He's actually chasing something that looks like a whale!"

Orca's aquatic drivetrain was maxed out, pushing his frame to nearly 30 mph. He wondered what they were waiting for. When were they going to attack? Right then, they launched a torpedo, and not just a rocket-propelled torpedo. Its acoustic signature indicated it was supercavitating.

With the torpedo doing close to 400 mph, Orca had to act fast. Angling his bow planes down, he plunged as quickly as he could. To accelerate even faster, he opened his internal space to the outside. Good thing his internals were waterproofed, but he could only hope the onboard supplies wouldn't get waterlogged. His descent helped him pick up speed, but more importantly, his evasive action worked. The torpedo couldn't make the same turn he had and ended up overshooting Orca's location.

Still, the Imperial submarine wasn't ready to give up. Seeing Orca's smart maneuvering had only confirmed their theory. They fired a second torpedo. This one succeeded in tracking Orca's dive. Now Orca had to race to the bottom, hoping the ocean floor would confuse the torpedo's guidance system. As the sea bottom approached, Orca looked up information on the Imperial supercavitating torpedo. Under guidance system, it said it had a neutrino sensor, so Orca tried a new tactic. He shut his fusion turbine down.

Without a neutrino signature to home in on, the second torpedo roared past Orca and slammed into the muddy sea floor. Successful, Orca pulled out of his dive and started pumping the water out of his internal compartments. Checking to see whether he was still being pursued, he could see the submarine was continuing to follow him, but if it tried to descend to Orca's depth it would implode.

"Sorry, guys, but I won't be picking you up," Orca lamented to himself.

"I can see it. It looks like a huge wall," Tomi commented.

"Yeah, mobile command post, my ass. The Imps decided to sink a flying building is more like it," Healy acknowledged.

The "huge wall" Tomi had observed was one of the broad sides of the Constantinople mobile defense station. The rangers started looking for the strategically placed gaps that allowed for suction and discharge of water from ballast tanks as well as thruster ports and weapon hatches. Locating one of the gaps, Tomi had to admire the engineers who designed this monstrosity. Just as the map in the briefing showed, the gap was angled so that only a shot from an extreme angle would get through. Anything else would hit thick armor and bounce right off.

"Hey, guys," she said, pointing toward it.

"Good job, ranger," Captain Guy said approvingly.

Traveling through the gap, it became apparent just how thick the station's armor really was. It was like traveling down a long corridor rather than descending into a trench. Reaching the outer hull at last, they searched for a door or hatch leading into the station's interior.

"Found something," Tomi said. "It's an outer door to one of the ballast tanks."

"I would rather an actual access hatch, but we're running out of time," Healy admitted. "Get your fusion cutter and get to it. I'll cover you."

Tomi nodded and ignited her fusion torch, switching it to an angled pistol position, and started cutting. Almost immediately, she was surrounded by what looked like dozens of long, slender fish sporting mouthfuls of sharp teeth. They kept swimming back and forth around her, not taking any action, but not losing interest in her either.

When one got too close, Tomi swung her fusion torch at it, cleaving it in two. The other fish didn't hesitate to pounce upon their stricken companion, devouring it in less than a minute. They seemed satisfied for the time being and swam off, so Tomi felt comfortable getting back to work.

She was surprised how she made short work of the metal door. The fusion torch was much hotter than even a plasma torch. It practically vaporized the enhanced steel alloy the door was made of, and in less than thirty seconds, a six-foot diameter hole had been cut through six solid inches of metal.

"Gentlemen, the door is open," Tomi announced.

Once again, Guy gave her an approving look. "You should have joined the marines, ranger."

Tomi laughed, not willing to admit she had actually considered it at one point. She was confident she'd made the right choice with the Federation Rangers. It really was the best fit for her, but she appreciated what Guy meant as a compliment.

"Ladies first, Ryan," Elba said. "No, wait. Send in a recon probe first."

Tomi pulled out a black sphere the size of an orange and tapped its activation stud. The probe sprang to life and dove through the hole in the ballast tank door. It started scanning with both sonar and lidar, quickly developing a 3D picture of what lay inside.

"Good, no surprise here. Just looks like a ballast tank more than halfway full of water," Elba said. "Let's get in there. We need to get inside above the tank's water level."

The rangers left their cyber dolphins just outside the door, swimming into the tank's interior using the hydro jets mounted on their lower legs. Tomi went in first and was surprised yet again. Anticipating tight quarters, she discovered the tank was huge, at least the size of a movie theater. When Zimmerman sped past her, she had to remind herself to keep moving and sightsee later.

"A ladder," Zimmerman pointed out. "Should we use it?"

"Affirmative. It's heading right where we want to go," Guy responded.

Swimming up to the ladder, Tomi reconfigured her boots from swimming to walking mode. Bringing her weapon to the ready, she proceeded upward. It was so steep, she knew all those hours on her StairMaster were finally paying off.

"According to the recon probe's map, this is where we should break through," Healy said, pointing at the bulkhead.

"Ryan, get to it," Elba said in a low voice.

It seemed strange to be so quiet and stealthy since they were the only ones in this vast space and there were no listening devices present. Still, sneaking around the inside of an enemy fortress had everyone including Elba on edge. Tomi fired up her fusion torch a second time, the stellar hot plasma sliced through the bulkhead just as easily as the tank door.

The other rangers moved into position and pulled the divot from its hole. Once more, the recon probe went in and did a full-spectrum scan. When finished, it reported back with an extension to the rangers' 3D map with no life signs. Any ranger would be getting a little antsy about now, especially one with experience.

"Can it really be this easy?" Zim voiced the concern all of them were having.

20

FORTRESS

"Easy?" Elba chastised Zim. "Son, we did an orbital insertion, narrowly avoided getting detected by an attack sub, swam ten klicks through predator-infested waters, and had to cut our way in here. Tell me, what part of what I just described sounds easy?"

Tomi wondered if Elba was merely trying to calm his own restless mind.

"I was wondering the same thing," Watry admitted. "Where are all the guards?"

"Who in their right mind would want to stay down here? Look around. If we weren't scared shitless right now, we would be comatose from boredom," Elba quipped.

The other rangers chuckled; it was nice to relieve some of the tension, though the stoic Captain Guy might have other thoughts on the matter. The rangers proceeded one at a time through the hole and into yet another huge space. This one was filled with a labyrinth of pipes and conduits interlaced with catwalks, which is what they now found themselves standing on.

"This place goes on forever," Zim commented.

It only seemed like it did. Once past the station's thick armor, most of the interior space consisted of tanks, open areas, or void spaces. It took several minutes, but the recon probe finally sketched out the interior layout for them. Generating the complete 3D map, all of the rangers could see their main target: the main power distribution systems.

"Smart. Triple-redundant systems. We'll have to take all of them out if we want to knock this bitch out of action," Watry commented.

"That's the weird thing about the Imperium. They either build huge, expensive contraptions like this or cheap units that can be cranked out by the thousands," Healy said.

"Yeah, it's like the Imperium applies hierarchy to everything. Big toys for the big wigs, small ones for the plebes," Watry answered.

"That's the Imperium in a nutshell," Elba agreed. "Status is everything, but most Imps don't have the resources to do much; only the more powerful can. Getting ahead means taking a risk, and when one of their governors does so, they take everyone else along with the gamble. Win and the rewards are great. Lose and everyone goes to the poorhouse."

"Enough civics. You have your assignments. Get moving," Guy ordered.

They split up into pairs, each heading to one of the three power distribution systems. Tomi and Healy set out, with Healy in the lead. Most of the time they were out in the open, so they were dependent on their optical camouflage. To increase its effectiveness, they moved at a slow-but-steady pace lest the distortion from sudden movement give them away.

Going slow was difficult since they all wanted to complete their mission and be done with it, but their patience paid off when they rounded a corner. Stopping short, Healy nearly bumped into an Imperial roving patrol.

"Balor is a filthy bastard!" Perrin swore.

"Now, now, Perrin, you shouldn't speak ill of our watch captain," Hampton, Perrin's fellow watch stander, said. His eyes darted around as though worried Balor would overhear.

"I don't care! He can suck my male member till next year. This duty is like descending into Hades itself," Perrin retorted, his words echoing off the metal walls.

"I'm sure he has a good reason for sending us down here. This is an important duty—" Hampton tried to reason.

"Wrong! The filthy, inbred bastard took just enough time off from licking the division commander's ass to send us down here so we could count ghost turds. It's busywork," Perrin lamented.

Hampton worried about his friend. They had both volunteered to serve in the emperor's legions with dreams of honor and glory. It was only when they reported to their first posting that they learned it was an "honor" to stand around on watch, and "glory" was cleaning the toilets every day. Hampton had taken it all in stride, but Perrin did not adapt to military life as well. Perrin's chances at getting promoted were declining as steadily as his mood.

The lift they were riding down to the lower levels came to a stop and the safety doors opened. Stepping out, Perrin hastily looked left, then right.

"Looks secure to me! Let's head back up," he announced.

"No, Perrin. We need to complete our security sweep. You know Captain Balor has a reputation for leaving something out of place to test a patrol's thoroughness," Hampton urged.

"Yeah, the last time, he left his half-eaten lunch on one of the engineering consoles, the sneaky shiteater! That smug bastard thought he was so clever."

"Yes!" Hampton agreed with his partner for the first time. "And he used it as an excuse to put you on restriction for a whole month.

You were also put on half-pay. Do you enjoy staying on base and losing money all the time?"

"Shut your damn mouth, Hampton. Your galaxy-class horseshit is giving me a headache," Perrin retorted.

"Okay, fine. Let's do a quick sweep to make sure Balor didn't leave anything behind, and then we can go," Hampton offered.

Perrin didn't answer, instead just walking off along the catwalk in the port direction. Hampton went to starboard. He'd rather not split up, but the sooner they finished, the sooner he could let Perrin go off and sulk. The man just didn't get it—the worse his attitude, the worse his situation.

As Hampton walked, he checked the pressure doors that led to the various access areas for engineering. Since he wasn't an engineer, none of the doors would open for him, so he quickly moved on. He walked around a corner and that's when he saw it: a cup sitting on the ballast control console. *Sneaky bastard, indeed,* he thought, heading to retrieve it.

Hampton picked it up at the same time that he sensed something was off. He didn't know what it was, but he could have sworn he saw something—a shimmer, a visual distortion, a shadow, some heat escaping, perhaps? Walking over to examine it more closely, he heard a faint hum coming from somewhere else nearby. Looking in the direction of the sound, he saw more shimmering.

His brows furrowed. "What the—" But before he could finish his sentence, a horrible pain shot through his body and he passed out, falling to the floor.

"Good shooting, Tom. He was right on top of me when I rounded that corner," Healy commented.

She thought it was odd, going from rookie to Ryan and now a more casual Tom. She took it to mean her increasing skills and experience were being recognized and accepted among her more seasoned partners.

"Yeah, this thing actually works," she said with a chuckle. "Should we keep moving?"

Just then, Perrin rounded the corner looking around frantically for the voices he swore he heard. Seeing his partner on the ground, Perrin's eyes widened.

"Hampton, what's wrong? Why are you..."

He trailed off as it occurred to him something was seriously wrong. Hampton would never just lie on the deck like that and there were no obvious signs that some crazy accident had happened. It occurred to Perrin that someone had gotten inside the base.

He narrowed his eyes and pulled his sidearm.

Tomi brought her weapon to bear, but it turned out Perrin had both sharp eyesight and fast reflexes. He started shooting at the shimmering that was her. His laser pistol unleashed a beam of coherent light that connected with Tomi's cyber armor, disrupting its optical camouflage. Once Perrin could see someone was truly there, he fired again, causing more damage to her armor and weapon. He made one crucial mistake though: he assumed Tomi was alone.

As the sayin goes, "Never assume; it makes an ass out of you and me." As Perrin reached for his communicator, a burst of 4mm fléchettes tore through his chest. With his spinal cord severed, Perrin fell to the deck next to his friend.

"You okay, Tom?" Healy asked.

"I'm okay, but my camo and weapon are fucked. This really sucks. I barely got to use the stupid thing," Tomi complained.

"Heh, them's the breaks, kid." Healy shrugged. "If you're going to suggest we hide the bodies, let's. When these two chuckleheads fail to check in, someone's sure as shit going to notice and send reinforcements."

Tomi agreed; they had wasted enough time. She grabbed Hampton's legs while Healy grabbed his arms. With no unlocked doors, they simply heaved each in turn over the catwalk's railing, letting them plummet into the water and sink to the bottom of the space.

"Hopefully it will take them a long time to find those two," Tomi said after they were finished.

"By then, we'll be long gone. Let's get moving."

Looking up, Tomi and Healy worked out the exact location they were going to place their limpet mines. Configuring their gecko gear, they climbed up the sheer surface of the bulkhead, easily fifty feet above the catwalk they had been standing on. Tomi placed her charge to one side of the main induction coils for the reactor, while Healy placed his charge on the pipe going to the reactor's primary heat exchanger.

Climbing back down, Healy signaled to Tomi to break out her fusion cutter. It was a little nerve-racking for Tomi to take the extra time to cut through the security doors that led into the reactor compartment, but there was a method to the madness. Once Tomi finished cutting through her designated door, she stood up and kicked the section loose, making a banging metal sound. A half a second later, she heard more metal clanging on metal as Healy did the same.

"Let's get the hell out of here," Healy said. "We've almost certainly set off a silent alarm by now."

"What do you mean they failed to report in?" Balor bristled.

"We haven't heard word from them since they were sent down there fifteen minutes ago. They haven't even responded via comm." Corporal Morrow knew he was going to get a reaming one way or another. He also knew it was better to get a bad reaming now, than a worse reaming later for willful blindness.

Balor was beyond upset; he was pissed. What should have been a simple security sweep to make sure the lower levels were secure was turning into a fiasco. To have a roving patrol not report in or respond to requests to confirm their status resulted in a full-blown security alert. Everyone was already on edge because of the earlier skirmishes in orbit with Federation forces, but this one hit too close to home.

"Is the full team assembled?" Balor demanded.

Morrow nodded and followed Balor into the assembly area where all available security personnel were waiting for further orders. Balor didn't even give the assembled men a pep talk. He simply ordered them to get to the lower levels and find their missing comrades. As his men scrambled to get to the elevators, Balor noticed the new administrative assistant standing by.

"You, private, what is your name?" Balor demanded.

"Private Petula Carver, sir. I'm your new admin—"

Balor turned away from her mid-sentence and ordered Morrow, "Issue her a weapon and send her down to the lower levels. I want Hampton and Perrin located immediately!" He turned and walked away.

Carver was stunned speechless. Looking to Morrow for guidance, he simply shrugged and motioned for her to follow him. She wanted to serve the emperor like so many others in the Imperium, but she didn't think she would ever be put directly into harm's way. Yet, even she could see something wasn't right about the missing duo and disobedience was not tolerated in the Imperium.

Carver steeled herself and followed Morrow to the armory.

The electromagnetic freight elevator glided silently down to the lowest level of the mobile defense fortress for the second time in a single day. Someone in engineering noted that the elevator hadn't been used so often since the fortress's construction. Arriving, the security personnel exited and established a perimeter, weapons drawn and eyes sweeping the platform and catwalks.

"Clear!" they all reported simultaneously.

"Fan out! Find our brethren. Locate those security breaches," Morrow ordered.

Pairing up, the men headed off in different directions searching crates, machinery, doorways, and any other place someone could be hiding. Morrow watched the men as they departed, and then looked at Carver. Taking a little pity on the clearly scared private, he gave her what he assumed would be the easiest of jobs.

"Stay here and watch the elevator. Make sure it doesn't leave this level. Use the security lockout I gave you. If you see Perrin or Hampton, call me immediately."

Morrow left so fast she didn't even have time to say, "Thank you," or, "Yes, sir!"

As things quieted down, the excitement eased and before long, Carver found herself getting a little bored. She tried pacing to and fro, then in circles, then in squares. She finally leaned up against the wall and was about to nod off when she heard multiple calls over the comm channel.

"I found blood!"

"Door 10-21-3-FR has been breached!"

"Draw weapons! Check your corners. All personnel, withdraw back to the elevator," said Morrow.

Carver perked up. Anticipating her comrades' return, she released the security lockout.

Shortly, they came within view, walking rapidly with flashlights alongside their laser pistols. Morrow opened his mouth to speak when objects the size of oranges landed on the deck beside him. He instantly recognized what was rolling around his feet and barely managed to yell, "Grenade!" before they activated.

Each repulsor grenade triggered, draining its power cell and sending out a repulsive force of dozens of Gs. While not producing any shrapnel, the concussive wave hit the Imperial soldiers like a tsunami, bowling them over and sending them flying away from the detonation points. Morrow was catapulted up into the air, coming down hard on the deck in a shallow depression in the deck plating, caved in by the repulsor field.

On a Constantinople-class mobile defense fortress such as the *Carthage*, the central control station was a whole room. A very large room at that. Different consoles controlled different areas—tactical, engineering, security, and so on—but like many ships in this day and age, the *Carthage* was extensively automated. With a computer network doing most of the "housekeeping" duties and every function remotely controlled, a minimal watch staff was needed to operate the fortress, whether the level of activity be peacetime or a full-scale war.

Lieutenant Gagley was manning the security console, but as it didn't need much manning, he was busying himself with a game of mahjong on his personal tablet. As long as the officer of the deck didn't notice, anything to keep the mind sharp and pass the time seemed to be acceptable. Gagley would periodically look around make sure the OOD wasn't looking. Seeing Colonel Thraxton's station vacant meant he was likely hanging out in the CO's ready room—probably watching videos.

Gagley's job wasn't that hard; the security systems did most of the heavy lifting. He just had to push the occasional button to give the computer consent to do something. On a typical day, he could kick back and take it easy for the most part.

But today was a bit unusual. Gagley had heard one of the

roving patrols had failed to report in today. They'd been sent down to do a security sweep on the lower levels and then lost all communication and contact. Balor didn't like loose ends, yet was too good to do the dirty work himself. Opposite to Balor, Morrow really was a good man and an excellent soldier. He did his job well, got along with everyone, and was well-respected. Now if only he could teach Balor some of those traits.

This missing couple was causing such a stir that Balor insisted someone go down and check on them and that poor bastard, Morrow, drew the short straw. If anything, this whole fiasco was a minor irritation for Gagley. It meant he had to push more buttons than usual, which meant continuous interruptions in his game. Then a door alarm went off.

Gagley sat up to check the security system. A secured door on the lower level showed a damage indicator. He relaxed; this was hardly a cause for alarm. Most likely, a sensor malfunctioned or the door jammed and someone tried to force it open. Probably Perrin and Hampton.

Morrow was already on his way down there or he may even be there by now. Either way, it didn't require any real effort on Gagley's part. All he had to do was update Morrow's orders with a simple a text message to his communicator, and Gagley could get back to his game like nothing happened. He sent the door ID to Morrow with a note to check it and picked up his tablet again.

The computer chirped another alert, causing Gagley to sigh heavily and roll his eyes. This time, there was a significant energy release on the lower level where Morrow had gone. Gagley furrowed his brows. Surely Morrow was handling whatever it was. But then some garbled comm transmissions came through.

"What the hell?" Gagley leaned forward, brows furrowed. Though annoyed at the inconvenience, he decided he'd better try to contact Morrow on the ship's comm system.

"Morrow, this is security central control requesting a status update." Nothing but static. "Morrow, please respond." Still nothing. "Anyone on the security team, respond. Sound off!"

Now Gagley actually was worried. It was bad enough to lose contact with a roving patrol, but a whole security team? Something wasn't right. He contacted Balor.

"The whole team? What's going on down there?" Balor demanded.

"I don't know, damn it. That's why I'm telling you!" Gagley retorted.

Gagley could hear Balor swearing under his breath, then he ordered a full security detail with full combat loadouts to assemble.

Morrow and the others caught in the blast radii were either stunned or in so much pain they could not speak. Those still standing swung their sidearms in the direction the grenades came from, somewhere above the freight elevator Carver was standing in. She was about to scream, thinking her comrades were going to shoot her by mistake, but before they could open fire, the whole area was illuminated by strobe lights. The men became too disoriented to even pull the trigger, desperately trying to cover their eyes. Then, it got really loud.

Staccato cracking sounds filled the air and the remaining men fell one after another. Carver could see a spectral cloud of pink floating over each crumpled body. She could only stare in horror. Not understanding what was happening to them, she assumed she was seeing each man's soul departing its mortal shell.

When the last man was down, the strobe lights went dark and all became silent again. Carver stood stock-still, trying to think of what to do. Looking up at the control panel, something told her, *Get the hell out of here...now!*

She dropped to her knees and crawled on all fours toward the panel, still looking for the unseen attackers. Remaining on her knees, she stretched, reaching up until she could reach the button. The safety gates closed and the elevator started to rise, leaving Carver trying to catch her breath.

After what seemed like an eternity, the elevator finally reached the top level. Carver was met by Balor and a fully equipped combat team wearing full-body armor and carrying plasma rifles. They had a team of ordinance specialists in tow as well, and every last one of them saw Carver cowering on her knees in the elevator.

"Report, private. What happened down there?" Balor commanded.

She slowly rose to her feet, considering how to answer. All hell had broken loose down there, and she was still trying to process exactly what had happened. Besides, all of the personnel who went down there were wearing body cameras. Balor should have seen and heard everything that happened from the safety of the central security console. She realized now that Balor enjoyed watching underlings tremble when he screamed at them.

Unfortunately, it worked on her in her broken state, and she couldn't bring herself to speak. Balor signaled for one of the members of the combat team to remove her. Grabbing Carver by the arm, the soldier pulled her roughly out of the elevator and shoved her to the side so they could file in.

Sinking down against a nearby wall, she watched as the safety gates and door closed. Now full of a new team, the elevator began its long and slow descent. In a matter of moments, Carver was alone once more.

What was a cute little thing like her doing down there? Gagley wondered to himself, having heard the whole interaction through the open comm.

Balor had clearly not wasted any time in abandoning her. Gagley could hear the many heavy footsteps of soldiers marching into the elevator, and the ding as the doors closed and it began transporting the men downward. *Why did Balor not call medical for Carver?* Gagley wondered. From what he heard, or rather didn't hear, Carver could barely speak. She might be seriously injured. *What an ass.*

Well, if Balor wouldn't be a gentleman, Gagley would. He cut the comm and ordered a medical tech to Carver's location.

An intense flame suddenly burned through the top of the elevator door into the room Carver was now the sole occupant of. It traveled in an oval, completing its circuit in a matter of seconds. With the edges still glowing, the section of door was shoved to the deck with a loud clang. First one, then a second person, emerged from the hole. Carver peered curiously toward them.

They didn't look like humans. More like one of the combat androids the commander kept around for protection. One was camouflaged so well it was practically invisible, but the other was covered with blast marks and could be seen more clearly. The more Carver looked, she could swear it was a machine—carefully articulated formfitting armor, a smooth visor with different eye-like structures spread across it. Though it was vaguely human with its feminine curves. Then it spoke, causing Carver to jump.

"Federation Rangers! You're now a prisoner of war. Do as you are told, and you won't be harmed. Try to do otherwise, and we will shoot you dead right where you stand. Now take us to the nearest vehicle bay."

Carver wanted to cry. Talk about a bad day! It had gone from bad to worse, and now she was being taken hostage and forced to betray the Imperium. Assuming she escaped the Federation rats, she would certainly be executed by her own if she so much as gave away one secret to them. The only question was would it be death by firing squad or hanging?

The woman helped Carver to her feet and, with a little prodding, they were on their way to vehicle bay A.

The truth was Tomi and Healy were just as scared as their new hostage. The original plan was to have left the target area the same way they came in, but one thing after another just kept going wrong. Orca was out of the picture, the interference from the security personnel meant the rangers wouldn't be able to leave through the holes they had made in the station's hull, and worse, they could accidentally lead the Imps to the other rangers. So, there they were again, doing what rangers do best: improvise, adapt, overcome.

"What's your name?" asked Healy.

"Private Petula Carver, service number—"

"Spare us the excruciating details. Just tell us what kind of vehicles you have in vehicle bay A."

"Something fast," Tomi added.

Carver swallowed hard. She was facing certain death no matter whether she acquiesced or not.

21

NO WAY OUT

"Morrow, Morrow! Can you hear me, son? Answer me!" Balor shouted into his subordinate's ear.

When Balor's team had arrived at the lower level, they saw men scattered all over the platform. Morrow was alive but unconscious. He had been in so much pain that he'd passed out sometime before Balor's arrival. The one medic they'd brought with them was already tending to those still alive. Most, like Morrow, had broken bones or internal bleeding; others had obviously been shot. But what had stirred up all this trouble?

Balor stood up and surveyed the carnage. His combat team had already fanned out and were continuing their sweep of the area, though not finding anyone who didn't belong left Balor unsettled with the whole scenario. Whoever or whatever it was, they could still be in here somewhere, lurking, waiting for the perfect opportunity to attack again. What were they after?

"Bloody hell," Bailor exclaimed to himself, "this has all the hallmarks of an ambush—deep inside a secure Imperial installation, no less!" He then shouted so everyone could hear him, his voice echoing in the cavernous room, "Keep searching! Any signs of Perrin or Hampton yet?"

"Sir, we found a blood pool over here away from the main battle," one of the soldiers called out.

Balor shoved his soldiers aside as he walked briskly over to see for himself. Sure enough, there was blood. It had started to coagulate, so whoever it belonged to had been shot much earlier than the big ambush that fell upon Morrow's charge. Perhaps it was one of the two missing guards.

Activating his bioscanner, a quick check confirmed Balor's suspicions: the blood belonged to Perrin. From the amount of blood here, the man was almost certainly dead. But where was the body?

"Sir, we have two separate door breaches!" announced one of the ordinance technicians. "One is going to the reactor's main control room and the other to the main fuel injection manifold."

"Get in there now! Start searching for any explosive devices. If one is found, everyone is to clear the area immediately and inform the ordinance technicians. Hurry, we have saboteurs loose inside the facility! They're most certainly still here somewhere, so keep a sharp eye," Balor urged.

He hoped he wasn't too late. Losing one of the station's three reactors would be detrimental, but not a total disaster. After all, the station had three. A would-be saboteur would need to disable all three reactors to truly cripple the station. Balor's eyes widened as his sudden realization left him in a cold sweat.

He accessed the emergency comm channel. "Central control, this is Balor. Send ordinance teams to the other reactor compartments immediately!"

"Hey, Gagley," a medical officer said over the comm, "we sent a med tech to the freight elevator FE-1A like you asked, but they said no one was there. This ain't the time for pranks, man. We've got a full security breach going on."

"What? What do you mean she wasn't there? I swear, I'm not messing with you," Gagley tried pleading his case. He had been known to pull some pranks for shits and giggles when boredom was really taking its toll, but this wasn't one of those times. "Balor left her sitting on the floor! Did the tech search the area? Maybe she went into one of the lavatories." Things were getting very strange.

"The tech already thought of that. She looked in both the male and female lavatories—no one was there. She did notice that the elevator door had been cut open. It looked like someone had burned through it," the doctor answered.

Two missing guards, gunfights in the reactor compartments, and now a hole in the elevator door with a cutting torch? I had better wake up the old man. Before he could contact Colonel Thraxton, another communication from Balor came in.

"Central control, this is Balor. Send ordinance teams to the other reactor compartments immediately! Search the whole compartment for any explosive devices. We have saboteurs on the loose. Lock the whole station down now and initiate a level-one security alert!"

Things were spinning out of control, taking his mind along with it. He was so out of practice of an actual emergency that Gagley blanked for a few seconds before jumping back into the game. He opened the comm channel to issue priority orders to the ordinance department when the whole fortress shook like Deus himself struck a blow. Alarms started blaring at the engineering console, and Gagley's jaw dropped as every muscle in his body tensed.

"Oh no, what now?"

"Doesn't the Imperium require you guys to stay in shape? With all of your huffing, I'm surprised you haven't gone into cardiac arrest already," Tomi chastised Carver.

"Oh, give her a break, Tom. The markings on her uniform tell me she's in some sort of support role." Looking at Carver, he guessed, "You're not dressed like a cook, supply, admin, maybe?"

"Administration, if you really need to know. But I'm telling you nothing!" Carver said defiantly, sticking her nose in the air.

"Don't worry, Carver. We're only interested in those 'sting rays' you mentioned in the vehicle bay," Tomi admitted.

Petula Carver was five-foot-four—a fairly average height for a woman. But with Tomi having an extra five inches on her and Healy eight, walking between the two rangers made her look like a runt. It didn't help that their cyber armor made them appear even taller, as well as making them stronger. They were practically dragging the Imperial admin clerk as they traveled down the passageway.

"Shit, a security door," Healy said.

"If you give up now, I'm sure my superiors will be merciful," Carver said hopefully.

"Sweetie, after what we've done to this place, we'll all be skipping the trial and going straight to the firing squad," Tomi commented, pulling out her fusion torch.

"What...what have you done?" Carver stammered.

"Oh, you'll know when it happens," Tomi said. She energized her fusion torch and got to work on the security door.

Within seconds, the fusion torch had done its work. The cut section fell to the deck, leaving a man-sized hole in the door. Tomi looked to Healy and was about to speak when he used a hand signal to alert her to a nearby enemy, pointing down the passageway. Without saying a word, Tomi grabbed Carver by the collar and started pushing her through the new doorway.

"Stop pushing me!" Carver demanded.

Tomi slapped Carver upside the head and pointed her

omniblaster in her face while pressing her finger to her own lips. Carver heard the rhythmic pounding of heavy feet: security robots. She struggled between her opportunity to call for help and risking the rangers simply shooting her in response. It seemed the choice was made for her when the automatons took notice of the rangers and started firing their plasma blasters.

Searing hot bolts of plasma struck the remaining portion of the door and surrounding bulkheads, resulting in explosions and showers of sparks. Only the lead bots were able to fire within the confines of the passageway without causing fratricide. Not only that, they were not deciphering between the rangers and Carver. She screamed, surprised to discover she couldn't even hear her own voice over the ensuing gun battle that drowned out anything else.

Healy returned fire with his repulsor carbine, the six-inch long fléchettes piercing the lead robot's torso armor. It staggered but didn't fall as its redundant systems kept it going. Healy shot slightly higher this time, finally hitting its power cell and sending the bot crashing to the floor. Its comrade immediately behind it took aim squarely at Healy's chest when a blaster bolt from Tomi took its head off. Healy took advantage of the bot's momentary distraction and retreated into the hole his partner had cut.

"Great shooting, Tom, but they're still coming," Healy told her. "We need to get rid of them or we'll be rushed into exposing ourselves to the Imps."

"Got it," she answered.

Tomi still had her fusion torch in hand, extended it to its full length. When the first bot stepped through the hole, she brought the two-and-a-half-foot-long plasma stream down on the robot, cleaving it in half with a single stroke. The following bot pushed its fallen comrade out of the way only to get its own head and arms severed next.

Imperial security bots were fearless, but not completely stupid. Knowing that an opponent was waiting on the other side of the door, they began concentrating their fire through the hole in an attempt to pin down the two rangers. Fortunately, the rangers were smarter. Both Tomi and Healy had stepped away from the seemingly endless shower of plasma bolts, but as the leading bot extended its arm through the hole, Healy shot it off with his carbine.

"We can't stay here forever. We need to do something to distract them," said Tomi.

"I agree," Healy said as he threw a repulsor grenade and a EMP grenade through the hole.

They grabbed Carver and ran in the opposite direction. Before the remaining bots could fire, the grenades detonated, the EMP stunning them while the repulsor grenade slammed them into the surrounding bulkheads and ceiling. The rangers allowed themselves a wolfish smile as they ran down the passageway.

Carver kept repeating the same phrase, "I'm going to die. I'm going to die. I'm—"

"What are you complaining about? We're not even out of the frying pan yet," Healy teased.

These Fed rats must be insane, she thought. She certainly did not want to give them any more information than she already had, though they weren't asking her any questions since the location of the vehicle bay. It seemed they just had a really urgent need to leave, which admittedly, made her anxious to leave as well.

"Shit! Those fucking robots are on the move again!" Tomi lamented.

Looking back, all three could see the security androids advancing one by one through the hole in the security door. The lead bot raised its arm-mounted plasma blaster and took aim. Then the whole fortress shook. The lights blinked and a level-one red alert was sounded. Emergency bulkheads slammed shut, blocking their path but also cutting off the robots' pursuit.

"May the emperor protect us!" Carver exclaimed. "What is happening to this contraption? What have you Feds done?" She was on the edge of hysteria now, but the rangers ignored her.

"Okay, now we have officially jumped into the fire," Tomi joked.

"And it's not over yet," Healy added. "Get your fusion torch energized. It's the only way we're getting through these barricades."

Tomi quickly cut through the emergency bulkhead. As the divot clanged onto the floor, they could hear noise coming from the other bulkhead.

"Ha! Looks like your engineers forgot to add fusion cutters to your new security androids," Tomi said to Carver.

"Enough chitchat," Healy said. "Let's get the hell out of here before—" He was interrupted when the station was rocked by another explosion.

Another fusion reactor was down. One more to go.

"Damn your father's loins, Overman. Where in the hell did they hide the explosives?" Balor screamed at the senior engineering officer.

"Damn *your* father's loins, Balor. Now, shut up!" Overman shot back. "The saboteurs did not make this easy. Their explosive charges aren't in the obvious places."

The hate between the two men was mutual. Maybe just dislike on a good day, but right now it was over-the-top loathing. Balor didn't like Overman's insolence. Engineers, even one as skilled as Overman, should show proper deference to warriors. On the other hand, Overman saw Balor as a pompous buffoon who was always making an ass of himself, and many agreed with him. The only difference was Overman had the spine to express his opinions. In terms of rank, they were, in reality, equal. Balor simply liked having his ass kissed, but Overman wasn't the type of man to do that.

And right now, Overman didn't have time for Balor's fun and games. He was busy frantically reviewing instrument readings to gain clues where the commandos might have hidden the explosives.

He knew it wasn't the red herrings they'd left behind, though the breached doors were a clever distraction.

Both the central control processor in the main control room and the main fuel manifold were the most obvious targets on a fusion reactor. Destruction of either one would immediately result in an automatic shutdown. However, those locations were eliminated as Overman noticed that two separate explosions had taken out reactor one. All readings from the main induction coil ceased and the coolant pressure to the primary heat exchanger crashed. *Clever*, Overman thought.

Modern ships, vehicles, and mobile bases didn't use wires for power or information transmission anymore. All of it was simply run through the metal frame of the construct—just run the power through an induction coil straight into the frame and you have power, control, and communication signals traveling throughout a ship or any structure without having to run a single wire. And if equipment needed to be replaced or added, it simply required attaching its induction coil to the frame, and poof, its ready to go.

For all the benefits this method offered, it also had one major downside. If the main induction coil was, say, vaporized by a one-ton-yield nuclear explosion, the power connection to everything would be severed. On cue, the fortress was rocked a second time with successive explosions. The second reactor was disabled. Lights blinked again, but since the emergency alarms were already blaring and the security lockdown had already been initiated, nothing else changed.

Overman studied the data. All fusion reactors created waste heat and lots of it. Without removing that waste heat, any fusion reactor would overheat and automatically shut down. Taking out the cooling system would not be the invaders' first choice, but until it was working again, the reactor it belonged to would simply become a giant paper weight.

Looking at the readings for reactor two, he saw the same thing as before. Overman concluded that one explosive charge was likely placed near the main induction coil, while the other was probably placed against the coolant inlet pipe as a backup. Within the chamber of the third and final reactor, he knew they had to act fast.

"Get to the coolant inlet pipe and the main induction coil now! The explosives are there!" Overman yelled to his fellow engineers.

Engineers and ordinance techs started climbing ladders to the specified locations without any hesitation. Reaching them before they were all vaporized was a great motivation factor. One of Balor's men climbed up onto the top of the induction coil's housing and called down to them.

"I found one! It's on top of the casing for the main induction coil!" the soldier exclaimed as he reached for it.

"Wait! Don't touch it!" Overman ordered.

But it was too late. The naive soldier seized the carrying handle and pulled the device free, inadvertently triggering its antitampering feature. The resulting explosion vaporized both the soldier and the main induction coil he was standing on. The overpressure instantly killed everyone else in the compartment, knocking Healy's explosive device loose and triggering its own antitampering mechanism.

With all three reactors now disabled, the *Carthage* lost all power.

Mission accomplished, sort of.

The entire station plunged momentarily into darkness. Fortunately for the rangers, their sensor visors allowed them to see in the dark. Carver, on the other hand, had no such advantage and complained. She moved much slower and more cautiously as a result, irritating Tomi.

"Damn it!" Carver said as she bumped into something. "What's going on? I can't see any—"

"Shut up and keep moving," Tomi said brashly. It wasn't like it was pitch black. Healy was still cutting, so the light from his torch illuminated their immediate surroundings...or their faces, at least. *Some people just can't be pleased,* she thought.

At the same time that Healy pushed the divot out of the way, the emergency lights came on. Carver, Healy, and Tomi all rejoiced, though for different reasons. While Carver was relieved to see more than six inches in front of her face, the rangers were excited to discover the final door to the vehicle bay at the other end of the proverbial tunnel.

"Hallelujah!" Healy proclaimed.

"Are you getting religious on me, Healy? Maybe you should switch to a desk job after this," Tomi ribbed.

"Shit, Tom, I know you're just as glad to see that door as I am. Let's get moving," Healy retorted.

Healy went down the passageway while Tomi grabbed Carver by the arm and pulled her along.

"Let go of me, you whore! Stop dragging me around like a rag doll," Carver complained.

Tomi didn't say anything. This woman whined a lot for an Imperial soldier. Then again, didn't she say she was admin? She must have thought she scored a cushy job. Too bad.

Tomi thought the sooner she and Healy got out of this floating deathtrap, the sooner they could dump the whiney broad. Healy quickly burst that bubble, insisting they bring Carver along. Tomi kept her mouth shut, given the direness of their situation with no time to waste, but she was certain the Imps would kill one of their own without hesitation to get two rangers out of the deal.

Dragging a fighting Carver slowed Tomi down tremendously. They arrived at the door just as Healy finished cutting it open, revealing a catwalk above the vehicle bay. The emergency lights illuminated numerous crafts, supercavitating submarines, submersible flare crafts, and autonomous underwater robots.

Tomi pointed at one of the flare crafts. "This one will do nicely."

"Why? Do you like the color?" Healy asked sarcastically.

"No, I just know how to pilot the damn thing," Tomi replied as she pushed Carver ahead of her. "Now let's get our hostage over to the control console."

All of the trouble the two rangers had gone through, dragging Carver with them through much of it, came down to this moment right here. They could only hope the other two teams had made it safely out as well, but this was a big ship and their possible locations were endless. Communicating via wrist comps would only give them away if they were still inside and they had agreed to radio silence.

Surprisingly, Carver let slip that her battle station assignment was this particular vehicle bay, which meant she was required to know how to operate the controls to open the bay doors. However, when Tomi shoved her toward the control panel, Carver looked at her captors sheepishly.

"The power is out," she said. "The controls won't respond even with emergency power."

"Should we shoot her now or drown her later?" Tomi asked.

The rangers started to weigh their options. They could try to jury rig the power so Carver could open the bay doors, but neither Tomi nor Healy knew enough tech—they weren't engineers. Should they cut the doors open with their fusion cutters? With the station sinking, it would take too long. Then Tomi remembered something she'd read about the war skate they were getting ready to "borrow."

"Get your butts into our new ride," she said. "I have an idea."

The command center was poorly lit. The emergency lights were just not adequate for a space this size. Though the light was limited, there was plenty of noise. There were so many alarms, klaxons, and sirens blaring that Gagley couldn't tell which particular systems were still working on the emergency power. Might as well be none of them.

Looking around, he noticed some of the workstations were empty. Some of his comrades had already deserted their posts. Desertion was an anathema to all those who serve the emperor; they swore an oath, but now they were just words. Looking over at the CO's station, Gagley could see the old man was still at his post —a true servant of the emperor.

Overman gave his last report from the engineering watch station. "Sir, we have lost main power, and auxiliary power is failing rapidly. It appears that along with the uncontrolled flooding on the lower levels, water is now reaching the MHD turbines. The station is listing to its port side; those turbines are already lost and we will inevitably lose the rest in less than thirty minutes. Once that happens, any remaining systems will power down and the station will sink within the hour. I am sorry that I have failed you, sir."

Colonel Thraxton stood up and addressed the remaining bridge staff. "All of you have done well. I could not expect a finer performance. If you have not already noticed, some have abandoned their posts and fled without permission. They will be deemed deserters and treasonous to the great emperor. But not you. You stayed and fulfilled your oaths, and for that, you will be rewarded.

"Unlike those who have fled and will feel the eternal shame of showing cowardice in the face of the enemy, I have entered all of your loyal and honorable names into the official records as heroes. As Overman has reported, this station is sinking and there is nothing more that can be done. Thus, I am giving the order: all hands, abandon ship! It has been an honor serving with you."

As others took their opportunity and fled, Gagley hesitated, disturbed by the fact that the colonel wasn't moving from his post. His feet remained planted, watching as everyone else left the command center.

Seeing that Gagley wasn't running off with the others, Colonel Thraxton tilted his head in question. "What are you waiting for, son?"

"I must apologize, sir. I have failed you. I should have done a better job of ensuring this station's security. I—"

"No, Lieutenant. It is my own fault. I am the commanding officer of this station, but it's not just that. I gave into the complacency that this mobile fortress was impregnable, that it would be the last asset to fall to the Federation. Now I alone must answer for that hubris."

Gagley bowed his head for a moment before asking, "Colonel, sir, are you going to leave with us?"

"The commanding officer is always the last to leave his post. You know that, don't you? The order has been given. Now, carry it out," Thraxton ordered.

Gagley hesitated just a moment longer, nodded his head, and then complied, leaving the command center and making his way to the escape pods with the rest of the command staff. As he progressed through the halls, he looked back to see if the colonel was following. Instead, Thraxton was busy transferring files to his personal tablet, and then, Gagley lost sight of him. As he boarded the nearest escape pod, he worried that this would be the last time he would ever see the old man.

"Get the skate ready to go. We're going to have to make a speedy exit," Tomi told Healy.

"What's with the attitude, Tom? Don't I still have seniority over you?" he asked, half-jokingly.

"Seniority went out the airlock a long time ago, Healy. Now shut up and let me save your ass for once."

Healy laughed, but Carver decided it was time to put her foot down.

As the ranger tried to get Carver to board the skate, she turned around and confronted him. It was time to start acting like a true servant of the emperor.

"No! No more, Fed rat. I am not helping you anymore," she said in defiance.

"Help? When the hell did you do that?" He took a step backward and put his hands in the air defensively. "If you want to go down with this sinking ship, you go right ahead, but the rest of us are getting our 'Fed rat' asses out of here."

Carver realized he had a point and looked around the room. She may know how to open the doors when the power was on, but she certainly didn't know how to pilot any of the vehicles. And she couldn't remember where the escape pods were located on this deck either. She pursed her lips, did an about-face, and climbed up to the vehicle's access hatch without another word.

Carver noticed the other ranger had boarded the adjacent supercavitating subfighter. *What is she doing?* she thought to herself. *Aren't we all taking the same vehicle?*

Healy powered up the skate's systems and the threat warning receiver started to beep instantly. Carver looked at the display. Multiple signals for supercavitating torpedoes were active, warning the pilot to clear the area. As Tomi climbed in and closed the hatch behind her, Carver understood exactly what the ranger had been doing.

"You armed those torpedoes! Are you trying to get us killed?" Carver exclaimed.

"No, I'm doing what rangers do best: improvise, adapt, overcome. Now get ready," Tomi warned.

She's crazy, Carver thought. *There's no two ways about it, that ranger is fucking psycho!* She climbed into one of the passenger seats, buckled up, and put her head between her knees. She started praying for the emperor's forgiveness since she was certain she had only seconds to live.

To their left, the subfighter's fire control computer finished its standby cycle and executed the instructions Tomi had entered. All of the torpedoes mounted on its hard points launched simultaneously, heading right toward the launch bay doors. With their range settings set to zero, the torpedo warheads immediately armed themselves in the split second it took to cover the distance.

They detonated just as they impacted with the door, and the searing hot plasma vaporized the doors along with several cubic feet of seawater on the other side. The flash was blinding. The rangers' visors darkened to shield their eyes and the shockwave rocked their skate. A split second later, the sea beyond flowed back, filling the vehicle bay.

Tomi checked the hull integrity display, the modern equivalent of the old "Christmas tree" that used to be used on submarines—all green. An explosion that powerful could have ruptured the skate's hull as well, but she breathed a sigh of relief. Everything appeared to be okay and they could finally get off this sinking graveyard.

Looking at the results of Tomi's plan, Healy expressed his disbelief. "Holy shit, Tom! Were you trying to blow us up or drown us?"

"Stop whining," she said, rolling her eyes. "We can leave now. 'Thank you, Tomi, for saving our lives.' Oh, you're welcome," she said in a mocking tone. "It was nothing, really."

Pushing the throttle forward, the war skate's engines cycled up, allowing it to lift off its launch cradle. With the launch bay flooded, all Tomi had to do was carefully pilot the vehicle through the hole blown in the bay door. It was just large enough; Tomi was certain she could hear the hull scraping against the ragged metal. Once clear of the door, Tomi accelerated away, putting as much distance as she could between them and the sinking station.

"We're clear. What heading should we—"

PING! The threat warning indicator went off.

"Oh shit, that submarine we passed with Orca is back!" Healy swore.

22

THE ENEMY BELOW

"Contact bearing 310, range 9,000 yards, speed 50 mph," Larsen reported. "Definitely originated from that last explosion on the *Carthage*."

"They are turning toward us!" Alonzo added in a state of panic. If whoever was on board had caused all that damage to the *Carthage*, he could only imagine what they could do to them. He'd much rather ignore them and continue on their way, so he wasn't too thrilled with Everson's next orders.

"Arm all torpedo launchers. Give me a firing solution on that contact." When Alonzo didn't move, Everson stared him down. "Now, Alonzo!"

"Yes, sir," Alonzo responded. With no other choice, he got to work and then reported, "Torpedo launchers armed and ready. Will have firing solution shortly."

Everson was not impressed with the CWO. "Move it or I'll put a boot up your ass! I do not want to suffer the same fate as the *Carthage!*"

Larsen switched on the submarine's lidar to supplement the other sensors. With gravitic and lidar sweeping the area, he double-checked the contact's acoustic signature just in case. Its profile gave him pause.

"Sir, the contact has been identified as a war skate," Larsen said.

"I can see that, Larsen," Everson said sarcastically.

"Yes, but...it's one of ours." Now he had Everson's attention.

"Oh, good," Alonzo said aloud by accident, his shoulders relaxing.

Everson gave him a dirty look before asking Larsen, "What does the IFF indicate?"

"None. No response at all, sir. Maybe their IFF has been disabled?" Larsen offered.

"Very well. Contact them."

Just then, they received an update on the *Carthage's* status. The information gained told them everything they needed to know —the *Carthage* was incapable of launching any craft at this time. Everson came to the conclusion that this craft was, in fact, stolen. Larsen had already opened a comm channel to the craft and a feminine voice responded.

"Ahoy, please don't shoot us. We're just trying to get out of there before it sinks."

"Ahoy?" Alonzo said, scrunching his nose. Nowhere in the Imperium's forces was that greeting used. "What is this? *Gilligan's Island?*"

"Identify yourself! What is your service number?" Everson demanded.

"Uh, four, six, three, seven—" the woman started to say.

Everson shook his head. "That doesn't make any sense! Start talking or we will open fire," he snapped.

Suddenly another female voice rang out. "Help me! These Fed rat commandos have taken me prisoner!"

The channel was closed abruptly.

"Alonzo, you had better have that firing solution ready. Well?" Everson asked.

"Firing solution ready, sir," Alonzo answered, nodding once.

"Shut up, you dumb bitch! Are you trying to get us killed?" Tomi screamed as she shoved Carver back into her seat. Tomi was furious. She knew the Imp submarine was already getting a target lock on them after that debacle.

"Forget about her, Tom," Healy said with a sigh. "The moment you said 'ahoy,' they knew you were bullshitting them. I mean, really, have you ever heard an Imp say 'ahoy?'"

"Oh, shove it! I was improvising. How am I supposed to know how Imps talk?" Tomi said defensively. "Besides, I didn't see you trying to do anything, Healy."

Before he could respond, the threat warning program started beeping. The rangers tried to figure out what it was telling them.

"What does this mean, Ms. I've-Been-Trained-on-This-Vehicle?" Healy said, dripping with sarcasm.

"It was only a basic course, smartass, but I can tell you that sub just locked on us."

With both the submarine and the war skate heading toward each other at flank speed, the once-large distance was closing fast. Tomi checked her war skate's fire control display. Two mini torpedoes and two Gauss machine guns. *Gauss guns? I thought Imps preferred plasma accelerators,* she pondered. *Then again, we are underwater.* Either way, both weapon systems were useless since they didn't have the range necessary to reach the submarine.

"What are you waiting for, Tom? Why don't you shoot?" queried Healy.

"We'll have to wait. The range on our torpedoes is only 4,000 yards."

The war skate's sensor display lit up; the submarine had launched two supercavitating torpedoes. *Of course, they have better weapons.* Tomi kept her lament to herself. Her sensors told her they were traveling over 300 mph and time till impact was less than a minute. Tomi was about to ask Healy for ideas, but he beat her to the punch.

"What are you going to do, Tom?"

Tomi rolled her eyes. *Gee, you're a real help, Healy.* Her mind raced for a solution, her eyes darting around the console. Time to use the very reason she'd chosen this craft—it was amphibious.

She pulled back on the control stick, sending the war skate into a steep climb. The torpedoes were almost upon them as the seconds ticked down. The skate broke the surface, causing the torpedoes to lose their guidance. They tried and failed to track their target as it flew out of the water and into the late afternoon sky. Tomi and Healy watched the torpedoes fly past on either side of the war skate.

"All right!" Healy cheered, throwing his fist in the air.

"Whew," Tomi said in relief. "They can't get us up here."

"Uh, Tom..." Healy pointed toward the sub as it began surfacing. "I wouldn't relax just yet."

"Why would they surface?" Tomi questioned.

The war skate's threat warning receiver answered her question, alerting them to another yet target lock coming from the submarine. Tomi let out a string of profanity that would make a sailor blush and prepared to take evasive action.

"Emergency blow completed; we are now surfaced, sir!" Larsen announced.

"Good. I want a target lock on that war skate, Alonzo." When Alonzo stood frozen in place, Everson barked, "As in yesterday!"

Larsen was secretly enjoying the fact that Everson was starting to lose his patience with the warrant officer. Everybody always liked Alonzo—he was popular, gregarious, and great to be around if you wanted to have a good time. But as an officer, he often left his load to be carried by his comrades and left his superiors wanting. Once the party was over, Alonzo was mediocre at best, even on a good day.

"Yes, sir!" Alonzo replied, struggling to carry out his CO's order. The procedure was further complicated by the fact that Everson wanted to simultaneously deploy the submarine's deck gun.

In training, the instructors had never asked him to do that, but then, Alonzo was always quick to whip out a bottle of fine liquor and turn on the charm to make things easier for himself. He'd been able to skate by pretty easily with his charisma, and he'd even managed to move up the ranks to attain officer status. Unfortunately for him, now his skills were actually being put to the test for the first time, and Everson was nowhere near as flexible or forgiving as his instructors had been.

"Today, Alonzo!"

"Yes, sir!" To Alonzo's relief, the fire control station chimed, at last indicating a target lock had been achieved. From inside, they could hear the laser turret swiveling to track the target.

"Deck gun ready," Alonzo announced.

"Fire!" Everson ordered.

Just after releasing the salvos, the war skate slowed and dove back into the water. The laser pulse created a burst of steam where the war skate had taken its plunge.

"Damn it! Track where it went," Everson said, raising his voice as the situation intensified.

It was Larsen's turn to shine now, and he worked quickly and skillfully to fix the war skate's new location.

"Starboard side amidship. They are coming straight toward us at over 50 mph," he said, struggling to keep his voice even.

"Full rudder right! All ahead flank! I want our launchers on them and ready to fire!" Everson ordered.

Larsen began carrying out Everson's orders just as the threat warning receiver flashed a warning. The war skate had launched two supercavitating torpedoes of their own.

"Target the torpedoes," Everson ordered Alonzo.

"What? Why?" he asked.

Everson kicked the back of Alonzo's seat so hard it shoved him into the console. "Do it!"

"Yes, sir. Targeting enemy torpedoes," Alonzo acknowledged.

Two torpedoes launched, their rocket motors igniting rapidly as they accelerated toward the incoming mini torpedoes. The wait wasn't long—the torpedoes collided in a spectacular explosion, but in the chaos, the Imperial soldiers lost sight of their enemy.

"Where is the war skate?" Everson questioned, scanning the stirred waters.

"Tracking now," he answered, but he was having a difficult time getting a reading.

When the torpedo warheads detonated, the energy release temporarily blinded the sensors as well. Larsen struggled through all the static, and as the sensor picture cleared, what he saw didn't make sense.

A half a second passed when Everson demanded, "Hurry up, Larsen!"

"Emperor's mercy! Sir, they are out of the water and they're almost on top of us," Larsen reported, eyes wide with fear.

Their submarine was raked from amidship back by the war skate's Gauss machine guns. Alarms blared as numerous hull breaches and equipment damage was detected.

"Emergency dive now!" Everson ordered.

"We can't, sir! The hull has been punctured in numerous locations. The diving controls and the sterling engine have been damaged. If we dive, we'll drown!" No longer able to control his volume, Larsen was yelling now too. He never imagined he would find himself fighting for his life in such an insane submarine battle.

"I don't give a shit, Larsen! Do it, now!"

Larsen peered at the sensor display, reluctant to follow

Everson's orders. He felt a sense of relief as he announced, "No need, sir. The war skate is withdrawing."

The next day, Sergeant "Rosey" Rosemont led his troop of four wild-turkey war walkers down the western beach of Pacifica's largest landmass known as New Washington. Contact with the *Carthage* fortress had been lost and now Imperial forces were struggling to hold territory. Without the *Carthage* to act as a command control communications center, the uncoordinated Imperial forces simply could not mount an effective defense.

Rosey and his troop had been skulking from one hiding place to another all night with hardly a moment to rest. It was getting to the point that they would have to stop to eat and sleep. He himself was just as hungry as he was exhausted, but survival took priority. Using his mecha's sensor periscope, Rosemont found a place to hide their mecha, and then noticed something else.

"What in the emperor's twenty names is that?" he said out loud. Some sort of vehicle was beached on the sand ahead of them. It had Imperial markings, but Rosey wasn't taking any chances. "Cogner, Smith, Brand, flanking positions. Brush, check out that vehicle. I'll cover you."

Despite their rough night, his last few men performed admirably. With only a few seconds' delay, all three mechs moved into position and neared the vehicle.

What greeted Brush was unexpected, yet anticlimactic. A young woman wearing a wrinkled and dirty Imperial uniform was sitting in the sand in front of the war skate. Through his mecha's sensors, Brush could tell she had been crying, further disarming him.

"Rosey, you need to see this," he called behind him to his sergeant.

Dismounting his walker, Rosemont approached and tried to

strike up a conversation with the woman, but for the first several seconds, it was rather one-sided.

Glancing at her name tape, he asked, "Private Carver?" She finally looked up at him. Still needing some time to get over her shock, he continued, "You're safe. We're with the Imperium also. Can you tell us what happened? How did you come to be here, Miss Carver?"

When at last she started talking, the tale she told was so unbelievable that Rosey had to confirm what he'd heard.

"Let me get this straight: two rangers kidnapped you, took down several combat bots, blew open the launch bay doors, and burgled a war skate, all after completely and utterly destroying our headquarters. Am I getting this right?" Rosey waited for Carver to respond, which came as a simple nod. "And, at any time, did you try to stop them?"

Her countenance turned harsh, full of exasperation and incredulousness. Using a tone that privates never used with sergeants, she rocked Rosemont on his heels with her sharp tongue.

"What was I supposed to do, shithead? Use the combat training I didn't need and never got to break their legs? I'm lucky to be alive. Those two literally scared the piss out of me the entire time they held me hostage!"

Rosey clenched his jaw and gave a single nod. Normally, he wouldn't stand for such insubordination, but it was clear the girl had just been through quite the ordeal. Unlike most Imperial troopers, Rosey had seen the results of the Federation Rangers' handywork before. From sentries to field officers, all shot through the head or the heart. Whole divisions vaporized by orbital bombardment directed by their unseen eyes.

Turning from Carver, Rosey looked at the tracks leading away from the war skate and into the tree line. *Federation Rangers*, he thought with a huff. *Improvise, adapt, overcome, my ass; more like win no matter what it costs.*

He sat down in the sand next to Carver and didn't say a word, trying to think of their next move. His limited troops were not anywhere near ready for a pursuit, and now he had this useless private under his charge as well.

"So," Carver prodded, "are you going to report me? Will I be court-martialed for treason?"

Rosemont shook his head. "You should have asked those rangers to stick around. We could have surrendered to them right away and gotten this over with."

She gave him a strange look, noticing that his shoulders slumped in defeat. "Surely, others will come and help us in the fight?"

"I'm afraid you're mistaken. My troop is all that remains of our division. The rest were destroyed in a Federation orbital strike. They didn't stand a chance, even with concealment."

Carver was regretting her decision to ever join the Imperial Army as the five soldiers waited on the lonely beach for someone to accept their surrender.

23

A CREDIT TO THE FEDERATION

With Tomi's chameleon cloak in need of repairs, the rangers relied on their fieldcraft skills to remain invisible to their enemy and avoid capture. Hiding among the trees, Tomi and Healy continued to observe radio silence and waited for orders to come over their comms to alert them to the status of the others and their next mission.

Moving around silently to get a lay of the land, they saw Imperial ground patrols and overflights every day, though their numbers did seem to be dwindling. It helped that more and more Federation aerospace fighters were overflying, indicating the Imperial garrison was, in fact, losing ground. Still, with two whole days behind them since they'd taken down the *Carthage*, Tomi was growing increasingly worried. Why had Federation command forgotten about them?

Zimmerman and Watry hung their heads in sorrow for their missing rangers. They still hadn't heard anything from Ryan or

Healy since the infiltration of the *Carthage*. When Elba and the other team members had succeeded in their missions and egressed before the first explosion even happened, they found Tomi and Healy's cyber dolphins, but no rangers.

Figuring the last pair had merely been detoured, the other four had cautiously made their way back to the ship, watching for the enemy sub as they used their dolphins since Orca had been compromised. Once back on board, they waited and waited for Ryan and Healy to show, but they never did. When the *Carthage* began sinking, it was assumed the duo had perished either in a gunfight, an explosion, or trapped in that watery grave.

"Such a shame," Lieutenant Elba said. "Ryan was on track for greatness."

If Tomi and Healy had not been so busy evading Imperial forces, they would have met up with Federation forces as planned and been discovered to be alive and well. As it was, they were assumed dead and waiting in the woods for someone to come, not knowing no one was. The snafu rule was in full effect.

A couple of days later, the order came down from the president of the Federation to "cease all combat operations," for their mission had been a success.

Tomi finally realized their dire situation. "What? Did those assholes forget we're out here?"

"See what happens when you talk too much? They were celebrating the silence," Healy ribbed in an attempt to keep the mood light, though Tomi wasn't laughing.

They had been out in the wilderness for several days now, living off their rations at first, and then the local wildlife. Sure, enough of each animal they caught was edible, but taste was another matter entirely. Well, at least now they could break cover.

"Should we travel to one of the Federation-held positions since we haven't gotten any further orders?" Tomi asked.

Healy nodded. "Hopefully there's room on one of the ships for us. If not, we can contact HQ to be picked up."

The two of them walked back to the beach where they had landed with the war skate. They were surprised to see it was still exactly where they'd left it, though it now had several new companions. Parked nearby were four Imperial war walkers with their cockpits open and completely powered down. Out in the surf was the mini attack submarine that had tried to destroy them, now beached as well.

Tomi scrunched her forehead. "Why have all these Imperial troops gathered in one place? It's almost like they're waiting for something."

Healy agreed. "They seem to have given up the fight knowing the Federation won."

About half a dozen people in all were gathered in front of the war skate. Most were reclining on the sand, some asleep. One man was standing, kicking something near the surf. A woman noticed their approach and began waving wildly. It was their old pal, Private Petula Carver.

Carver yelled to them impatiently, "Will you two Fed rats get over here already? We need someone to surrender to. It's been nearly a week and we're all starving!"

Two of the men stood and stepped forward, one wearing the uniform of an Imperial Army sergeant, while the other's uniform indicated he was a lieutenant with the Imperial Maritime Forces. The lieutenant spoke first.

"I am Lieutenant Everson, commanding officer of the attack submarine *Uranus*."

Tomi started to laugh because it reminded her of the old joke involving that planet's name, but Healy elbowed her in the ribs. This was hardly the time for jokes. She sobered up and stood tall and confident as the sergeant stepped forward.

"Sergeant Rosemont," he said, introducing himself. "Since you two are the first and only Federation personnel we have encountered so far, please accept our formal surrender." He extended his hand as if to shake Tomi's.

"Uh, sure. Your surrender is accepted." She took his hand, but he looked like he was waiting on something more. *Oh, duh.* "Uh, Tomi Ryan…er…Lance Corporal Federation Ranger Tomi Ryan," she stumbled.

Shit, I fumbled my first formal surrender. I will not hear the end of this, she thought to herself. *Oh, well.* Tomi smiled anyway, proud of how much she had accomplished over this last year. She had survived her first war, although she secretly hoped it would be her last.

With Imps now under their charge, Tomi and Healy decided it would be best to call for a dropship to pick them up. Unfortunately, it wasn't that easy. Even with all of the Federation surveillance overhead both in air and in orbit, Carver and the other Imperial soldiers had been sitting out on that beach unnoticed for days. Or perhaps they were simply deemed not a threat and, therefore, not a priority.

Between that and the rangers' assumed deaths, Federation command didn't believe Tomi at first when she called in. Command kept insisting that Ranger Tomi Ryan was dead. Even Healy tried hopping on and affirming that they were both still breathing and they even had some surrendered Imps with them, but the Fed on the other end assumed it to be some prank made in poor taste.

Several calls had to be made, but they finally reached Elba who confirmed they were talking to the real McCoy. When it was realized an error had been made, HQ immediately authorized a dropship with Elba, Guy, Watry, Zimmerman, and a small contingent of Federation Marines to secure the Imperial prisoners and equipment.

A mere hour later, the dropship landed on the beach nearby. Their mission team all debarked and came jogging toward them.

"Holy shit, you two are some of the luckiest bastards I have ever had the sorry pleasure to meet!" Watry exclaimed, breaking protocol by embracing each of them in turn, much to Captain Guy's displeasure.

Zimmerman nodded enthusiastically. "Yeah, when you go on leave, be sure to hit the casinos! We thought you were goners, for sure."

"What the hell happened?" Elba asked.

Healy told them the whole story of how they had to improvise when they encountered a roving patrol, and how things escalated from there. Tomi pointed out their prisoner, Private Carver, and how they escaped from the *Carthage* using the war skate that was now parked on the beach. Even Guy looked impressed now.

"You should put these two in for a medal, Elba," Guy acknowledged. "Talk about improvising."

"Damn right, Guy. That's a great idea. It's the least the Federation could do for you two in honor of your service, your skills, and your ability to think on your feet."

Guy's wrist comp chimed with an incoming comm call.

"Captain Guy," the marine on the other end said, "I've been told Healy and Ryan need to be debriefed back at headquarters. I've also been informed that all of you are required to attend an awards ceremony."

Tomi's jaw dropped.

"Awards ceremony? Isn't that a bit much?" Tomi asked on the dropship.

"We blew up the enemy's HQ, Tom," Healy answered. "We're a big reason the Federation won the war."

Watry added, "About damn time they give the rangers some credit. We're always out there on the edge of the frontier pulling someone's fat out of the fire, and if we're not doing that, then we're cleaning up someone else's mess."

Tomi agreed with Watry. After all, her first real mission had been babysitting...er...escorting a Survey Service mission with no acknowledgment of their efforts. The expedition had proved difficult when some of the survey scientists decided to act like adolescents. Tomi had even saved Albertson's life but didn't get any gratitude then either. Not even a simple thank you. It would be nice to have her efforts acknowledged for once.

"Maybe they need some live heroes to pin some medals on? Hasn't it been a while since the Federation had a real war?" Healy queried sarcastically.

"No way," Elba said. "They have plenty of marines to do that. No offense," he added, seeing Guy side-eyeing him. "Besides, approving those medals usually takes time. No, kids, I think you're forgetting a long-standing tradition," Elba pointed out.

When Tomi and the others looked at him with quizzical looks, Captain Guy jumped in. "Just wait, you'll see."

Did Tomi see a smile breaking through the marine's stoic countenance?

The dropship arrived aboard the Federation's flagship: the *Olympus*, an Asgard-class fleet carrier. Tomi thought it was strange that they were brought aboard the flagship and not the orbital assault carrier they had deployed from. Elba and Guy were right, it seemed; the brass had something planned, but what? She racked her brain trying to remember what the "long-standing tradition" was that they were referring to.

The rangers were allowed to shower and were given crisp, clean dress uniforms to wear, which was a little off-putting for Tomi. It had been so long since she had worn her dress uniform, instead practically living in her exosuit. The Federation Ranger dress uniform was a similar cut to the Space Patrol's, except it was green and black instead of the patrol's blue and silver. Getting all dolled up, so to speak, definitely made it feel like something big was in the works, especially when they made sure to remind the rangers to don their badges.

Each ranger always kept their badge with them as both tradition and professionalism, but they rarely wore it out in the field. Between that and the fact that hers was not quite a year old, her badge was hardly tarnished, but Tomi still made sure to polish it now. She admired the way in which the titanium sparkled as she studied the five-point star superimposed over a ring with holographic embossing. If she were to admit it in the privacy of her own mind, Tomi was rather proud of herself.

A knock came at her door and Healy peaked his head inside. "It's time, Tom."

She exited the room to find Watry and Zimmerman waiting for her also. This group had become like a second family to her, and she was proud to have them by her side, whatever came next.

They walked together into hangar bay one, where they found the embarked marines awaiting their arrival. The rangers walked to the front of the formation and it suddenly struck Tomi what the long-standing tradition was supposed to be. Seeing Captain Guy next to the five-star general of the Federation Marines, her heart pounded in her chest as the general began to speak.

"Good afternoon. As many of you already know, I am General Warnock, commandant of the Federation Marines," he began, receiving many whoops and oorahs in response. "Even in times of peace, Federation Rangers regularly face many unspeakable dangers with little or no support, often numbering just a team of four. And yet, the rangers never fail to offer their support to other services when needed, including to the marines."

Chills ran up and down Tomi's spine. *Oh my Deus, it's actually happening!*

"Long ago, the Federation Rangers promised to always answer the call to work alongside the Federation Marines in times of war as pathfinders, pararescue jumpers, and commandos. Not once have the rangers failed to answer that call, and answer they do without hesitation."

Tomi tried to subtly wipe her palms on her pants. *I've faced enemies that would send most people packing. Why are my palms so sweaty now?*

"It has been a tradition, going back nearly a hundred years, that any ranger who serves with a marine detachment during wartime will be presented with a symbol of the highest honor and of our acceptance of said rangers as our very own."

Don't pass out. Don't pass out.

"And so, on behalf of the Federation Marines, as a sign of gratitude and our utmost respect, I would like to bestow upon these rangers you see before you the very same black beret that our Federation Marines wear with pride." At General Warnock's signal, five marines stepped forward and handed each of the rangers a beret. "You are a credit to your service and the Federation," Warnock concluded as applause broke out.

Tomi laid hold of her beret from the marine's hands and feasted her eyes upon it. Dark in color, bearing the emblem of the Federation Marines: a globe, wreath, vertical path, and three stars. She placed it reverently upon her head as her fellow rangers did the same. Once all of the rangers had their new covers on, General Warnock saluted them, and they returned the gesture.

"Welcome to the brotherhood of the Federation Marines."

"So, what are you going to do next, Tom?" asked Healy as they headed back to their temporary berths.

"I don't know," she admitted. "Haven't thought about it. I'm thinking of trying out for the Hostile Environment eXploration suit training course—"

"No, no," Healy laughed. "I don't mean that. We're all due for some leave after that war. I'm asking where you will go on leave. What will you do with all that free time?"

Leave. The word almost seemed alien to Tomi. She'd been granted a brief leave after she graduated from the pipeline before receiving her first mission. She'd used it to go home and see her family, but this time felt different. After having been through so much, she wondered how she could possibly describe the experience to anyone, let alone her family. How would they understand?

Tomi had quite a bit of leave saved up at this point. Maybe she needed some time alone to process and unwind before going home —a true vacation. After all, there was a place she had always wanted to visit.

"I think I'll spend a little time with my family, but first, I'm going to Hawaii," she answered.

"Hawaii? Oh, that's right. You're from Earth," Healy said.

Tomi gave him a look that questioned why he was judging her decision.

"No, no. That's great," he added, "it's just, usually everyone goes off to Eden or Utopia or even Olympus, not the Hawaiian Islands. Just...do me a favor, will you?" he asked. "Go ahead and check Hawaii off your bucket list, but then make sure you expand your horizons. You're a ranger, for Deus's sake! You can go anywhere you want, Tom."

Tomi nodded. "I'll keep that in mind for next time, Healy."

24

WELL DESERVED REST

The sun was warm on Olin's back, the sky clear and bright blue, and the beach had beautiful women as far as the eye could see. *This truly is paradise,* he thought as he walked along the beach and took in the sites, mostly of the human kind. He deserved this though; Tomi had broken up with him after she'd been with the rangers for a mere month.

"With me traveling the universe, we won't get to see each other much," she had told him. "It's not fair for me to hold you back."

Olin rolled his eyes at the memory. More like she'd found a new stud who knew how to shoot an omniblaster and could travel with her to all those faraway places. No matter, there were plenty of pretty ladies to check out here on Earth, and who knew? Maybe he'd even get lucky.

There were definitely some women here who grabbed his attention. Still, he found himself sighing. This was supposed to be his and Tomi's honeymoon spot, back when she still wanted to marry him. If he was being honest, maybe his heart was still a little broken. Perhaps keeping in touch even after they'd broken up hadn't been the smartest move, but Tomi had always been more than just his girlfriend. She was his best friend.

He couldn't deny that his heart still skipped a beat whenever Tomi's name came up on his personal comm, but they hadn't spoken since he'd told her he planned to sign up with the Federation Survey Service. She'd told him he was crazy and that he should reconsider, but when he admitted that he had already signed the paperwork to begin the testing, she'd lost it on him and then hung up. She hadn't answered his calls since.

Secretly, Olin envied her. Tomi knew what she wanted and she went for it, not letting anyone stop her or get in her way. College was fun and all, but when Tomi had joined the rangers and started telling him of all her adventures and experiences, he realized that he needed the same thing, just maybe not on quite that extravagant of a level. He'd always been skilled at science, geology in particular, and he was getting tired of going to school. He was also getting tired of constantly being broke. The Survey Service seemed like perfect solution for all of that.

So, Olin signed up. Actually, he'd already taken the written entrance exams. In addition, the bigwigs in charge really liked him. So far, he stood out from many of the others—his academic qualifications were solid and he'd gotten good scores on the test for intelligence.

With all of the written tests out of the way, what was left were the physical requirements, obstacle course, and psychological evaluation. These were much trickier, or so he'd been told. Olin had heard of people breezing through the written tests only to be crushed when it came to the physical tests, and still others who had barely squeaked through the IQ test only to excel later. Olin figured theory really was different from actual practice, and everyone had their strengths and weaknesses.

There was a two-week break between the written and physical exams, so Olin decided it was the perfect opportunity to go to Hawaii after all, even if it meant going alone. As the sun began its descent, he walked through the parking lot toward a restaurant. His stomach told him it was time for some dinner.

He passed a few aerocars, hovercycles, hoop bikes, even a couple of flitters. The flitters were the more insane since that's what you had to be to ride one. They essentially had an advanced jet turbine. Some were even fusion-powered with repulsor ring lift thrusters, complete with wings and control surfaces. Olin thought of them as miniature VTOL jets with a motorcycle seat.

The ones he saw here were street-legal versions, as fast as aerocars, but with speed-limiting electronics, an autopilot, and danger-avoidance sensors. The military and racing industry had special mechanics who knew how to either shut the safety features off or have them removed altogether. Olin had heard the rangers really like them, and he found himself wondering whether Tomi had gotten to ride one yet.

He turned his focus toward the door to the restaurant but did a double-take when he recognized one of the hoverbikes in the parking lot. It looked like the motorcycle Tomi had bought just before she'd left for ranger school. He paused before walking up to it, circling it. Olin could see where one of the panels had been replaced and repainted, but the decal was the same. Either she had sold it or...she's here.

Her bike was parked in the furthest row from the restaurant, closer to the beach than the door. Dinner would have to wait. Olin walked out to where pavement met sand and scanned the area, but there were so many girls on the beach it was difficult to narrow down where she might be. He quickly eliminated the shorter ones; Tomi was almost as tall as Olin. There were plenty of blonds, plenty of curly and straight hair, but Tomi's was brown and wavy.

He eyes landed on a girl who stood out from the rest and he strolled over to where she was playing volleyball with some guys. Her hair was cropped short now, but he would have to be blind to not see her familiar curves. She was wearing a sporty blue bikini with a red waistband, and then he heard her laugh—it was definitely Tomi.

He watched for a moment. It was quite a game as Tomi didn't slow down, single-handedly holding down her team. It wasn't too long before the guys needed a breather. Being a ranger had clearly been good for her stamina, strength, and fitness. She had always looked good to Olin, of course, but he couldn't deny that she had somehow become even sexier. She walked over to her backpack and took out a cropped shirt with blue and white stripes. He watched her skin glisten under the golden sunset as she pulled her shirt on, facing away from him. He couldn't wait any longer.

"Tomi!" he called out. She turned around, seeing him as he ran and embraced her in a hug. "I can't believe it's you!" Olin spun her around in a circle before setting her back down.

Tomi laughed. "Olin! What are you doing here? Aren't you on your fourth major by now, or have they finally kicked you out of college?"

Snarky as ever, he thought with a smirk. *The rangers must love her attitude.* "No, remember? I told you that I was joining the Survey Service." He held his breath, waiting for her wrath.

"You're still doing that?" she screamed, slapping her forehead. "Olin, are you nuts? You don't like going camping. Why would you go on a survey mission? It's basically a giant camping trip full of science nerds, only there's more than just bears in those woods."

Even though she was yelling at him, Olin couldn't help but smile. Tomi had always been direct.

"You do realize you will be out in the middle of nowhere going primitive? No sink, no shower, no toilet...the only civilization is what you can carry on your back."

"Hey, I went primitive during field camp. It wasn't so bad," he said lightly. "Besides, I already started the exams process."

Tomi rolled her eyes, obviously not impressed.

"What? Is it really that bad?" he asked.

She shook her head and stared at the ground.

"If you know so much then why don't you enlighten me," he demanded. Now he was feeling a little defensive. If she could do something crazy like joining the rangers, why couldn't he carve his own path?

Normally ready to fight back, Tomi recognized the need to change the subject matter if she didn't want this rendezvous to end so quickly. She picked up her backpack and said, "Dinner?" When Olin nodded, she asked, "Aren't you going to compliment me?"

They started walking off the beach and onto the walkway. He knew what she wanted him to say, but he was confused.

"You always said it's condescending to objectify women like that," he countered.

She smiled without looking at him. "I saw you looking at my ass, and I've already checked out yours too." Tomi looked directly at him now. "You still have some cute buns, Olin."

Was she flirting with him? It was hard to say. Sometimes Tomi liked to say shit just to get a rise out of you. Then again, they were on the romantic island where they had planned to say their vows, the sun was setting on the horizon behind them, and they had a long history together.

He followed her to her hovercycle. "I thought we were going to have dinner," he questioned, looking at the restaurant.

"Not here," she said. "Where's your ride?"

Busted. "I don't have one," he admitted. "I...I rode the autobus here." He knew there was no shame in taking public transportation, but his mind always went back to the old stereotype of the guy with the nicest car getting the girl.

"No problem," she said as she swung her leg over the bike. "My hovercycle has a passenger seat." Tomi patted the bitch seat behind her.

Olin swallowed hard, hoping Tomi's driving was good as he remembered, and that riding all those military vehicles with no limitation controls hadn't changed that. He hopped on behind her and she fired up her hovercycle.

"Hold on," Tomi said with a smirk before gunning it out of the parking lot.

Olin wrapped his arms tighter around her waist as the hovercycle shot forward. *Holy shit, what the fuck have I gotten myself into?* he thought as Tomi barreled out into traffic and raced through the streets.

She deftly maneuvered between cars at breakneck speeds. If Olin could have watched from afar, he would have thought it looked like a scene from a movie, the hero slaloming effortlessly through an obstacle course. When they rounded a corner, Olin braced for impact with an oncoming automated garbage truck, but there was no need. Tomi's instincts and reaction time had enhanced with her ranger experience, and she easily swung out in front of it before speeding around another corner.

"Hey, Olin, you still alive back there? I didn't scare you too bad, did I?" she teased.

"Holy shit!" he exclaimed. "Yes, I'm still alive, smartass, but I don't know for how much longer with the way you're driving."

"You're squeezing me so tight it's starting to hurt," she admitted.

Tomi came up to a red light and Olin was surprised when she actually stopped at it. He loosened his grip just a little.

"So," she said, looking over her shoulder flirtatiously, "your place or mine?"

Olin had thought they were going to dinner, but he didn't mind putting that on hold a bit longer if she really meant what he thought she meant. Still, he didn't want to take her back to his hotel room. He had gotten the cheapest one he could find and was surprised to discover that even Hawaii had sketchy neighborhoods.

"Yours," he answered.

"Let's clean up first," Tomi said, pulling Olin by his hand toward the shower.

Her hotel room was definitely nicer than his own, and he didn't mind a quick shower to get the sand off before rolling around in the sheets, especially if she planned to help soap him up. They shared some unexpectedly tender kisses as the warm water ran over their bodies and down the drain. When things really started to get heated, they quickly toweled off and stumbled into her bed, no longer able to keep their hands off each other.

Olin was shocked at Tomi's stamina. When he became fatigued, she got on top and kept things going a bit longer. He certainly didn't mind, nor did he mind the fact that she laid her head and hand on his chest once they finished. He'd really missed her.

During their pillow talk, he played with her hair as Tomi revealed she had become a corporal and was receiving some pretty significant pay these days—free fall pay, dive pay, vacuum pay, and hazardous duty pay, just to name some of the extras she received every month. Tomi was earning so much money these days that she could afford her own room, ride, travel expenses, and so on. Olin was impressed, though also a bit jealous.

He was beginning to regret following his parent's advice. Go to college, they'd said. Get a degree, they'd said. *It will pay off, trust us.* Yeah, right! He felt stagnant as Tomi and everyone else moved on with their adult lives. Never mind the massive debt he now had to pay off with no job opps in the "real world" to show for it. And his parents wondered why he'd signed up with the Survey Service.

"Oh, don't blame them, Olin," Tomi said. "They're parents—they had good intensions. They only want what's best for you. Sometimes you have to go through some bullshit to find out a particular path is not the best investment for you."

"You're telling me," he said, rolling his eyes. "I just feel frustrated, you know? I see how far you've come since joining the rangers, and I guess I just feel a little left behind. Like I'm stuck in our teenage years."

"I get it," Tomi said. "But we all have our own paths, Olin."

He peered down at her and stopped playing with her hair.

"So, are you going to try talking me out of joining the service?" he asked.

She lifted herself up and straddled him, giving Olin a perfect view of her bust. "I'm not thrilled that you decided to join the rangers' sworn enemy," she admitted in a teasing tone, "but since you did, let me give you some advice." She paused a moment and he relaxed at her response. "I just want to make sure you know what you're getting yourself into. I've been out there on the wild frontier and I've seen grown men shit their pants."

Olin didn't know how to respond, so he kept his mouth shut.

"If you pass your physical exams, you sure as shit better pay attention to the survival training afterward," she warned him. "A lot of things get overlooked by trainees or underestimated even." Tomi peered at her nightstand that held her bush knife. "What they teach you in there can mean life or death out in the field."

"Yes, ma'am," he answered dutifully.

She slapped him on the chest. "Olin, I'm serious. And by the way, my eyes are up here, dickhead!" She pointed to her eyes and then, in one fluid movement, hopped off and rolled Olin onto his belly with alarming strength. "Are you more focused now or are you planning to get by on your good looks?" she said, slapping his ass.

"Ow!" Olin jumped and then laughed. "Watch it or I'll keep these good looks out of your bed," he teased back. Then, getting more serious, he rolled back over and looked deeply into Tomi's eyes. "I'm really determined to do this. I need to feel important and purposeful."

Tomi nodded, knowing exactly where he was coming from as she remembered herself just a year prior.

"And hey, if you can do it, I can do it better!" he said, lightening the mood with another joke.

Tomi smiled, smacking him lightly. "Seriously, Olin, if you get in trouble, I will be the one who has to come rescue you. I know you like your lessons from the school of hard knocks, but if that happens, I'll put my boot up your ass."

They smiled at each other in silence for a minute, and then Tomi lay down beside him again. *He's a lost cause,* she thought. *Bound and determined to go off on an adventure.* She just prayed to Deus that the next time she saw him, it would be under benign circumstances.

She jumped out of bed and started to get dressed.

"Where are you going?" he asked, not wanting to leave their little love nest.

"Get dressed—I leave tomorrow morning. Let's go and have that dinner we talked about, my treat."

The rising sun peered through the curtains and poured over Olin as he lay alone in Tomi's bed. He had a moment of panic that he'd missed her departure—he had promised to go to the spaceport to see her off. Then he heard some movement coming from the bathroom.

When she emerged, he found it shocking to see Tomi in her ranger uniform. It was quite the contrast to the skimpy bikini she had been wearing just yesterday. His eyes landed on the new addition on top of her head as she straightened it.

"When did you join the marines?" he asked.

"I served with the Federation Marines on Pacifica," she answered.

His eyes widened. He'd heard about that war on the news, but he didn't know Tomi had been there. "You never mentioned you went to war," he said with concern.

Tomi laughed. "Don't worry, Olin. The war is over." Glancing at the clock, she said, "We'd better get going. I don't want to be late." She tilted her head playfully and added, "And you'd better get used to waking up earlier if you want to be a scientist in the Survey Service."

When Tomi's shuttle arrived at the spaceport, she wrapped her arms around Olin and gave him a lingering kiss goodbye.

Still holding onto him, she leaned back to say, "If this is something you really want to do, Olin, then I will support your decision. Just don't go getting on any of my fellow ranger's bad sides, got it?"

He smiled and nodded. She let go of him and stepped back, straightening her uniform and grabbing her bag. Entering the line for the shuttle, she turned and waved goodbye. Olin could see her mouthing something.

See you soon.

Made in United States
Troutdale, OR
06/04/2023